The Breadstealers

The Fight against the Corn Laws, 1838-1846

NORMAN LONGMATE
THE BREADSTEALERS

St Martins Press · New York
Temple Smith · London

First published in Great Britain in 1984
by Maurice Temple Smith Ltd
Jubilee House, Chapel Road
Hounslow, Middlesex, TW3 1TX

Longmate, Norman
    The breadstealers: the fight against the Corn
Laws, 1838-1846.
    I. Title
    344.103'851311   KD5662.C6

ISBN 0 85117 245 8
Typeset by Tellgate Limited, London WC2
Printed in Great Britain by
Billing and Sons Ltd, Worcester

First published in the United States of America in 1984.
For information write: St Martins Press Inc.,
175 Fifth Avenue, New York, NY 10010. All rights reserved.
Library of Congress Catalog Card Number 84-40142
US ISBN 0-312-09511-2

Contents

Illustrations

Acknowledgements
Punch Frontispiece, 14, Endpiece
BBC Hulton Picture Library Title page, 1, 3, 4, 5, 6, 7, 11, 12, 13, 15, 19, 20, 21, 25, 27, 29, 30, 31, 32, 33, 34, 35
Manchester Public Libraries 2, 9, 10, 17, 18, 22, 23, 24, 26, 36
The Author 8, 16, 28

Foreword

The struggle to achieve the repeal of the laws designed to keep up the price of bread appears at first sight remarkably remote from the problems of the present day. It began in earnest in 1839 and ended in triumph seven years later in 1846, so that very few of those involved lived on into the twentieth century. It was the fact that this seemed a limited, self-contained subject, with a clear beginning and end, which originally attracted me to it. Further reading, however, soon made clear that even if the Corn Laws are dead beyond recall the issues they raised are still topical and important. A tax on imported wheat seemed inconceivable in the immediate aftermath of 1846 but the possibility was raised again only a few years later and, under the name of 'Tariff Reform', was advocated by the Conservatives during the famous election of 1906, when it resulted in a landslide victory for their opponents. Interestingly enough, the propagandist phrase 'the Big Loaf', coined sixty years earlier by the Anti-Corn-Law League, was employed again in 1906, but on an even wider scale.

Today the extent to which British agriculture and the price of food should be subject to outside political control is again a live issue, with the two major parties in the state divided, not on simple free trade versus protection lines, but over the extent to which a foreign-dominated organization in Brussels, which the British public agreed that its government should join, should dictate not merely the price of food and other commodities produced within Great Britain but even their nature and amount. The European Economic Community imposes upon the British economy far greater restrictions, and subjects it to a far greater degree of external interference, than the Corn Laws ever did, though whether Cobden and his colleagues would have hailed its emergence as a step towards free trade, or have denounced it as an intolerable barrier to international commerce, one can only speculate.

The story of the League evokes, too, other echoes in contemporary political life. The League was, thanks to the penny post and the railways and the efficiency of the men who directed its affairs, the first truly modern political organization in this country. It was also a body rooted in one particular section of society. 'I will admit that, so far as the fervour and efficiency of our agitation has gone,' said Richard Cobden, 'it has eminently been a middle-class agitation. We have resorted to tea parties and taken those pacific means for carrying out our views which mark us rather as a middle-class set of agitators.'

Another parallel with the present day is the extent to which the League, in a phrase not then current, broke the mould of existing political allegiances. Its chosen path was always the middle one and it suffered the inevitable fate of the moderate, reasonable party in being simultaneously attacked by those of more extreme views, whether the aristocratic and conservative, who argued that it was indirectly encouraging revolution, or the proletarian and radical, who denounced it as traitorous to the progressive cause. The League's most bitter opponents were the most active sections of the working class whose cause it claimed to champion and its spokesmen were subjected to violence in public. They were also sometimes shouted down in the House of Commons by the hooligan element which still disgraces that assembly today, though in the 1840s it spoke with a more aristocratic accent.

The Breadstealers forms to some extent a sequel to my earlier works on nineteenth-century social history and especially to the last such book, *The Hungry Mills*, which dealt with the area which formed the League's heartland, Lancashire, though at a period twenty years later. If the theme of that book was one of courage and charity in the face of adversity, the message of *The Breadstealers* is of the remarkable results that a group of dedicated, determined and resourceful men can achieve by making full use of the opportunities a free society provides for publicizing opinions in an orderly way. The repeal of the Corn Laws was a triumph for the political institutions — inadequate as they then were — which people of intrinsically undemocratic temper, in the 1840s as now, professed to despise. It revealed that the reasonable man can, with patience, defeat the extremist and that moderation is not a reason for apology but, at least in this country, a formula for success.

As in my earlier books on Victorian England, I have made extensive use of the contemporary sources, believing that wherever possible the League and its opponents should be left to speak for themselves, through their own speeches and through the pamphlets and newspapers of the time. To avoid distracting the reader, this has meant introducing consistency into spelling, punctuation and capitalization — in the mid-nineteenth century no two printers seem to have followed the same house-style. The chief such problem was presented by the Anti-Corn-Law League itself, for its supporters rendered its name in a variety of ways and I have adopted a common form throughout, irrespective of the capitals and hyphens used in the original.

In a book which inevitably contains a great many prices the

change to decimal currency and other measurements presented particular problems. I have retained the currency figures used at the time — indeed to have altered them would have misrepresented what was actually said or written — but give below a summary of the principal equivalents, to which the reader unfamiliar with the pre-1971 terminology can refer.

I am grateful to Mr Stanley Williamson, who undertook research on my behalf in the Central Reference Library in Manchester; to my daughter Jill, for her extensive research in the British Library in London; and to my secretary, Miss Julia Arrowsmith. I have endeavoured throughout, as in earlier books, not to reveal my own views and attitudes, at least until the closing sentences, though I confess to being on the side of argument rather than violence and to feeling more sympathy for the poor and under-privileged than for the rich and powerful. These are postures of which, I am sure, both the principal heroes of this book, Richard Cobden and Sir Robert Peel, would have approved, even though they sat on opposite sides of the House of Commons.

NRL   August 1983

Note on Currency

Old	New
One pound (£1)	£1
One shilling (1s)	5p
Sixpence (6d)	2.5p
One penny (1d)	0.4p (approx.)
One halfpenny (½d)	0.2p (approx.)
One farthing (¼d)	0.1p (approx.)

PAPA COBDEN TAKING MASTER ROBERT A FREE TRADE WALK.

PAPA COBDEN.—"Come along, MASTER ROBERT, do step out."

MASTER ROBERT.—"That's all very well, but you know I cannot go so fast as you do."

Punch took a constant interest in the Corn Law controversy, especially in its later stages. This cartoon, published during 1845, shows an eager Cobden dragging a reluctant Peel towards total abolition of the Corn Laws and universal free trade.

CHAPTER ONE

The Price of Corn

'For what were all these country patriots born,
To hunt, and vote, and raise the price of corn?'
— Lord Byron, *The Age of Bronze*, 1823

When, one evening towards the end of July 1838, the citizens of
Bolton assembled in the local theatre to attend a lecture, they did so
in no great spirit of expectation. The subject, though often discussed
in politically-conscious Lancashire, was hardly a burning question
at that moment, but there was — noted a journalist from Manchester
— 'a good attendance and the lecturer was well received'. Soon,
however, he had stretched his audience's goodwill almost beyond
endurance. 'He had provided himself with a great bundle of papers
and he could not readily find those to which he wished to refer.
When he did find them he read them badly, his connecting
observations were not understandable and, the meeting expressing
its impatience, he came to a complete standstill.'

The occasion was saved from turning into a complete fiasco by a
young medical student, who had watched the proceedings from a
box with growing dismay and was finally urged by his companions
to 'get on the stage and say something'. He responded to such effect
that 'the people . . . called "Hear! Hear!" and "Go on!"' and,
having spoken for twenty minutes, 'created a wish that he should be
heard at more length'. A week later, on Monday 6 August 1838, the
young man, Abraham Paulton, duly responded to these requests
and secured the rapt attention of another crowded meeting in the
same place thanks to 'his earnestness and energy and . . .
combination of argument, with appeals to high moral principle,' a
mixture that was to become a feature of the campaign now
beginning.

In this manner, initially so inauspicious, was launched an
agitation which was to engage the sympathy and efforts of
thousands of solid citizens and to split one of the two great political
parties. Its subject was the Corn Laws, the statutes which restricted
the free flow of grain and other cereals between Great Britain and
foreign countries, to protect the British farmer from possible
harmful competition.

By 1838 the principle of interfering with this most basic of
commodities already had a history stretching back to the Middle

Ages, but the systematic involvement of government in the corn trade only began with the Restoration in 1660. In 1663, to encourage home production, a duty was placed on all imported grain unless the price of home-grown wheat had risen above a certain level; and in 1670 a sliding scale of duty was introduced, related to the prevailing price level at home. In 1673 another Act provided a bounty of 5s for each quarter (28lb) of wheat exported, with lesser sums for rye, barley and malt, when the price at home fell below a certain level. This Act was revived in 1689 to help reward the 'landed interest' for supporting the 'Glorious Revolution' which placed William III on the throne.

The eighty years which followed came to be regarded as the golden age of British agriculture, but in 1751 the policy of protection was challenged by the great agricultural reformer, Charles Townshend. He argued in favour of the doctrine of free trade, which held that it was in every nation's interest to impose as few barriers as possible between itself and its neighbours, and that national wealth was to be secured by exporting manufactured goods rather than raw materials. The farmers were not slow to respond and in the following year the *Gentleman's Magazine* reprinted a number of articles from country newspapers whose readers were shocked at this threat to their income. Naturally enough, they regarded the waving fields of ripening corn, which they both saw and profited from, as a better measure of the country's prosperity than the wagon-loads of manufactured cotton goods which failed to benefit them. 'Our wise ancestors, when they gave us the bounty,' wrote one dedicated agriculturist on 4 January 1753 in the *Stamford Mercury*, which spoke for rural Lincolnshire, 'expected it would make us a corn nation, which we were not at that time. Experience hath convinced us of the rectitude of the measure.' In 1753 the Prime Minister, Henry Pelham, assured an audience of his constituents at Lewes that they need have no fear about the future:

> The bounty for debenture to encourage the exportation of corn having been falsely reported to be taken off, I must beg leave to assure you that no such thing was intended. Well must I consider what the consequences of such an act would be, which must reduce the rent of lands a third in value, greatly lessening the estates of all landed gentlemen, impoverish gentlemen and yeomen of small fortunes, and farmers of long leases must be inevitably ruined. As trade and particularly the corn trade is the chief concern of the County of Sussex, it shall be my constant care to encourage and support the same by encouraging our farmers in their agriculture and extending our commerce abroad, we have no

reason to fear being what we have ever been, a rich and powerful people.

Here was a classic statement of how the government identified itself with the farming community, or at least the better-off part of it; the needs of the farm labourer, it may be noticed, were not mentioned, but assumed to coincide with those of his betters. This attitude was to persist in varying degrees for almost another hundred years, although it became less and less related to the facts as the factories and mills spread across the Midlands and the North and agriculture was first challenged and then deposed as the nation's major employer and source of wealth.

Apart from the quantity of bread eaten, the quality was also a useful index of prosperity. In 1755 appeared Dr Johnson's *Dictionary* with its famous entry defining oats as 'a grain which in England is generally given to horses, but in Scotland supports the people'. 'It is certain,' wrote Charles Smith in 1766, in the last of his *Three Tracts on the Corn Trade and Corn Laws*, 'that bread made of wheat is become much more largely the food of the common people since 1689 than it was before that time, but it is still very far from being the food of the people in general.' He estimated that fewer than four million of the estimated six million people in England and Wales could afford wheaten bread, the rest, especially in Wales, relying on flour made from rye and barley. By the end of the century, however, in most places rye was eaten only under protest and in 1802 a writer in the *Farmers' Magazine* was able to assert that 'nearly twice as many persons now eat wheaten bread as formerly' ('formerly' apparently referring to half-a-century earlier). Even in Scotland, revealed the same author, 'the great proportion of the inhabitants subsist chiefly on wheat'.

The eighteenth was a somnolent century. Its prevailing political philosophy, from indolence rather than conviction, was *laissez-faire*, but bread was always an exception. Charles Smith, in the second of his *Tracts*, published in 1759, summed up the government's duty as being to prevent 'grain from being at any time either so dear that the poor cannot subsist or so cheap that the farmer cannot live by growing of it'.

The whole subject was constantly debated in the House of Commons. In 1766 the duty on imported grain from the American colonies was briefly lifted, and the export of grain and flour was forbidden; and from 1 January 1774 a full-scale Corn Law established the principles which were to govern legislation for the next half century. When the domestic price, as paid to the farmer by the baker or dealer, fell below £2. 4s, he was encouraged to sell his produce abroad, to prevent the market falling still further, by a bounty of 5s for each quarter exported. When it fetched £2. 8s export was forbidden to ensure that the price was not kept artificially high. At prices in between these levels there was a nominal duty of sixpence a quarter. The system was later refined, with elaborate regulations specifying precisely how and in what town the price was to be measured, with special procedures for reporting it and making allowance for regional differences.

The new law, known as Governor Pownall's Act after its principal sponsor, Thomas Pownall, a former governor of both Massachusetts and South Carolina, was widely praised by the two great contemporary arbiters of agricultural and economic policy, Arthur Young and Adam Smith. Young, himself a practising, experimental farmer, wrote between 1768 and 1771 a series of books describing his visits to the rural areas of his native country, and in 1793 became secretary to the Board of Agriculture. His verdict on the Act of 1773 was entirely favourable, and even more significant was the endorsement given by Adam Smith, whose *Inquiry into the Nature and Causes of the Wealth of Nations*, published in 1776, was to dominate economic thinking until well into Victorian times. He believed that the 1773 Corn Law, 'though not the best in itself . . . is the best which the interests, prejudices and the temper of the time would admit of'.

> The laws concerning corn may everywhere be compared to the laws concerning religion. The people feel themselves so much interested in what relates either to their subsistence in this life, or their happiness in a life to come, that government must yield to their prejudices, and in order to preserve the public tranquillity, establish that system which they approve of. It is upon this account, perhaps, that we so seldom find a reasonable system established with regard to either of those two capital objects.

Adam Smith considered agriculture as the most important of all occupations for, he suggested, 'nature labours along with man,' and 'No equal capital puts into motion a greater quantity of productive labour.' His message was basically optimistic but the melancholy cleric Thomas Malthus, in his *First Essay on Population*, published in 1798, took a gloomier view. The growth in the population — estimated at 6,500,000 in England and Wales in 1751, and known to be 9,100,000 in 1801, when the first census was taken — must, argued Malthus, inevitably outrun the ability of the land to support it. His predictions were to be invoked for at least the next half century as an excuse for doing nothing, such as reducing the price of bread, which might cause the poor to adopt more profligate ways, although he was by no means an unqualified defender of the Corn Laws. 'Feed the people from home-grown wheat if you can,' he summed up, 'but feed them' — if necessary, he implied, by cheap imports.

The Act of 1773, designed to stabilize the price of corn by encouraging its export when prices were low and its import when they were high, proved hard to operate. It was strengthened in 1781, and replaced by an even harsher statute in 1791. Petitions against the new law were still pouring in from the expanding manufacturing areas when, in 1793, the whole situation was changed by the outbreak of war with France. The war, and the first of a series of bad harvests, sent prices soaring. By August 1795 wheat stood at the unprecedented 'high' of £5. 8s. 4d a quarter, having almost doubled in price in eight months, and the government briefly contemplated a system of public granaries, where grain would be stored for sale at subsidized prices, only to abandon the scheme following opposition from rich politicians like Edmund Burke. 'The moment that government appears at market,' wrote Burke, 'all the principles of market will be subverted. . . . The capital to be employed in the purchase of grain would be enormous. The waste, delay and corruption would be a dreadful drawback to the whole dealing.' Instead, Parliament took a whole series of other steps designed to make life a little easier for the poor. The use of grain in making starch and hair powder was forbidden, a bounty was paid on imported wheat at various periods, and both Houses carried a resolution pledging themselves, and recommending their neighbours, to reduce the amount of wheaten bread their families ate by at least a third. At the same time bakers were encouraged to sell a coarser type of bread made from a mixture of types of flour and labelled 'M', but — perhaps suspecting an attempt to poison them to reduce the population — the poor refused to buy it, its brown colour being regarded with distrust.*

None of these devices made any real contribution to starving off the revolution which the governing classes feared. Instead the powder keg of discontent was defused by subsidizing wages, under the soon-notorious Speenhamland system, first practised in 1795, under which any man whose income, even when in work, was inadequate to support his family had it made up to a specified minimum out of the poor rates, the amount being related to the number of his dependants and the price of bread. This cumbrous,

*This fear seems hard to credit, but was widespread when bread replaced monetary relief under the 1834 Poor Law Amendment Act. See my book *The Workhouse*, p.73.

intrinsically unsatisfactory device was only ended by the Poor Law Amendment Act of 1834 and the general introduction of the workhouse.

Meanwhile bread became ever dearer. Wheat stood at £7.3s. 2d a quarter in March 1801, a new record, prompting many riots, and Parliament that November formally suspended the laws permitting the export of grain and imposing a duty on imports. Peace, agreed in March 1802 but lasting only to May 1803, was too short-lived to bring an enduring respite and, following a new crop of petitions, this time from the rural areas, pleading for the protective laws to be restored, a private member's Bill imposing a new and heavier scale of duties was hurried through the House of Commons in less than a week. It became effective on 15 November 1804.

The law did not pass without protest, including a vigorous outburst from William Cobbett, who denounced the Prime Minister for having 'listened . . . to the advice of contractors and corn merchants . . . and . . . speculating farmers' whose 'object was to obtain a law . . . for the sole purpose of advancing their own interest, though the well-being of the whole nation should thereby be hazarded'. In the event, the law had hardly been passed when it had to be suspended.

In 1809 and 1810 there was a further, unexpected twist to the already tangled story. Napoleon finding himself with a huge surplus of wheat, and Great Britain finding herself with an inadequate harvest, the British government agreed to import a large quantity of wheat from its enemy across the Channel. These two years apart, little corn was imported during this period and in April 1814 the war with France ended, though it was briefly resumed between March and June 1815. Even before Waterloo, however, the price of corn had tumbled, from £5. 17s. 10d in June 1813 to £3. 9s. 7d in May 1814, and the farmers and landowners were clamouring for Parliament to help them. The result was predictable. A Bill preventing the sale of corn from abroad unless the price of home-grown wheat rose above £4 a quarter was introduced on 1 March 1815, achieving a second reading two days later.

The Bill's opponents made much of its unpopularity in the country, and the London mob, prompt to respond to its cue, provided ample confirmation of their dislike of it. On 6 March 1815 the crowds thronging the road outside the Mansion House to sign petitions against the Bill were so huge that many had to go away frustrated, and that evening the windows of some of its known aristocratic supporters were smashed and vast crowds blocked the roads leading to the House of Commons. The following night it was the turn of the homes of the Prime Minister, Castlereagh, in St

James', and of the Vice-President of the Board of Trade, Frederick Robinson, who in introducing the Bill into the Commons had rashly declared that opposition to the Corn Laws had declined. The angry mob surging outside his own front door demonstrated the contrary in no mean fashion and only dispersed after three soldiers and the butler had opened fire and killed several rioters. That same evening the crowds smashed the windows of a pro-government paper, the *Morning Herald*, in Catherine Street off the Strand, and gave three cheers outside the offices of the more sympathetic *Morning Post* nearby. The homes of suspected supporters of the Bill were ransacked, and the diarist (and later pro-Corn-Law propagandist) John Wilson Croker complained that on his way to the House he was 'surrounded by a tumultuous mob who demanded his name and requested to know how he had voted on the Corn Bill'. Another MP reported that he had been 'assailed with sticks and his friend had his coat and waistcoat torn,' while a third had been 'carried above a hundred yards on the shoulders of the mob just like mackerel from Billingsgate market'.

> The mob is particularly enraged against the three great parishes of St Marylebone, St George, Hanover Square and St James', which comprehend the town houses of nearly all the great families of the United Kingdom [reported the *Morning Post*]. They complain of these parishes for not having called a Vestry [i.e. a meeting of the representative body of ratepayers] to petition against the Corn Bill; and hence it is that they direct their course up among the great squares after Parliament rises, or when driven away from the vicinity of the Houses of Parliament.

With the House of Commons unsympathetic to the Anti-Corn-Law cause some newspapers appealed for support to the peers or even to the Crown. The *Brighton Herald* reminded their Lordships of the petitions against the Bill now heaped upon their table from 'so great a portion of the well-informed and well-disposed part of the community'. The *Statesman* suggested that the Prince Regent should simply refuse his assent if the Bill were carried. All such pleas proved in vain. The Lords, a week after the Bill had reached them, spent two hours receiving petitions against it, but remained unimpressed by them, one peer even arguing that signatures on such a scale could only have been secured by compulsion. The Bill was then given a third reading by 128 votes to 21. Eleven of the minority exercised an ancient privilege and entered a written protest recording their reasons, providing an admirable summary of the case against the Corn Laws at that time:

1   Because we are adverse in principle to all new restraints on commerce. . . . We think it certain that public prosperity is best promoted by leaving uncontrolled the free current of national industry. . . .

2   Because we think that the great practical rule of leaving all commerce unfettered, applies more peculiarly, and on still stronger grounds of justice as well as policy, to the corn trade than to any other. Irresistible indeed must be that necessity which could, in our judgement, authorize the legislature to tamper with the sustenance of the people and to impede the free purchase and sale of that article, on which depends the existence of so large a portion of the community.

3   Because we think the expectations of ultimate benefit from this measure are founded on a delusive theory. We cannot persuade ourselves that this law will ever contribute to produce plenty, cheapness or steadiness of price. . . .

On 23 March 1815 the Bill received the royal assent and entered the statute book as 55 George II Cap. 26, 'An Act to amend the law now in force for regulating the Importation of Corn.' It was relatively brief, running to only twelve clauses, covering three printed pages, and its heart lay in clauses three to four. Here was the actual 'Corn Law' against which so many protests were to be made:

And be it further enacted, that such foreign corn, meal or flour, shall and may be permitted to be imported into the said United Kingdom, for home consumption, under and subject to the provisions and regulations now in force, without payment of any duty whatever, whenever the Average Prices of the several sorts of *British* corn, made up and published in the Manner now by Law required, shall be at or above the Prices hereafter mentioned; (that is to say) whenever Wheat shall be at or above the price of eighty shillings *per* quarter; whenever rye, pease and beans shall be at or above the price of fifty-three shillings *per* quarter; whenever Barley, Beer, or Bigg [Beer and Bigg were varieties of barley] shall be at or above the price of forty shillings per quarter; and whenever oats shall be at or above the price of twenty-seven shillings per quarter.

And be it further enacted, that whenever the average prices of *British* corn so made up and published, shall respectively be below the prices herein-before stated, no foreign corn, or meal, or flour, made from any of the respective sorts of foreign corn herein-before enumerated, shall be allowed to be imported into the United Kingdom, for the purpose of Home Consumption, or taken out of warehouse for that purpose.

Special provisions were made for 'corn, meal or flour' produced in Canada, but with this exception the Act effectively and totally prohibited the importation of corn unless the price of the home-grown variety rose to a level which, when translated into the cost of a loaf, was likely to cause real hardship. Eighty shillings a quarter was an extremely high price, only twice exceeded between 1815 and 1820, namely in 1816 and 1817 when post-war distress was at its height.

The 1815 Act satisfied no one. The farmers continued to complain that they were badly off, because of the burden of taxation and of tithes; their labourers, with more reason, protested because they so often went hungry. In the cities, working-class feeling was increasingly concentrated on the campaign to extend the franchise, reaching its bloody climax in St Peter's Fields, Manchester, on 16 August 1819, in the notorious Peterloo Massacre, when a holiday crowd demonstrating peacefully for electoral reform were cut down by the dragoons, leaving eleven dead or dying and hundreds wounded. To most working-class leaders the Corn Laws seemed an irrelevance compared to the real struggle, for political freedom. There was little outcry when the Corn Law of 1815 was in 1822 amended by a new Bill, which passed the Lords on 10 June. This revived the idea of a sliding scale of duty. Foreign corn was now excluded when the home-grown variety was available below 70s a quarter. When it cost more, imports were allowed but with a declining scale of duty, according to the domestic price; 12s when wheat cost between 70s and 80s, 5s when it cost from 80s to 85s, and only 1s when it rose above 85s. This attempt proved no more successful than its predecessors and achieved the distinction of being scourged by Byron in his long poem *The Age of Bronze*, first published in 1823, and later quoted on many a platform:

Alas the country! How shall tongue or pen
Bewail her now *un*country gentlemen,
The last to bid the cry of warfare cease,
The first to make a malady of peace.
For what were all these country patriots born,
To hunt, and vote, and raise the price of corn?
But corn, like every mortal thing, must fall.
Kings, conquerors, and markets most of all.

In 1827 the law was, though only temporarily, changed again, to allow foreign wheat already in British warehouses to be released for consumption on a lower scale of duties, and in 1828 there was another major statute, 9 George IV, Cap. 60, which became law on 15 July 1828. Its forty-eight clauses, spread over twenty-one pages of text, went into enormous detail about precisely how the current cost of corn was to be calculated, specifying the towns from which weekly details of the prevailing price being paid to farmers were to be supplied by a local Inspector to the central Controller of Corn Returns in London, and even setting out the wording of the oaths these officials were to take on appointment. The heart of the Act, however, lay in the sections which specified what duties imported corn should pay, on a sliding scale based on the home price of British corn; 'corn' for this purpose also included, though with a different level of prices and duties, oats, barley, rye, peas, beans, maize, oatmeal and flour.

The scale of duty was set out in great detail, and was based on the expectation that corn would normally cost between £2. 12s and £3. 13s a quarter. When it dropped to £2. 12s the duty, of £2. 0s. 8d, would almost double its price. The duty then dropped gradually to £1. 4s. 8d at £3, 14s. 8d at £3. 5s and 2s. 8d at £3. 10s. From £3. 11s and above it was 1s, a token amount designed merely to preserve the principle of taxation.

Some dire predictions as to what would happen if the Bill were passed were made in the House of Commons, especially about the fate of 'our unoccupied and famishing artisans' in time of scarcity, but in neither House was there as much opposition as in 1815. The principle of taxation was by now well established and the Act did at least allow the importation of corn at any time, at a price, and did not, unlike the Act of 1815, exclude it altogether at certain price levels.

The comparatively peaceful reception of the 1828 Act gave little hint of the bitter controversy which was so soon to surround it. When 'the Corn Laws' were denounced in the next twenty years it was the 1828 Act which was primarily meant, although some provisions of earlier laws on the subject had also been retained. Already, however, the voices of the critics could be heard, the most powerful being that of a Member of Parliament, Colonel T. Perronet Thompson, who issued a new edition of his popular *Catechism on the Corn Laws*, which will be quoted later. Few of those who attacked the Corn Laws had mastered all their details to the same extent, but all understood the fundamental truth which no amount of oratory could conceal, that their purpose was to keep up the price of bread — a realization sufficient in itself to ensure that they would not be accepted without a struggle.

CHAPTER TWO

Stable and Regular Government

'With the return of stable and regular
government . . . the Tory Party will gradually
regain its political ascendancy.'
— *Morning Post*, December 1832

Like every earlier Corn Law the Act of 1828 was neither as beneficial
nor as disastrous as had been predicted. In 1831 imports amounted
to more than 3,500,000 quarters, the largest amount so far, out of a
total United Kingdom consumption of 52,000,000 quarters. By
now public and politicians alike were preoccupied with a far more
immediate and exciting struggle, for what later became known as the
Great Reform Bill, though this was closely linked to the Anti-Corn-
Law cause. 'From 1815 to the period when some considerable
parliamentary reform was seen to be inevitable,' wrote Archibald
Prentice of the *Manchester Times*, 'its necessity was mainly argued
from the impolicy and the injustice of the corn laws.' Concentration
on the one, however, tended to divert attention from the other, as a
contemporary historian explained:

> When the Sheffield Mechanics' Anti-Bread-Tax Society was first
> instituted [in 1831], the members, in common with most of their
> countrymen, had almost ceased to hope for a reform in
> Parliament. Determined to invite the legal cooperation of all the
> oppressed throughout the kingdom they formed themselves into
> an association, with the design of attacking a particular point in
> the enemy's line. By overthrowing the Corn Laws, they knew
> they would compel their enemies themselves to become
> reformers. The announcement of the Reform Bill, in the infancy
> of their union, induced them to suspend their operations.

The First Reform Act proved, once passed into law in 1832, a
bitter disappointment to most of those who had fought for it.
Although it removed many of the more picturesque electoral
qualifications and corrected the worst injustices in the distribution
of seats, such as the non-representation of Manchester — the fifth
greatest city in the kingdom, with a population in 1831 of 182,000,
or close on 200,000 including its environs — it still increased the
electorate of the United Kingdom only from 510,000 to 720,000, in

an adult male population, aged twenty and upwards, of 10,200,000. Until 1831 one in twenty adult males had had the vote; now it was one in fourteen. The vast majority of working men, especially in the rural 'county' constituencies, were still disenfranchised and, with voting public, intimidation or indirect influence by landlord or employer remained easy. This had indeed been the government's deliberate intention, and though Manchester and other important places, like Birmingham, now returned two Members of Parliament, they still possessed only a meagre electorate in relation to their size.

Although the Act was a disappointment, the way a Member had voted on the second reading of the Reform Bill became the test of his commitment to the popular cause, especially in the next General Election, which continued from 8 December 1832 until 15 January 1833. (At that time the poll took place on different dates in different places and a man could stand in several constituencies at once.) Manchester was one of the first places to vote, with five candidates competing for its two seats. When the poll finally closed, on Friday 14 December 1832, after three noisy days, about 10,000 votes had been cast and a known opponent of the Corn Laws topped the poll with 2,923 votes, followed by Charles Poulett Thomson, Vice-President of the Board of Trade in Grey's government, with 2,069. (Poulett Thomson should not be confused with Colonel T. Perronet Thompson, who also at various times sat in the House, though as a backbench MP.) The 'Whig-radicals', as Prentice described them, thus secured both Manchester seats, pushing an old-fashioned Whig, who favoured a moderate duty on imported corn, into third place, and an acknowledged Tory into fourth. More surprisingly, an out-and-out Radical, the legendary William Cobbett, came bottom of the poll, though comfortably returned for Oldham, where he was also standing.

Using the test of who was elected as a government supporter, the House of Commons which assembled on 29 January 1833 contained 483 Whigs and only 175 Tories, but about 300 of the former were 'old-style' members of their party, and no fewer than 217 of the Tories were the sons of peers or baronets. The membership of the new Parliament seemed reassuring to the traditionalists. The *Morning Post* predicted that, with the excitement of the Reform Bill behind it, the country would now go back to its natural allegiance:

> With the return of stable and regular government . . . the Tory Party will gradually regain its political ascendancy . . . simply because it has a great, manifest, and indestructible superiority over every rival party in its association with the historical glory of

the nation, in its possession of large masses of property, and its insuperable connection with the education, the intelligence and the respectability of the country. . . . Neither vote by ballot, nor universal suffrage, nor both of these combined, would retard this restoration.

But the effects of 1832 went deeper and wider than was apparent on the surface. Parliament was now sufficiently representative to make a sustained campaign for some specific change in the law worthwhile, though for the moment those seeking to see the Corn Laws repealed were disappointed, as Archibald Prentice observed:

> The King's speech on the opening of Parliament did not contain any allusion to an improved commercial policy. . . . The cry of 'Do not embarrass the ministry' had already been raised. It was found exceedingly effective in repressing the impatience of those who had thought that the Reform Bill was but an instrument for the attainment of other necessary reforms. . . . When the instrument was obtained, there was a reluctance to use it immediately, as if the axe would cut more effectively after it had rusted.

The new government had plenty to occupy it, in particular the Poor Law Amendment Bill, which aimed to set up the new workhouse system, and the Municipal Reform Bill, introducing a more representative system of local government. When the issue of the Corn Laws was finally raised, on 17 May 1833, the Leader of the House immediately replied that Parliament had more urgent business to attend to. 'The country,' confessed Archibald Prentice, 'showed little disposition to urge ministers forwards. The "not-the-right-time" plea was admitted.' In his paper he urged the formation of local associations devoted to stirring up 'a systematic opposition to the continuance of the bread tax,' but had little success. Nor did another Manchester man who published a pamphlet urging reformers everywhere to take a formal pledge rather like that which the teetotal movement, also established in 1832, was currently promoting against drink. 'We this day,' read the free traders' vow, 'commence a system of agitation against the iniquitous Corn Laws, which we solemnly pledge ourselves shall terminate only with their abolition.'

There was, however, a pretty general belief that ministers, 'at the right time', would be faithful to their free-trade professions. Even Manchester, Archibald Prentice complained, reacted only 'listlessly' to those efforts. Nor did a private meeting of merchants and manufacturers held on 29 January 1834 to promote repeal, achieve anything. 'The sun was shining,' commented Prentice caustically, 'and there was never to be a rainy day again.'

Fine weather meant good harvests, which made foreign imports unnecessary, and between 1832 and 1835 the price of wheat dropped steadily, from £2. 18s. 8d in 1832 to £1. 19s. 4d. When the issue was raised in the House of Commons, on 6 March 1834, even the modest, half-way proposal of a fixed duty in place of the sliding scale introduced in 1828 was vigorously opposed. One of the Manchester MPs, Poulett Thomson, a junior member of the government, strongly criticized his ministerial colleagues and urged the House not to wait until a bad harvest meant that 'a change of the Corn Laws would be called for in much less respectful language,' but he spoke in vain; the motion to set up a committee to examine the proposal was thrown out by 313 to 155. Three months later Poulett Thomson was promoted to a Cabinet post, as President of the Board of Trade, where he made a start on demolishing the network of duties behind which British manufacturing industry sheltered. Agriculture remained sacrosanct and unaffected.

For the moment all was tranquillity, as Archibald Prentice acknowledged:

> One could . . . draw the curtains and wheel round the sofa nearer to the cheerful fire, and the more enjoy the social meal, from the conviction that there was comfort also in the cottage, and no wailings in the street. It was worth something on the Saturday night to see the working man's wife need her husband's help to carry home the heavy basket, filled with bread and beef, and flour and suet. But then came the reflection that the Corn Law was unrepealed, and that a single bad harvest might mar all this comfort.

In July 1934 Lord Melbourne succeeded Grey as Prime Minister and in November the Whig government fell. A brief caretaker administration under the Duke of Wellington was succeeded in December 1834 by a new ministry under Sir Robert Peel. A General Election followed, in January and February 1835, in which the Conservatives made some gains, but when Parliament met, on 19 February 1835, they were still in a minority, with 273 Members against the Whigs' 385. Lord Melbourne now returned to Downing Street, and Poulett Thomson to the Board of Trade. However, far from any change in the law being contemplated, the government, according to Prentice, found Whig Members from rural constituencies 'complaining of the "distress" occasioned by the

plentiful harvest and demanding more protection. . . . Much
outcry came from the landowners at the cheapness of provisions, as
if heaven-sent plenty was a curse.' The reformers' efforts to secure
support prompted the reply 'Why should we agitate for cheap food
when wheat is only four shillings and sixpence a bushel?'

Despite such discouragements the opponents of the Corn Laws
remained active, especially in Lancashire, and during 1835 the man
whose name was ever after to be associated with it, the thirty-one-
year-old Richard Cobden, a calico-printer already making his name
for a combination of 'good taste and . . . business ability,' first
appeared on the political stage. Cobden made his debut
anonymously, in unsigned letters to Archibald Prentice's
Manchester Times, but later that year he produced a pamphlet
entitled *England, Ireland and America* which was 'circulated in tens
and thousands' and was one of the first to argue that 'the doctrine of
free trade and non-intervention in the affairs of other states' went
hand in hand. Cobden sent similar articles to the *Westminster
Review* and *Tait's Magazine*, as well as to the newspapers, while
Prentice distributed with the *Manchester Times* four thousand
copies of the *Catechism on the Corn Laws*. Late in 1836 an Anti-
Corn-Law Association was founded in London. Its committee, 74
strong, contained no fewer than 22 MPs, among them Thomas
Wakley, founder of the *Lancet*, and the temperance reformer James
Silk Buckingham. Non-MP members included the veteran radical
Francis Place, Archibald Prentice from Manchester, and repeal
enthusiasts from other provincial towns. The Association, which
should not be confused with the body of the same name founded
later, achieved little other than keeping the subject alive, and when
in March 1837 another attempt was made in the House of Commons
to impose a single fixed duty (of 10s a quarter), only 89 Members
supported the motion while 223 were against it.

Queen Victoria's accession, in June 1837, on the death of William
IV, meant a dissolution and a General Election in July and August,
which reduced the government's support in the House to 345,
against the Opposition's 313. Poulett Thomson and his fellow
Whig-radicals were comfortably returned for Manchester. Another
'advanced Whig', Joseph Brotherton, was returned for Salford, and
protectionists at Wigan and Oldham lost their seats to free traders,
though Richard Cobden just failed to gain election at Stockport.
The results demonstrated once again how effective the Reform Act
had been in weighting representation in favour of the status quo. It
was the small, ancient boroughs — fifty of which, as Archibald
Prentice complained, contained only as many electors as
Manchester — which overwhelmingly returned protectionists. The

great cities, Glasgow, Leeds, Birmingham, Nottingham and Leicester, all returned known opponents of the Corn Laws as did seven London constituencies. All told, Archibald Prentice identified thirty-eight MPs as unquestioned repealers, representing about five-million people (though only a small fraction of these had votes). But the faithful thirty-eight had to wait before raising their voice in the new Parliament, for it 'did not meet till November. There was the grouse shooting and the partridge shooting to be attended to.'

In March 1838 the radical MP Charles Villiers, of whom more will be heard, began his long parliamentary campaign against the Corn Laws by calling for an enquiry into their working. 'The House,' complained Archibald Prentice, 'would not inquire — would scarcely even listen,' though the ninety-seven votes he mustered included some from members of the government. On 2 July 1838 the subject was reopened with the presentation in the House of Lords of a repeal petition from Glasgow. This time the Prime Minister himself made the government's position clear. It would not, he assured the House, come down on one side or the other until certain that the majority of the people desired a change — though how they were to express their wishes, with an electoral system deliberately loaded in favour of the small, overwhelmingly Tory, boroughs, was not apparent.

By the time the House dispersed for the long recess Charles Villiers was close to despair, as he revealed in a letter dated 15 August 1838 to a sympathizer in Birmingham, Joseph Sturge, of whom more will be heard later:

> Before I left London I put a notice on the books to the effect that I would call the attention of the House to the taxes that raised the price of food, contracted the commerce of the country, limited the demand for labour, lowered the profit upon capital, and yielded nothing to the revenue. I will take the earliest opportunity in the next session to bring the matter on with a view to a motion for the total repeal of such taxes . . . I am determined to ask for nothing short of this, because they are *in principle* opposed to justice and sound policy and are really threatening this country with tremendous evils.

CHAPTER THREE

Vile and Silly Laws

'I hereby constitute and appoint you my
lieutenant-general against those equally vile
and silly Corn Laws.'
— Lord Brougham to Joseph Sturge, 29
September 1838

The first signs of progress in mobilizing opinion against the Corn
Laws came from outside Parliament. Two months after Abraham
Paulton's first public appearance at Bolton, Archibald Prentice
arranged a similar meeting in Manchester, on learning that a well-
known traveller and advocate of free trade, currently in the news,
Dr John Bowring, was passing through the city. In spite of the short
notice sixty people, out of a hundred invited, turned up at the York
Hotel on the evening of Monday 10 September 1838.

They were not disappointed. Bowring was an interesting,
colourful personality. The son of an Exeter wool merchant, he had
an astonishing aptitude for foreign languages, including such
obscure tongues as Arabic and Chinese, and a rare mixture of
business acumen and literary talent: his doctorate was an academic
honour not a medical qualification. On his travels to negotiate with
foreign governments he had also collected material for anthologies
of foreign poetry, and had got himself imprisoned by the Bourbons
while assisting the anti-monarchist cause in France. Having stood
unsuccessfully for Parliament in 1832, he was elected in 1835 for the
Clyde Boroughs, as an 'advanced Radical', and sat till 1837,
returning to the House in 1841 as MP for Bolton. Like many
opponents of the Corn Laws, Bowring was an all-round reformer,
voting the progressive 'ticket' on education, the Factory Acts,
slavery and the abolition of flogging in the army. Still only forty-five
in September 1838, Bowring delighted his audience with a rousing
attack on the Corn Laws and a vigorous panegyric on free trade:

It is impossible to estimate the amount of human misery created
by the Corn Laws, or the amount of human pleasure overthrown
by them. In every part of the world I have found the plague-
spot. . . . When I went into Normandy and Brittany, what said
the Normans and the Britans [i.e. Bretons]? 'Why,' said they,
'admit our corn and then we'll see whether anybody can prevent

the importation of your manufactures into France.' (Cheers.)
'We are millions,' said they, 'willing to clothe ourselves in the
garments you send us, and you have millions of hungry mouths
to take our corn.' The same language is held by every nation in
trade. . . . Why England, if once she pleased, might become the
universal benefactor! Ask the Duke of Wellington, and the other
advocates of the Corn Laws, as to what would be the
consequences of a war? Do you believe that war would be
possible when we had universal trade? . . . Who would seek to
quarrel with those who were perpetually communicating to them
benefits and blessings?

Two weeks later, on Monday 24 September 1838, seven of those
present returned to the York Hotel to form the Anti-Corn-Law
Association. A French visitor to Manchester, writing seven years
later, described these pioneers as displaying 'that manly
determination which characterizes the Anglo-Saxon race' and their
names certainly suggested impeccably British origins: Archibald
Prentice, Edward Baxter, W.A. Cunningham, Andrew Dalziel,
James Howie, James Leslie and Philip Thomson. The subscription
was fixed at a low-enough level, 5s a year — a third to a quarter of a
loom-minder's or mechanic's weekly wage — to ensure 'that all
classes should be included as members'.

Within a week Prentice was able to announce a membership of
'nearly one hundred' and he urged each existing member to bring
with him in future 'a list . . . of the names of half a dozen friends'
who might also be recruited. Prentice himself was already emerging
as a militant in a basically peaceable movement and his report in his
newspaper of this first, key meeting struck a typically combative
note:

> We believe that what might be thought to be apathy on the part of
> the merchants and manufacturers of Manchester upon the subject
> of the Corn Laws, has arisen from there being no organization for
> the expression of their opinions. They have expected that the
> Chamber of Commerce would commence the movement, but
> that self-constituted body, having satisfied itself with a single
> petition in seven years, seems to have fallen into another seven
> years' sleep.

By 13 October 1838 Prentice was able to announce the formation
of the Provisional Committee of the Anti-Corn-Law Association,
thirty-seven strong. It included a wealthy local businessman
Thomas Potter, soon to become Manchester's first mayor, and the

son of a Rochdale mill-owner, John Bright, aged twenty-six, who had already made his name both as a temperance orator and as a successful calico-printer. A week later the name of Richard Cobden, eight years older than Bright, was added. The whole Committee lacked as much as a single 'honourable' between them, though a comparable body in a rural area would have been loaded down with earls, marquesses and baronets. Here was a new phenomenon in British history, a middle-class organization that neither sought nor needed upper-class patronage, but if its supporters lacked social distinction they were not short of money. 'You will soon need more than such sums. Put me down for ten pounds,' said one when Prentice called to collect his 5s subscription, and eventually the Committee alone contributed more than £10,000 to the new movement's funds.

The first general appeal for public support came with a meeting at the Corn Exchange, Manchester, on the evening of Thursday 25 October 1838. The star attraction was the young Bolton medical student, Abraham Paulton, and the chairman was John Benjamin Smith, a local businessman and treasurer of the Provisional Committee. He had for years campaigned so ardently for free trade that he had been nicknamed 'Corn-Law Smith' or, less flatteringly, 'mad Smith'. The spacious building was packed and Smith's introductory remarks explaining why the Association had been founded nicely matched the mood of the meeting:

It had been established on the same righteous principle as the Anti-Slavery Society. The object of that society was to obtain the free right for the negroes to possess their own flesh and blood. The object of this was to obtain the free right of the people to exchange their labour for as much good as could be got for it; that we might no longer be obliged by law to buy our food at one shop, and that the dearest in the world, but be at liberty to go to that at which it can be obtained cheapest. It was an object in which men of all political opinions might unite without compromising those principles and it was a fundamental rule of the Association that no party politics should be mixed up in the discussion of the question.

This last assertion, his hearers may have reflected, was somewhat unrealistic, but, for public consumption, 'no party politics' had the right high-minded ring, and Smith went on to publicize a phrase that was to epitomize the whole campaign:

It might seem to be a work of supererogation to prove that a man had a right to a big loaf, but when we saw the nobles of the land, the majority of our senators, and men of wealth and education contending that the indulgence of an appetite for big loaves was fraught with consequences no less serious than the ruin of the landowner, the farmer, the labourer and ultimately of the nation, it was then that lectures like these became necessary to show the absurdity and fallacy of such assertions. Mr Paulton was a big-loaf man, but if any of the little-loaf men, or any of the noble lords who occasionally came amongst us on visits of humanity, to inquire into the condition of the poor factory children, or the wretchedness of the hand-loom weaver, would favour us with a lecture to make us sensible of the benefits we derive from little loaves, as friends of free discussion as well as free trade, he thought he could promise them from the meeting a fair and patient hearing.

Smith's introduction was followed by a two-hour lecture by Paulton which produced, as Prentice claimed, 'not the slightest appearance of weariness on the part of the audience'. A return appearance, a week later, brought in 'a still more crowded audience' and J.B. Smith, again in the chair, revealed that Paulton, who had so far given his services free, was in demand by 'other towns' and that 'the Committee were endeavouring to effect an arrangement with him for this purpose'.

From the first a strong element of support for the movement was provided by the Quakers. The Friends, as they preferred to call themselves, opposed the Corn Laws both on moral grounds, believing that restricting international trade encouraged war, and because many of them objected in principle to governmental interference in commerce. John Bright was typical of the group, but far more influential in the early days was Joseph Sturge of Birmingham, already famous at forty-five as an indefatigable campaigner in the causes of peace and social justice. The son of a Gloucestershire farmer, Sturge had refused, as a pacifist, to pay a proxy to serve for him in the militia and had, at eighteen, seen his sheep driven off to pay the resulting fine. He next, as a successful corn dealer, refused to handle malting barley, destined to be turned into whisky or beer, but having moved to Birmingham, continued to prosper and became an alderman. The first major cause to attract his attention was slavery, and with its total extinction throughout the British Empire he looked around for a new cause to champion. What more natural then that he should follow the lead of Charles Villiers MP, indeed was there not a debt to be repaid? As Sturge's biographer explained, 'Mr Villiers had been one of his most faithful associates in his struggle for the liberation of the slave. It was very natural therefore that he [Sturge] should be anxious to do all in his power to strengthen the hands of that gentleman in those assaults upon the Corn Laws which for some years he so gallantly sustained.'

Sturge's support was also considered important by the veteran reforming statesman and former Whig Lord Chancellor, Lord Brougham, who on 29 September 1838 wrote to him in encouraging terms:

I heartily rejoice at your coming into the Corn Law controversy. I regard you as already a veteran and a veteran who has gained a great victory; and I hereby constitute and appoint you my lieutenant-general against those equally vile and silly Corn Laws. I am ready, of course, to do my duty, but I much doubt if my going to Birmingham would serve the cause so well as presiding at a London meeting, which I am quite ready to do, and had promised to do before getting your letter.

Though rarely prominent in public, Sturge now became, and remained, an elder statesman of the movement. Villiers, Cobden and 'Corn-Law' Smith all regularly consulted him and in Prentice's words he placed 'the whole question upon the eternal principles of justice and humanity which, he said, were shamefully outraged by a tax on the food of the people'. It followed that no compromise was possible. 'Mr Sturge,' his biographer recorded, 'strongly urged them to take, as the ground of their appeal to the country, nothing less than the total and immediate abolition of the Corn Laws,' with results which one of those involved later described:

I remember how little the great majority were prepared for anything so strong and uncompromising, and how gladly nine-tenths of us would have avoided the question at the time. But I believe that it was our late friend who, fresh from the experience of the anti-slavery struggle, pointed out the necessity of taking our stand on the rock of abstract truth and justice; and I must say we found it our rock of safety during our . . . struggle.

The League's leading parliamentary spokesman, Charles Villiers, had, as already mentioned, left London when Parliament adjourned in August 1838 in despair of gaining support there, but, not for the last time, the vagaries of the British climate now came to the reformers' aid. As one wet week followed another, beating down the corn standing ready for harvest, the price of wheat rose, until by the end of the month it stood at more than double the level of the same date two years before. Whatever its effect in the agricultural counties the miserable weather that autumn must have raised the spirits of the free traders of Manchester as they splashed through its grey, ill-paved streets, for there could be no better recruiting sergeant than a bad harvest and dearer bread. By 10 November 1838 Archibald Prentice, ever optimistic, declared in the columns of the *Manchester Times* that a new spirit was abroad:

> The movement against the Corn Laws is likely to be the most formidable ever. The apathy for which we have blamed the population of large towns has not existed, for all that has been wanted has been concentration of opinion, and this will be obtained by associations such as the one of which Manchester has set the example. There needs but a spark to ignite the mass of smouldering discontent. To supply this, let lectures be delivered everywhere, bringing into one view all the mischiefs that are occasioned by the starvation-creating laws and the certain ruin of our manufacturers and workpeople. . . . The landlord papers in the metropolis have taken alarm and are abusing Mr Paulton in good set terms for the boldness with which he denounces the robbery. We rejoice to think that he will soon deserve a larger share of their abuse. On Monday the 26th, and Wednesday the 28th instant, he will lecture in the Birmingham Town Hall, a magnificent building, capable of containing from 4,000 to 5,000 persons, and we have no doubt that it will be filled on each occasion. In the meantime invitations pour in upon the eloquent lecturer from the large towns in our neighbourhood, and he has been pressingly requested not to omit the agricultural towns in Norfolk, where the opinion's fast spreading that the Corn Laws are injurious rather than beneficial to the farmers, the farm-labourers and all with whom they expend their money.

Paulton's debut in the Midlands, at Birmingham Town Hall, proved, as his companion J.B. Smith recorded, very encouraging, for 'a crowded audience filled the place,' and at Wolverhampton next day 'we had a crowded and enthusiastic audience'. A return visit to Birmingham a day or two later, however, provided the first experience of opposition from the Chartists, who considered the real remedy for all the nation's ills to be universal male suffrage. 'At the close of the lecture in a motion of thanks, an amendment was carried in support of the Charter which it was contended would settle the grievance of the Corn Laws and all other grievances. The amendment was carried by [an] overwhelming majority.'

The meeting was presided over by the mayor, who . . . was so astounded by what he called the violent language of the lecturer that he hastily left the meeting at its conclusion; declaring that he had been imposed upon and that nothing would have induced him to preside at a meeting of Chartists. The next day we heard from all our friends that the mayor was denouncing us in all quarters and had created a great prejudice against us among [the] respectable classes. . . . The fury of the mayor caused such an excitement that at the time of [the next] meeting the place was immediately filled and there remained as many people as would fill two other rooms of the same size. . . . We were received with loud applause but there was no chairman . . . I thought it . . . best . . . to take the chair myself . . . and Paulton proceeded with his second lecture. . . . The mayor having denounced us as Chartists had the effect of rallying the people round us. The meeting from the beginning to the end was one of the most exciting I remember. . . . When I left the chair people crowded round me to shake hands and one respectable-looking old gentleman shook me with both hands and with tears in his eyes exclaimed 'God Almighty bless you. You are the real friends of the poor and industrious classes!'

The real proof of the successful foundation of the movement came from Manchester. In the first-ever borough elections, held in 1838, following the Whigs' reform of municipal government, the Anti-Corn-Law Liberals carried all before them, securing a large majority on the Borough Council, where Thomas Potter became mayor. Even more remarkable, however, was the conversion of the Chamber of Commerce, representing all the leading businessmen in the area. Ten years earlier J.B. Smith had moved a motion in favour of free trade but could not find even a seconder. 'When,' recorded a retrospective newspaper article a few years later, 'he brought the self-same motion at other periods, members of that drowsy Chamber took to shaking their heads and wondered if he were quite right in his mind' — hence the nickname 'Mad Smith' already quoted. For ten years Smith had tried, and failed, to persuade the Chamber to send a petition to Parliament against the Corn Laws. As late as February 1838 it repeated that decision but during the autumn the President was called on to summon a special meeting on the subject. When held, on 13 December 1838, it attracted the largest turn-out on record. J.B. Smith, his hour come at last, expressly disassociated himself from the feeble draft petition — which implied approval of a moderate, fixed duty on corn — and with the help of Richard Cobden, by now a Manchester alderman, secured an adjournment for a week.

In the intervening period the results of the municipal elections proved, as already mentioned, a triumph for the free traders, and on 20 December 1838 the resumed meeting of the Chamber of Commerce agreed enthusiastically that something even more sacred than corn was at stake, namely, cotton. The cotton trade, a new petition pointed out, owed 'no sort of allegiance to the soil of England' and potential competitors were springing up everywhere with the help of 'skilled English mechanics,' while the growth of railways all over Europe and the United States had removed 'the superiority we have hitherto possessed in our unrivalled roads and canals'. The only security for the future lay in free trade, for no foreign country was going to go on buying Manchester's textiles if Great Britain refused to accept its corn.

As one successful cotton merchant or spinner after another declared that 'the repeal of the Corn Law had been so long delayed that the country must gradually sink into utter ruin without an instant change,' Prentice observed that 'a great impression was produced on the assembly,' and after five hours' debate, when the vote was called at last, only four or five hands were raised against the motion, which supported an outspoken and explicit petition:

> Your petitioners cannot too earnestly make known that the evils are occasioned by our impolitic and unjust legislation, which, by preventing the British manufacturer from exchanging the produce of his labour for the corn of other countries, enables our foreign rivals to purchase their food at one half the price at which it is sold in this market; and your petitioners declare it to be their solemn conviction that this is the commencement only of a state of things which, unless arrested by a timely repeal of all protective duties upon the importation of corn and all foreign articles of subsistence, must eventually transfer our manufacturing industry into other and rival countries. . . . Maintaining the practice of protecting one part of the community at the expense of all others to be unsound and unjustifiable, your petitioners earnestly implore your honourable House to repeal all laws relating to the importation of foreign corn and other foreign articles of subsistence; and to carry out to the fullest extent, both as affects agriculture and manufactures, the true and peaceful principles of *free trade*.

The Prime Minister, Lord Melbourne, though not yet familiar with the precise terms of the Manchester resolution, was well aware that trouble was brewing for his government over this issue. On 29 December 1838 he wrote to his most important subordinate, Lord

John Russell, the Home Secretary, after what seems to have been a somewhat miserable Christmas — 'I have been ill these two or three days, and almost unable to do anything — gout, or bile, or both' — giving a private explanation of his own position:

> I suppose the present high prices will make the Corn Law a serious question, which it never has been since the year 1815. I own I dread it very much, not so much from either the difficulty or the danger of the question itself, as from the conviction that it will not be settled either one way or the other without a very severe struggle, a struggle which will increase all the evils of the present day by leaving behind it more animosity, discord and alienation than even prevails at present. Nothing is so bad in my mind as abuse and condemnation of classes of society, and this question naturally produces it.
>
> There are some who hold that a freer importation of foreign corn would not cause a single grain less to be grown in this country. I cannot be of this opinion. If it would diminish the home growth, I cannot but doubt whether a large labouring population, dependent in any considerable degree upon foreign corn, is in a safe position, and whether it is not worth some sacrifice to insure a supply within ourselves, as far as it can be insured. . . .
>
> Thomson's idea is prohibition up to an average price of 35s, a fixed duty of 10s from thence to 70s, and after that free importation . . . if there is to be a change it appears to me the best that can be made. But, depend upon it, any advantage that can be gained is not worth the danger and evil of the struggle by which alone it can be carried.

CHAPTER FOUR

The Great Object

'And to adopt any other measures to secure the great object of the Association which they may think fit.'
— Resolution setting up the Anti-Corn-Law League, 20 March 1839

The old year had ended in triumph for the free traders of Manchester; the new one, 1839, began with promise. On 10 January 1839 a meeting was held in the York Hotel to 'consider the proper mode of carrying forward the proceedings of the Anti-Corn-Law Association in a manner commensurate with the magnitude of the obstacles to be surmounted, and worthy of the object for which it has been established'. After the Chairman, a Conservative — a word now replacing the older 'Tory' — had declared that protection threatened his business, Richard Cobden suggested that those present should regard donations to the Association as an investment, and a flood of gifts followed, with one man promising 'half of all he possessed if it were needed'. £1,800 was collected that evening, and a finance committee was set up to launch an appeal for further funds. Week by week lists of subscribers, many of them local companies, were published in the local newspapers, until by 9 February 1839 the Association's bank balance had reached £6,136.10s.

Meanwhile, on 22 January, a public dinner in the Corn Exchange had attracted eight hundred people, including the mayors of Leeds, Hull and Bolton. This was no mere social occasion. Even the royal toast had a propagandist ring: 'Our Queen, Duchess of Lancaster; may she long reign over an industrious people, unshackled by Corn Laws, or any other monopoly'; it was followed by two even more pointed: 'The total and unconditional repeal of the Corn and Provision Laws,' and 'A cheap loaf for the people.' A whole series of toasts then ensued, each progressively more ambitious, until the company was drinking to 'Peace and free trade with all the world'.

Next morning the delegates got down to business, listening to reports from various parts of the country. In Glasgow, it appeared, eighty thousand people had already signed a repeal petition; in Leeds fifteen thousand; in Liverpool a resolution at a public meeting had been carried by fifty to one. Everywhere, the 'gradualists' who favoured a step-by-step lowering of duty, or a small fixed tariff, had been routed, just as in the Manchester Chamber of Commerce — with which, however, the reformers still had a score to settle.

The Manchester members reassembled a week later, on 28 January 1839, to put their own affairs on a more formal basis. The Manchester Association's aims were declared to be to 'obtain by all legal and constitutional means, such as the delivery of lectures, the distribution of tracts, the insertion of articles in the public papers, and forwarding petitions to Parliament, the total and immediate repeal of the corn and provision laws'. The five-shilling subscription and the rule banning 'party political discussions' were confirmed. The Association's organization was also agreed, with a large Council of 'not less than one hundred . . . to be chosen by the members out of their own body,' specialist committees for Finance and Petitions respectively — Richard Cobden sat on the former and John Bright on the latter — and a twelve-man Executive Committee, to manage day-to-day affairs. This included both Cobden and Prentice, though the President of the Association, and its nominal head, was J.B. Smith.

The Prime Minister, meanwhile, had determined only to be indecisive. On 11 January 1839 he had written from Downing Street to his President of the Board of Trade, Poulett Thomson, to praise a speech about the Corn Laws which the latter had submitted for his approval, though questioning whether it would be wise tactically. 'Telling people that they have been hitherto silent,' Melbourne commented shrewdly, 'is exciting them to make a noise in future. But I do not see how this can be helped. Whether the address is prudent or not is another matter. . . . There is in it a good deal of sarcasm. The middle and lower orders are very touchy and above all things hate to be sneered at.'

To his Home Secretary, Lord John Russell, who sent him the text of a declaration he was about to make favouring a fixed duty on corn, Melbourne was even more candid:

I think this letter will do very well . . . as an expression of your opinion, which I do not think a very tenable one. If there are no other reasons for a duty on importation except the *peculiar matters* [Melbourne's italics] and the land, I doubt whether it can be maintained in argument. I should wish some words or a sentence to be introduced which should guard against your letter being taken as the opinion of the government. . . . I am not prepared, on account of the present high prices, to put myself at the head of this Corn-Law movement. If the feeling and opinion are weak, we shall fail. If strong, we shall still only carry it by the same means as we carried the Reform Bill, and I am not for being the instrument . . . of another similar performance.

Melbourne's reference to 'peculiar matters' echoes the famous euphemism of the 'peculiar institution' of negro slavery and, recognizing a potentially damaging division in the government's ranks, he returned to the subject only a week later, in another letter to Russell:

I am quite convinced and, as far as I can determine it, determined that the Corn Law should remain open. The present outcry is raised evidently by the master manufacturers, taking advantage of the present dearness of corn, and with the object of lowering wages. It is not at present very strong; but if we, the government, adopt it, as we shall do by making it a government measure, we shall strengthen it at once to such a degree that we shall be ourselves carried away by it. Keeping it open will give us time to see what the real feeling is both in and out of Parliament. I am not prepared to give my voice for a free importation of corn. I doubt whether the property or the institutions of this country can stand it.

Collective Cabinet responsibility was not yet an established constitutional doctrine and it does not seem to have occurred to Melbourne to drop his Board of Trade President because he disagreed with him. 'With respect to P. [i.e. Poulett] Thomson and the Corn Laws,' he wrote to the Home Secretary on the following day, 21 January 1839, '. . . I do not see why P. Thomson should not move upon the question as Member for Manchester, just as Plunket, when Irish Attorney-General in 1825, moved the Roman Catholic question [i.e. lifting the legal disabilities on Roman Catholics] whilst Lord Liverpool was against it.' In further letters during the next week Melbourne repeated his desire not to commit himself. 'I do not care how open the question is left, but I am not prepared to pledge myself to a fixed duty,' he wrote to Russell on 23 January. 'I hope you will be able to persuade Thomson and Howick [Viscount Howick, Secretary at War, another member of the Cabinet] to acquiesce in this.' On 29 January he wrote to Russell: 'I have no objection to inquiring into the operation of the Corn Laws, if that course is thought prudent or would be in the least satisfactory.'

Melbourne's unwillingness to give a firm lead seems to have accurately reflected the mood of his colleagues. There was a disarming candour about the letter sent to him on 3 February 1839 by Lord (John Charles) Spencer, who as Viscount Althorp had formerly served as Chancellor of the Exchequer, but who, on succeeding to the family earldom in 1834, had retired with relief to his estate in Northamptonshire and to his real loves of hunting, racing and prize-fighting. If his Party needed him, he was, he revealed, even prepared to abandon his beloved Pytchley Hunt in the very middle of the season:

> The state of the Corn-Law question, and the certainty . . . that it will be discussed in the House of Lords have frightened me from coming up. I could not avoid stating my opinion upon it if I was in the House of Lords . . . and . . . my opinion — which is against the Corn Laws altogether — would do you no good. . . . My opinion is that, if there are to be any Corn Laws at all, the present system is as good as any that can be devised.

On the very Sunday that Lord Spencer was writing this letter the delegates of the local Associations which had met at Manchester during January were making their way to London, to assemble on Monday morning at Brown's Hotel in Palace Yard, Westminster. Some of those expected did not turn up on time, it being against their religious principles to travel on a Sunday. Those who did arrive soon discovered that the Corn Exchange, Manchester, and the House of Commons were two very different places. The Corn Laws were, once again, not even mentioned in the Queen's Speech but the seconder of the humble address of thanks was the President of the Manchester Chamber of Commerce, George Wood, a half-hearted 'gradualist'. Dutifully, as his constituents had urged — he was MP for Kendal in Cumberland — he criticized the harmful effects of the Corn Laws, but 'elated by the honour conferred upon him by ministers', Prentice believed, he went on to praise the peaceful and prosperous state of the country. The visiting 'strangers' listened in growing indignation, consoling themselves, a reporter from the London *Examiner* commented, with 'whispered assurances . . . that "Wood was a deep fellow and would wind it all round before he sat down."' Instead, the *Examiner* man noted, carried away by 'the respectful attention of Sir Robert Peel' and 'the startling applause of the country gentlemen . . . the orator himself continued, brick by brick to demolish the foundations of the castle he was commissioned to garrison'. The dismay of 'the advocates of free trade in the House' and 'the nervous anxiety of the delegates under the gallery' was, thought this journalist, so 'irresistibly droll' as to be worthy of the Adelphi Theatre. Peel confounded them still further by commending Wood 'for the very able speech he had delivered in favour of the existing system' and thanking him, as 'the President of the Chamber of Commerce at Manchester' for 'the account which had been given them of the stable and secure position of our commerce and manufacturers'.

The Times next day rubbed salt in the wounds of the disappointed delegates with a typically facetious 'colour piece' about the previous day's proceedings:

> Not a word of the Corn Law in the speech [i.e. the Speech from the Throne], not a word of that question which has of late so much disturbed the kingdom. . . . The fact is, that between the opposite terrors of the landed interest and the commercial, the ministers have no pluck left in them. As a Cabinet they dare not budge an inch. Lord Melbourne gave an explanation of his own Corn-Law intentions, which would have better become the namby-pamby neutrality of a bedchamber-woman. [This was a reference to the Queen's Ladies of the Bedchamber, who were traditionally of the same political complexion as the government. The Queen's refusal three months later to replace her Ladies when there was a change of Prime Minister led to a constitutional crisis.] 'I am not prepared to bring in a bill for repealing the Corn-Law Bill . . . nor will I bind myself on any future occasion to give my vote against it.' A nice way this of splitting the difference between the manufacturers and landlords — a kind of bidding for whosoever shall turn out to be the strongest. Ministers . . . wishing to curry political favour with the opposers of the existing law by the assumption of a vast eagerness for its repeal, yet shrink from incurring the disapprobation of their own Whig aristocracy by tendering that repeal as a government measure.

The Times scornfully accused the Home Secretary, Lord John Russell, of having 'found it necessary to sop [i.e. give a sop to] the manufacturing interest by pledging himself to vote for a Corn-Law modification,' a comment vindicated by events that very day. 'It would be his duty,' Hansard reported Russell as saying, 'to oppose the motion as to hearing evidence at the Bar [of the House]. . . . At the same time . . . when a mode was proposed which he thought was confirmable to precedent, and not inconvenient to the House, by which these facts could be ascertained he should be willing, although not ready, to propose it himself, to support a motion so to ascertain the facts.' This elaborate double-talk infuriated even such a loyal Whig as the writer Harriet Martineau, who recalled that Lord John Russell had declared to his constituents 'that the existing Corn Laws were indefensible'. His position, she commented, was that of a man who 'disapproved [of] the Corn Laws in the abstract — just as the Carolina planters disapprove of slavery in the abstract'. The result of Russell's attempt to have it both ways, declared Miss Martineau, was to 'weaken him . . . in every one of the various positions in regard to the Corn-Law question, in which he afterwards endeavoured to establish himself'.

The repealers' chief fury, however, was reserved for their supposed spokesman, George Wood. At a meeting at Brown's Hotel on Wednesday 6 February 1839, *The Times* reported next day, it was 'contended that he had the previous night proved himself to be a most unworthy member' of the Chamber of Commerce of which he was President. That weekend a public meeting in Wood's own constituency passed a resolution condemning their Member's behaviour and anyone with a business connection with Manchester was urged to join the Chamber of Commerce for the express purpose of giving its President his come-uppance. When, six days after Wood's disastrous speech, the annual election of directors of the Chamber was held, the Anti-Corn-Law Association swept the board. At a meeting of more than a hundred strong 'only about twenty hands' were raised in support of Wood, who was deposed and succeeded as President by 'Corn-Law' Smith, the directors who had supported him also being rejected in favour of out-and-out free traders.

While in London the Anti-Corn-Law delegates did their best to press their views upon influential people, but had little success. Lord John Russell said he was too busy to see a deputation, and the Duke of Wellington, with soldierly forthrightness, turned them down flat. 'I am not in the habit,' he wrote, 'of having interviews with, or even receiving the visits of gentlemen with whom I have not the honour of being acquainted, much less of deputations.' Advancing their cause in London, wrote J.B. Smith despairingly to Cobden, was 'like descending into an ice-box compared with Manchester,' and even that star of the northern circuit, Abraham Paulton, failed to make much impression. 'I went last night to hear Paulton lecture at the *Crown and Anchor,*' the Vice-President of the Manchester Association, C.J.S. Walker, wrote home to a sympathizer there on 14 February 1839. 'The audience did not amount to one hundred persons, although the admission was free. So much for the excitement here.'

The visit to London was by now proving an expensive, as well as an unproductive, business. Paulton's expenses, for which he had to produce detailed bills, came to £84. The delegation as a whole, it later emerged, had spent at least £500, much of it on press advertisements and on hidden subsidies to newspapers, of which they promised to buy a large number of copies of any issue containing a pro-repeal article. In Parliament they had had no

success at all. Wood's inept performance in the House and private
hostility — he had, they learned, told Poulett Thomson that they
were only a set of noisy agitators who had no influence — had for
the present crippled their chances.

A motion moved by Charles Villiers, on Monday 18 February
1839, that a number of petitions should be referred to a committee of
the whole House was rejected without a division. On the following
day, armed with 'a vast number of additional petitions', he tried
again, proposing that J.B. Smith and others 'should be heard at the
Bar of the House'. A debate followed, which ended in the motion
being rejected by 361 to 172, a majority of 189, 'and this',
despairingly commented Archibald Prentice, one of those waiting
to give evidence, 'in a House in which the Whigs, professedly the
friends of free trade, had yet a preponderating majority'. Among
those voting in the majority were Lord Palmerston, Lord John
Russell, and the Conservative leader Sir Robert Peel, who declared
that 'the repeal of the Corn Laws would be grossly unjust to the
agriculturists'. Two members of the government supported Villiers,
Poulett Thomson and Sir John Hobhouse, President of the Board of
Control — an example of 'the agreement to differ' accepted by
Melbourne in operation. When the disappointed free traders
flocked to Brown's Hotel to voice their indignation, Richard
Cobden did his best to raise their spirits. Their allegiance, he told his
audience, would be a Hanseatic League* against their feudal Corn-
Law plunderers. The castles which crowned the rocks along the
Rhine, the Danube and the Elbe had once been the stronghold of
feudal oppressors; but they had been dismantled by a League; and
they now only adorned the landscape as picturesque memorials of
the past, while the people below had lost all fear of plunder and tilled
their vineyards in peace. No doubt gratified by these metaphors, the
repealers dispersed. Their departure, Harriet Martineau noted,
delighted their opponents who had greatly disliked seeing 'the train
of delegates going down to the House', but, observed one
journalist, 'The departure of the delegates was like the breaking-up
of a Mahratta camp† — the war was not over, but only the mode of
attack was about to be changed.'

The subject was certainly not considered closed by the men who
now left London, by train and stage-coach and private carriage, to
bear their dismal tidings to their own Associations, though the

---

*The Hanseatic League was formed by the merchants in ports around the
Baltic in the fourteenth century. The members accorded each other trading
privileges and imposed their own terms on outside towns and rulers.
†The Mahrattas were an Indian tribe perpetually at war with the British.

reporting-back session in Manchester was a fiasco. At the Corn Exchange, on 28 February 1839, the Chartists successfully wrecked the meeting and were able to carry instead a motion congratulating the delegates to the National Chartist Convention. More immediately important, however, was the opposition in Parliament. On 12 March C.P. Villiers again tried to get the House to agree to examine the Corn Laws; observing the dictates of parliamentary procedure, MPs spent five sittings debating whether or not to do so. Eventually, on 19 March 1839, came the division, with a slightly smaller majority, 147, than the 189 recorded a month earlier, with 342 MPs going through the 'No' Lobby and 195 'Ayes'. The Anti-Corn-Law lobby therefore needed either to convert at least another 140 MPs to their cause, or else to produce a change in public opinion that the House could not ignore. As Harriet Martineau put it: 'The delegates had offered to instruct the House; the House had refused to be instructed; the House must be instructed; and the way now contemplated was the grandest and most unexceptionable and effectual — it was to be by instructing the nation.'

The process began in earnest the following day, 20 March 1839, when the delegates endorsed the decisive resolutions which were to transform the previously sporadic, localized efforts into a coordinated and sustained national campaign:

> The formation of a permanent union, to be called the Anti-Corn-Law League, composed of all the towns and districts represented in the delegation and as many others as might be induced to form Anti-Corn-Law Associations and to join the League.
>
> Delegates from the different local associations to meet for business from time to time, at the principal towns represented. . . . The central office of the League shall be established in Manchester, to which body shall be entrusted, among other duties, that of engaging and recommending competent lecturers, the obtaining the cooperation of the public press, and the establishing and conducting of a stamped circular [i.e. a regular news-sheet liable to Stamp Duty. The later history of this publication is given in Chapter 11], for the purpose of keeping a constant correspondence with the local associations.
>
> That, in addition to the funds subscribed for local purposes by the several Associations, at least £5,000 should be raised to defray the expenses of the general League for the ensuing year, and that every sum of £50 entitle the individual, or Association subscribing it, to one vote in the appropriation of the funds of the League, and that on all other questions the votes of the persons present be equal. That this meeting adjourn, subject to the call of

the Manchester Anti-Corn-Law Association; that it be left to their discretion at what time to bring forward the substantive question for the total abolition of the Corn Laws before Parliament, and to adopt any other measures to secure the great object of the association which they may think fit.

The League's first president was, almost inevitably, J.B. Smith, with, as chairman of the League Council which managed day-to-day affairs, George Wilson, a professional organizer, until recently secretary of the group formed to secure Manchester's charter of incorporation as a borough. The third of the men effectively directing the new League was Richard Cobden. These three, and the thousands who supported them, set out to change the whole structure of British political and economic life, and to demonstrate that the decisive factor in the political and economic life of the nation was no longer the 'agricultural' and 'landed' interest, but the manufacturing and commercial section of society.

CHAPTER FIVE

The League is Manchester .

'You speak of the difficulty of getting on
without funds from the League. The League is
Manchester.'
— Letter from Richard Cobden to Taunton
man, 1840

From first almost to last the heart of the struggle against the Corn
Laws lay in Manchester, the symbol and citadel of the new industrial
age. The foundation of the Anti-Corn-Law movement coincided
with Manchester's incorporation as a borough. Its royal charter was
received on 1 November 1838, and on 15 December the newly-
elected Council met for the first time and chose Thomas Potter as
mayor. Economically and educationally, too, 1838 was a landmark.
In May the ten-mile-long railway linking Manchester with Bolton
was opened, in July the *Jack Sharp*, a steam-operated canal boat
carrying 150 passengers, began to ply upon the River Irwell. In
February the Manchester School of Design was opened, in May the
Zoological Gardens, in June the Salford Mechanics Institution. The
city was traditionally regarded in London as a hotbed of
revolutionary sentiment, but the meeting in Manchester in May of
the Fourth Socialist Congress attracted little attention, while the
Coronation of the young Queen Victoria, in the following month,
was enthusiastically celebrated.

Politically, however, there was never much doubt where
Manchester's sympathies lay. Hitherto, the city had lacked a cause it
could make supremely its own: the fight against the Corn Laws was
to provide one. In no other place could leadership and objective,
temperament and tactics, have been so ideally matched. In no other
area were so many people, of such similar background and opinions,
in almost daily contact with each other, united, despite their
business rivalry, by a recognition of common interest. The leaders
of the cotton industry were aware, whatever anachronistic illusions
the farming community might cherish, that the country's wealth
increasingly depended upon their skill and enterprise. In 1815
cotton manufacture had contributed about 7–8 per cent of the whole
national income; by 1830 it accounted for half the value of all British
exports, produced by a mere half-million people, almost all of them
living within a day's ride — by horse not railway — of Manchester,

with perhaps another million in related occupations such as transport, building and engineering. The city's rapid expansion had taken its population from a mere 20,000 in 1750 to nearly 90,000 in 1801 and 300,000 in 1841.

The filthy rivers, the close-packed houses, many with cellars crammed with Irish families, the mill-studded skyline, with tall chimneys pouring forth black smoke: all were famous throughout the kingdom. A character in one of Disraeli's novels, published in 1844, spoke of 'the grandeur of Manchester' and even compared it with Athens. However, a visitor who toured the town in 1841 found it a sobering experience:

> It is essentially a place of business, where pleasure is unknown as a pursuit and amusements scarcely rank as secondary considerations. Every person who passes you in the street has the look of thought and the step of haste. Few private carriages are to be seen; there is only one street of handsome shops, and that is of modern date; there are some very stately public buildings, but only one of them is dedicated to recreation, the rest are devoted to religion, charity, science or business. . . . The men are as business-like as the place. . . . Were I asked how a stranger could best form a notion of the character of the Manchester manufacturers, I should recommend him to visit the Exchange of Manchester at the period of 'high change' . . . noon on a Tuesday. It is the parliament of the lords of cotton, their legislative assembly, which enacts laws as immutable as those of the Medes and Persians; but, unlike every other parliament in the world, very much is done, and very little is said.

Manchester in 1844, published that year by the French writer Leon Faucher, gives a detailed picture of the area at the height of the Anti-Corn-Law agitation:

> Manchester . . . is . . . an agglomeration the most extraordinary, the most interesting, and in some respects the most monstrous, which the progress of society has represented. The first impression is far from favourable. . . . Amid the fogs which exhale from this marshy district, and the clouds of smoke vomited forth from the numberless chimneys, labour presents a mysterious activity, somewhat akin to the subterraneous action of a volcano. . . . All the houses, all the streets, resemble each other; and yet this uniformity is in the midst of confusion . . . Manchester is situated at the confluence of the little river, the Irwell, swollen by the waters of the Irk, and of a brook called the

Medlock. The manufactories and machine shops form, as it were, a girdle around the town, and follow the courses of the streams. Factories, seven stories in height, rear their lofty fronts along the banks of the Irwell, and along the borders of the canals. . . . The waters of the Irk, black and fetid as they are, supply numerous tanneries and dye-works; those of the Medlock supply calico-printing establishments, machine shops and foundries. The banks of the Irwell, which appear to have been the principal seal of this civilization, still form the centre of it. The primitive municipal buildings are scattered along its course. Descending from the hill where the workhouse has its situation, you come to the buildings of the College, the Old Church, and the Exchange, and upon the other side, the Court of Sessions, and also the Gaol.

The 'Exchange', of course, was the Cotton Exchange, heart and centre of Manchester's business life, but these buildings apart, the town seemed given up to industry and commerce:

From Pendleton to London Road is one great thoroughfare, crossing the town from east to west. At its extremities are ranged the shops which supply provisions and the necessaries of life; and, at the centre, in Market Street, the shops are devoted to luxuries, the libraries and newspaper offices, etc. The aristocratic quarter called Mosley Street, which joins Market Street at right angles, contains the warehouses of the principal manufacturers; and in the angle of the two streets are concentrated the storehouses for raw material and manufactured goods. The railways, being of recent formation, terminate at the exterior points of the circumference; those of Liverpool, and Bolton to the west, and those of Leeds, Sheffield and Birmingham, to the east. . . . The railways penetrate the town upon immense arcades to the points where it ceases to be inconvenient to load the merchandise upon them, and the canals pass under the streets, and thread their sinuous way in every direction, conveying boat-loads of coal to the doors of the manufactories and even to the very mouths of the furnaces. . . . There is perhaps good reason for complaint that too little attention has been paid to the health and convenience of the inhabitants; the want of public squares, fountains, trees, promenades and well-ventilated buildings; but it is certain that it would be a difficult task to devise a plan by which the various products of industry could be more concentrated, or by which the manufactories could be brought nearer to the fuel which feeds them, or more accessible to facilities for disposing of the goods when manufactured.

One curious feature of Manchester was the appearance of inactivity which the streets often presented:

> During the greater part of the day the town is silent, and appears almost deserted. The heavily-laden boats glide noiselessly along the canals . . . between rows of immense factories. . . . The long trains roll smoothly along the lines of the railway. . . . You hear nothing but the breathing of the vast machines, sending forth fire and smoke through their tall chimneys. . . . At certain hours of the day the town appears suddenly animated. The operatives going to, or returning from, their work, fill the streets by thousands; or it is perhaps the hour of 'change and you see the chiefs of this immense population gathering to one common centre.

The character of the city was altering as the more successful manufacturers, instead of living close to their mills and warehouses, moved out into the suburbs. The working people remained behind, although catered for by a growing range of amenities. Between 1839 and 1846 a whole series of new schools, adult-education institutes and scientific academies were opened, along with humbler premises for public wash houses and baths, a new post office and the Lyceum Theatre. Even more plentiful were the public houses and beerhouses: Manchester and Salford in 1841 had between them 1,267 to serve a population, as revealed by the census that year, of 288,362 for the two municipal boroughs, or 309,607 in the two parliamentary constituencies. The most numerous new buildings of all were places of worship. Most of the leading citizens were Anglican, and 30,000 of the 34,000 Irish were Roman Catholic, but all denominations shared in the building boom. 'Even the Quakers,' complained one member of the Manchester Athenaeum — which itself moved into impressive new premises, designed by Sir Charles Barry, in 1839 — 'have been infected with the prevailing fashion; and . . . the spirit moves them in a building so heathen in its architecture that Jupiter . . . would not be disgraced by it.' To the existing twenty-two Anglican churches, two more were added in December 1839 and no fewer than ten after 1841, the most impressive, Holy Trinity, Hulme, which was designed by the future Sir Gilbert Scott, costing more than £18,000.

Although what it got was churches, what Manchester really *needed* was paving-stones, sinks and water-closets. Even allowing for the notorious deceptions of nostalgia, the evidence given by a 51-year-old mechanic, Titus Rowbotham, to a government committee during this period undoubtedly contained an element of truth:

When I came to Manchester in 1801, the operatives, like myself, were better fed, better clothed, more moral, and of a more vigorous constitution. . . . They were joiners, carpenters and colliers, who were induced, by the higher wages, which spinning yielded, to abandon their handicraft trades, and become spinners. These men brought their wives with them, women who had been accustomed, like themselves to outdoor employment. Their children, reared in the manufactories, had much more feeble constitutions. . . . Their mothers have neither time nor instruction to give them, and they grow up more vicious and demoralized . . . I have seen three generations of operatives. I know men who are of my age . . . who have passed their lives in tending the mule jenny. Their intellect is enfeebled and withered like a tree. . . . The long hours of labour and the high temperature of the factories produce lassitude and excessive exhaustion. The operatives cannot eat, and seek to sustain life by the excitement of drink. . . . This is the first step; they finish by abandoning themselves to drunkenness and gambling; their health decays, their intellect is depraved, and the money which is spent in such degrading pursuits is abstracted from the food and clothing of their children.

For this gloomy view the statistics provided some support. 'No town,' wrote M. Faucher in 1844, 'contains so large a proportion of widows and orphans.' The death rate among children was even higher: 'out of 1,000 infants in the labouring classes, 570 die before they have completed their fifth year'. Those who survived, he believed, tended to be weak and undersized. This last charge was reaffirmed in the *Manchester Guardian* in August 1843, where it was stated that 'the Army recruiting officers found great difficulty in obtaining men of the minimum height,' but there could be a very different explanation, as Faucher's translator pointed out: 'Is it,' he asked, 'that men are not big enough, or that they are too big to stoop to the degradation of selling their liberty and becoming instruments of slaughter for eighteen pence a day?' This question remained unanswered, but Manchester was, Faucher discovered, overwhelmingly working-class:

The town strictly speaking . . . is only inhabited by shopkeepers and operatives; the merchants and manufacturers have detached villas, situated in the midst of gardens and parks in the country. . . . At the very moment when the engines are stopped, and the counting-houses closed, everything which was the thought — the authority — the impulsive force — the moral order of this immense industrial combination, flies from the town, and disappears in an instant. The rich man spreads his couch amidst the beauties of the surrounding country, and abandons the town to the operatives, publicans, mendicants, thieves and prostitutes, merely taking the precaution to leave behind him a police force, whose duty it is to preserve some little of material order in this pellmell of society.

Faucher thought the 'operatives' accounted for 'at least 70 or 75 per cent' of the residents and he was fascinated by the way of life of this teeming mass of men and women:

How does this immense population employ the few hours left between the seasons of labour and repose? One would think that after fourteen hours of separation during the hours of labour, the husband and wife, and other members of the family, would be glad to spend the evening hours together at the domestic hearth; but . . . partly from the force of circumstances, partly from bad habits, home has no charms for the operative. After a hasty meal, men, women and children sally forth to saunter in the streets, or to lounge in the beerhouses. If you traverse the poor quarters of the town — Angel Meadow, Garden Street, Newtown St. George's Road, Oldham Road, Ancoats and Little Ireland — you perceive the doors of the cottages open and you are jostled by the crowd of loiterers; but if the weather be cold or rainy the streets are abandoned in favour of the beerhouse and gin shops.

By ten o'clock most people had gone home; with the factory whistles calling their hands to work at 6 a.m. there was little temptation to stay out late, and overall Manchester was a law-abiding place, its occasional turbulence being inspired by political conviction, not by drink or crime. The exception, however, was the Irish population. All told, Lancashire contained 105,000 Irish, in a population of 1,667,000, and almost 35,000 of them lived in Manchester. Their English neighbours tended to take a disapproving view of them. 'The extensive immigration of poor Irish,' considered the translator of Faucher's book, 'has inflicted a deadly blow upon the health and comfort of the working classes in Manchester.' Many were crowded into cellar dwellings, from which, when in funds, they escaped to the public house; the number of children taken to the police station after being temporarily 'lost or abandoned by their parents' averaged more than two thousand a year, though almost all were claimed once the parents had sobered up.

But it was not only the Irish who were badly housed in Manchester. The local Statistical Society discovered in 1836 that more than 12,500 people, in Manchester and Salford combined, lived in lodging houses, which were often breeding grounds for disease and promiscuity. Manchester also contained a considerable number of families just above the vagrant class, who, in Faucher's words, wandered 'from town to town, from factory to factory, seeking work. . . . These unfortunate operatives live in furnished rooms, where several families are often crowded together in a single bedroom, at the rate of threepence each for bedding'.

The drunken and the destitute apart, the wages and living conditions of Manchester's working class were by no means a bad advertisement for the prevailing economic system, as Faucher discovered. 'Factory girls, such as throstle-tenders,' he wrote, 'who in the neighbouring towns earn 5s. 6d to 6s. 6d per week, can get from 7s to 9s in Manchester. The same proportion applies to journey [men], tradesmen, and indeed, to almost every other department of labour.' It was, Faucher thought, possible for a really careful and provident family to live on 10s or 12s, and since the mills could employ the whole family there were many homes with more than 15s coming in — the dividing line, most studies suggested, between a hand-to-mouth existence and reasonable comfort. Some families, indeed, earned as much as £1. 5s to £1. 10s. 'There are,' confirmed one Anti-Corn-Law-League publication of 1842, 'large numbers above want and some who enjoy small luxuries, such as houses with three sleeping rooms enabling them to cultivate habits of delicacy in their families.' Some even had 'a good stock of books, furniture and clothing, and . . . educate their children even at some sacrifice of their wages,' the usual charge being from 2d to 6d a week.

With so much needing to be done in Manchester, abolishing the Corn Laws might have seemed of low priority, but Faucher's editor, a local man and dedicated free trader, disputed this:

> At no previous period in the history of the town, have a greater number of extensive improvements been projected and carried out. . . . The Town's Improvement Bill; the project for providing Public Parks; the improved machinery for the cleansing of the streets . . . the bold project for supplying the whole town with abundance of pure water from the Swineshaw hills . . . the marked attention and labouring investigation devoted to all questions relating to public health and social economy . . . all attest the healthy state of public opinion in Manchester, and confirm the high eulogium which M. Faucher has passed upon its inhabitants when he says 'There is no portion

of society which struggles with greater avidity for a better future'. . . .

But much remains to be done. It is noble to hold out the hand of charity to our suffering fellow townsmen, but would it not be nobler still to raise them above the necessity of imploring it? Is it not better to prevent misery than to console? . . . We have regarded too exclusively the effect; we have been too indolent in tracing the cause.

What then was the true remedy for poverty?

Firstly the attainment of entire FREEDOM OF TRADE . . . to prevent the recurrence of those frightful periodical crises which, like hurricanes of tropical climes, convert the most smiling prosperity into sudden desolation.

Secondly, a comprehensive system of SANATORY REGULATIONS to secure healthfulness, cleanliness, and order in our vast urban population. . . .

Thirdly, a comprehensive and liberal system of SECULAR EDUCATION, combining moral training with intellectual instruction, and open to all classes without distinction of sect or party.

Here was a programme on which liberal and progressive opinion everywhere could agree. Thus it was that the Anti-Corn-Law League set up its offices in Manchester, selecting premises in the very heart of the city, at Newall's Buildings on the corner of Market Street and Cross Street, subsequently the site of the Manchester Exchange and the Royal Exchange Theatre. Newall's Buildings adjoined the Manchester Arcade, a shop-lined passageway which provided 'one of the very few places,' according to a local resident, 'where covered walking shelter could be obtained in wet weather' and 'ladies and gentlemen could walk up and down and have a little social intercourse'. At election times 'this old smoke-begrimed building . . . was a hive of excitement,' and 'as each fresh instalment of the state of the poll was posted up, the populace shouted themselves hoarse with delight,' or engaged in 'the free fights which often accompanied a difference of opinion as to the merits of a candidate'.

Close by stood 'the calendaring warehouse of Goodier, Krauss and Co' and the League official or Council member on his way to a meeting could stand and look 'through the cellar windows' to see 'the large rollers revolving and doing their work'. More important, perhaps, for the busy officials was 'Wheeler's the newspaper shop,' at the Arcade entrance. 'A busy scene it was,' remarked the local writer quoted above, 'when the London newspaper arrived, to see stout old Wheeler in his shirt sleeves, struggling manfully and quickly with the huge pile of papers which were before him,' although the most important, *The Times* — highly priced at 5d (an hour's pay for an unskilled workman) — did not arrive, like the other London papers, until around 1 p.m.

To those who had not visited it, Newall's Buildings sounded a reasonably imposing address, but the League's actual office was unimpressive. 'We sat,' recalled Richard Cobden later, 'in a small room . . . and we had a dingy red curtain drawn across the room, that we might not be chilled by paucity of numbers. Two or three were all that were here on one occasion and I recollect saying to my friend Prentice, "What a lucky thing it is the monopolists cannot draw aside that curtain and see how many of us there are, for if they could they would not have been much frightened".'

CHAPTER SIX

What Plans for London?

'You ask me "What are your plans in London?"'
— Letter from Francis Place to Richard Cobden, 29 September 1840

The euphoria created by the foundation of the Anti-Corn-Law League in March 1839 soon faded. The first and most urgent problem was that many of those who had promised financial support failed to pay up. The Manchester men kept their word, contributing £2,000 of the £5,000 needed to launch the League, but the Scottish Associations failed to contribute a penny of their pledged £2,000 by the end of May, and two lecturers, as will be described later, were despatched to Scotland to shame them into paying up, though without much success. What money the League did receive was spent wisely, but all that the Council's scrupulous accounting achieved was to reveal that it was sliding steadily into debt. Hardly had operations begun than retrenchment was the order of the day. Henceforward lecturers, it was decided, would be sent to places where League supporters would guarantee to pay their expenses, and in November 1839 a fixed scale of fees, related to distance from Manchester and the number of lectures to be delivered, was laid down. There were also economies in the modest headquarters staff. The first secretary of the League was dismissed and replaced in July by Sidney (sometimes spelt 'Sydney') Smith, who was expected to combine with the post the editorship of the League's journal. He was also warned that his 'services would at an early date be dispensed with, as the League was likely soon to break up'; the salary offered was a mere £200 a year, about the pay of a junior curate. Changes were also made in the *Anti-Corn-Law Circular*, to make it at least partly self-supporting. It had been launched, as a fortnightly, on 17 April 1839 but during the summer began to carry advertisements for patent medicines and other distinctly non-political products. The circulation, 15,000 by the end of the year, sounded respectable but sales were small, for any contributor donating £1 or more was put on the 'free' list, and many copies were distributed free to public reading rooms or sympathetic newspapers.

In November 1839 the League's own president, J.B. 'Corn-Law'

Smith, suggested that the League be dissolved; his colleagues decided to hang on, however, for there remained one encouraging sign: the unwavering loyalty of Manchester itself to the cause. A meeting of citizens in the Town Hall produced an overwhelming vote in favour of repeal. The sole opposition came from a Conservative notorious for his involvement in the 'Manchester Massacre' of 1819, who was interrupted by cries of 'Peterloo!' Seconding his resolution were two Chartists; hostility to the League was producing some strange bedfellows. More significant was the formation of a Working-Man's Anti-Corn-Law Association, with its own officers and lecturers, which invited outside speakers to enlighten its members on basic economics, from a free-trade point of view.

A timely test of public opinion as a whole was provided by the by-election which followed the appointment of one of its MPs, Poulett Thomson, as Governor-General of Canada. He gave up his seat, and his ministerial post at the Board of Trade, without regret. 'There is,' he confided to his journal that September, while on board ship, 'no chance of carrying the House with one for any greater commercial reforms, timber, corn, sugar etc.; party and private interest will prevent it.' As for his constituents, 'One could not help feeling nervous and irritated by the constant complaints of not going far enough or going too far.' This stalwart pro-trade Whig was more hopeful of the Leader of the Opposition than of his own party. 'If Peel were in, he might do this' — i.e. reform the tariff laws — 'as he could muzzle or keep away his Tory allies.' His health wrecked by the bickerings of the past three years, Poulett Thomson lived only until 1841, when he died at the early age of forty-two, the first martyr in the Corn-Law struggle.

While Poulett Thomson was on the high seas, Manchester was going to the polls. From the first there was only one real issue. The unfortunate Conservative was forced early on to acknowledge himself in favour of 'a moderate fixed duty,' and when the polls closed on 5 September he had received only 2,762 votes against the 3,156 cast for the successful Liberal, Robert Hyde Greg, a well-known Manchester manufacturer and an active member of the League.

That Manchester should return a repealer was, perhaps, no surprise. But what of opinion elsewhere in the country? The *Anti-Corn-Law Circular* on 29 October 1839 reported a wide-reaching survey of the national and provincial press which revealed that, in a single week, thirteen London newspapers and magazines, including *The Times* and the *Spectator*, had expressed sympathy with the League's cause, and no fewer than forty-five in the provinces —

ranging from the *Aberdeen Herald* to the *Wiltshire Independent* and the *Yorkshireman* — though the latter was less impressive than it sounded, since most sizable towns supported two or more local papers, and Manchester itself had four. In truth, most of the press was still hostile. The *Morning Post*, much read by the aristocracy, suggested that if that vulgar new element in society, 'the manufacturing people,' did not like their country's institutions they should emigrate. 'Take your manufactures away with you by all means, and exchange them anywhere you will, from Tobolsk to Timbuctoo,' its leader-writer wrote scornfully. 'But do not insist on bringing your foreign corn here untaxed, to the ruin of your countrymen. If nothing will serve you but to eat foreign corn, away with you, you and your goods, and let me never see you more.' The London *Standard* also cautioned its readers against being deceived by the current agitation:

> The present cry against the Corn Law is, at bottom, the work of a few commercial swindlers, though aided, no doubt, by the exertions of political swindlers who see the benefit of an agitation calculated to disturb public attention from the misconduct of the Whig government. It is well, however, to remember that the commercial swindlers are the prime movers; because the honest class of traders, who would be the very first victims of a repeal of the Corn Laws, may be entrapped into joining the suicidal movement by what they believed to be good commercial names.

The year ended on a more hopeful note than had earlier seemed possible. Manchester itself presented the most encouraging picture. By now the membership of the local Association had outgrown the capacity of any existing building to accommodate it and a special temporary pavilion was erected on land owned by Richard Cobden at St Peter's Fields, the site of Peterloo in 1819. The significance of the area was not lost on Archibald Prentice:

> The survivors of that fatal day have seen the Reform Bill passed; and many of them, seeing on that blood-stained field a great place of assemblage rising up, to be devoted to the purpose of abolishing, by peaceful and temperate discussion, the oppressive monopoly against which the older radical reformers were all united, began to entertain the hope that . . . the time was coming when selfish monopolies would share the fate of the rotten boroughs.

A hundred men laboured for eleven days to erect the building where this new revolution was to begin, and when finished it was, briefly — before being replaced by the first Free Trade Hall — one of the wonders of the age, at least according to the *Manchester Times*:

> The length is 150 feet; width 104; area 15,750 square feet. In its framework, pillars etc., 4,500 cubic feet of timber have been used; in the flooring of the pavilion and its anterooms 17,100 square feet of three-inch plank; there were twenty-five tables from side to side; it was seated for 3,800 persons, and 500 more found entrance after the dinner. It was lighted by twenty-four chandeliers of twelve burners each, eight chandeliers in the roof of the three aisles, and there were three others at the entrances. Besides these was a device in gas upon the wall above the president's chair, consisting of the word JUSTICE in letters of a yard in length. About 20,000 yards of white and pink calico had been used in the drapery. The whole had a very light appearance, the ground of the draperies forming the walls and roofs of the pavilion being white, panelled by broad bands or fillets of pink and white drapery within, which gives the form of a coned roof to each of the aisles, at a height from the floor of from twenty to twenty-four feet. A striking relief to the almost uniform colour was given by the draperies which cover the front of the galleries. These were of a deep crimson, having mottoes inscribed on them in letters of large dimensions. The one along the principal gallery, directly facing the chair, and extending the whole length of the pavilion, is 'Landowners! Honesty is the best policy.' That on the gallery at the east is, 'Total and Immediate Repeal' and that at the west, 'A fixed duty is a fixed injustice.'

Monday 13 January 1840, when the pavilion was to be opened, took on the air of a public holiday in Manchester, with huge crowds at the Liverpool Road Railway Station to greet Daniel O'Connell and lining the streets to watch the arrival of other delegations. By 5 o'clock the hall was already almost full as J.B. Smith led the mayor and other important guests to the platform, while cheers rose to the tented roof and the band played *God save the Queen*. It was said that ten thousand tickets could have been sold and the successful applicants had their money's worth, politically if not gastronomically, for even the grace was pressed into service, expressing the hope that 'God would bless the great council of the nation' and spare them 'the curse of those who withheld bread from the poor'. Later, the loyal toast was followed by another calling for the 'Immediate and Total Repeal of the Corn and Provision Laws,'

and a third to Charles Villiers MP. Villiers responded on behalf of
the twenty-six MPs present, proclaiming their intention 'to rescue
the country from a law which makes them the scorn and the
mockery of their neighbours. . . . Gentlemen, do fling away this
badge of iniquity, English servility and ignorance'.

All in all, it was a moving occasion, and the caterers were kept
busy for the following evening five-thousand working men from the
Operative Anti-Corn-Law Association filled the hall, with their
women folk in the gallery. 'Although the guests,' commented
Archibald Prentice in the *Manchester Times*, 'did not disperse until
two in the morning nothing untoward occurred. Their scrupulous
decorum at the dinner table, their rivetted attention to the various
speakers, their knowledge of the subjects discussed . . . proved the
gross falsehood of the assertion that they regarded with indifference
the efforts of other classes of society to procure for them the full
reward of their industry and skill . . . which are wickedly
intercepted by the legislation of the selfish landowners.' The
'reward,' he continued, should clearly include 'the elective
franchise, unjustly withheld by Tory obstruction and Whig
finality'.

The Manchester meetings had been merely a preliminary to the
spring offensive in London. What was needed, the League realized,
was a well-known figure to launch a broadly-based organization,
and so they turned to Francis Place, the Grand Old Man of the
Radical movement. The first approach to him, directly after the
Manchester banquet, was unsuccessful, but following the next —
from Charles Villiers, who had worked with Place in the campaign
to secure the penny post — Place did finally agree to attend a
meeting at 154 The Strand, on Monday 24 February 1840. He now
for the first time met Richard Cobden and J.B. Smith, as well as
Sidney Smith and Abraham Paulton. The chairman inevitably
proposed that Francis Place be elected to the Provisional Committee
then set up. 'It would,' felt Place, 'have been absurd of me to have
declined,' and he soon discovered that his colleagues were 'all real
good men of business with zeal for the cause, but most of them
unused to the means of getting up such an association' — the very
expertise he could provide himself.

Place was confident of success in the area he knew best, the trade
unions. 'We have,' he informed Colonel Thompson, 'lists of Trade
Clubs [and] Societies and arrangements are being made to have them
visited.' About the business world he felt less optimism, warning
that 'The great obstacle to a rapid progress in the City of London is
that very many of the influential men are either for a fixed or a
sliding duty.' By August other problems had emerged. 'At the

commencement of their labours,' the first report of the Metropolitan Anti-Corn-Law Association acknowledged, 'the chief difficulties the Committee had to contend against arose from the general apathy which they found to exist among a large portion of the middle class and from the absolute hostility of the working class.'

The Provisional Committee's first action was to try to recruit known sympathizers for a General Committee and the Provisional Committee also contacted every MP who had supported Charles Villiers' motion. As in Manchester, the minimum subscription was fixed at five shillings a year, but those 'to whom the payment of five shillings would be inconvenient' could acquire working-class membership, at one shilling. Another enterprising move was to send a circular to the heads of factories and other large establishments. One man who, with management approval, canvassed factories in Southwark 'disposed of a thousand tickets and handed the Secretary a cheque for the amount'.

This recruitment drive was only just beginning when, on 4 March 1840, Francis Place sent a long progress report to Richard Cobden:

> We have done an immense amount of business, but it is all preparatory — all absolutely necessary.
> 1. We have sent out some six-hundred notes to as many persons requesting permission to put their names on the General Committee list. About 250 are to MPs. . . .
> 2. We have issued in like manner a much larger number to persons requesting them to become members of the Association. . . .
> 3. Time has unavoidably been consumed in discussing Rules and Regulations.
> 4. The same in preparing an address to the people.
> 5. In procuring places in which to hold lectures and discussions.
> 6. In obtaining the consent to Bankers to receive subscriptions.
> 7. In endeavouring to persuade a considerable number of persons of the right sort to consent to work for us in various ways.

Place was apologetic that even more had not been done, but admitted that his real troubles were only just beginning:

> London differs very widely from Manchester and indeed from every other place on the face of the earth. It has no local or particular interest as a town. . . . Its several boroughs in this respect are like so many populous places at a distance from one

another and the inhabitants of any one of them know nothing or next to nothing of the proceedings in any other; and not much indeed of those of their own. . . . [There is] a very remarkable working population, also — each trade divided from every other and some of the most numerous even from themselves . . . [they] are a quiescent inactive race so far as public matters are concerned. The leaders, those among them who do pay attention to public matters, are one and all at enmity with every other class of society. . . . They call the middle class 'shopocrats', usurers . . . money-mongers, tyrants and oppressors of the working people and they link the middle class with the aristocracy under the dignified appellation of 'Murderers of the People'.

There was an even more fundamental difficulty, as Place, a Londoner to his fingertips — his home was at Charing Cross — readily acknowledged:

The people here differ very widely from you at Manchester. You, some of *you*, at Manchester resolve that something shall be done and then *you*, some of you set to work and see it done, give your money and your time and need none but more servants to carry out the details. Our men of property and influence never act in this way. . . . Of the committee of eleven appointed at the meeting which you attended, and half a dozen whom we put on the next day, we have met no more in committee than three four or five until yesterday when we met to discuss our constitution, when seven attended.

The League's provincial supporters knew that the decisive battlefield lay in London. 'A pistol discharged in the metropolis would produce as great an effect as a cannon here,' one in Leeds wrote to J.B. Smith in February. In March 1840 delegates from all over the country once again convened at their old stamping-ground, Brown's Hotel in Palace Yard, before sallying forth in strength — variously said to be sixty and more than two hundred — to tackle the Prime Minister himself. The meeting, on Friday 27 March in the Colonial Office in Downing Street, was described by the sympathetic *Morning Chronicle* on the following Tuesday, 31 March 1840:

The deputation having been received by Lord Melbourne, Messrs Cobden and Sturge entered into various details to show the injurious effects of the Corn Laws. . . . Lord Melbourne then asked what was the object of the delegates — was it a total repeal or an alteration only of the present system? Several delegates answered that 'Our object is a total repeal.' Lord Melbourne: 'But you know that is impossible; you may be assured of that. . . . It would create great disturbances in the state of the country and would violently change our present condition.'

Melbourne's parting words, though courteous, were far from encouraging:

I am very glad to have seen you. It is impossible not to be struck with the intelligence and respectability of such a meeting as this and with the facts that have been mentioned detailing the distress of the country. My own opinion on the present subject has already been declared . . . but you may be assured that I will give all the attention in my power to the information and suggestions you have offered.

A deputation which went to see Lord John Russell on Tuesday 31 March 1840 had even less success, for Russell failed even to appear, pleading an indisposition; they had to be content instead with Sir Francis Baring, the Chancellor of the Exchequer, whose office they 'completely filled,' reported Archibald Prentice, and Labouchere, President of the Board of Trade. Once again the carefully-orchestrated tale was told, until J.B. Smith introduced the 'worthy Borough reeve of Manchester' who 'stated unmoved many instances of serious depression in the property of men of his own class'. But as Prentice recounted:

When he came to . . . detail . . . the distresses of the working classes and to describe one particular family, the members of which, after a life of economy and industry, had been compelled to pawn articles of furniture and clothes, one after another, till nothing was left but bare walls and empty cupboards, his feelings completely overpowered him, convulsive sobs choked his utterance and he was obliged to pause till he recovered from his deep emotion. The tears rolled down the cheeks of Joseph Sturge; John Benjamin Smith strove in vain to conceal his feelings; there was scarcely a tearless eye in the multitude; and the ministers looked with perfect astonishment at a scene so unusual to statesmen and courtiers.

In the House of Commons the following day, Charles Villiers once again called for a Committee of the whole House to 'take into consideration the act of George IV regulating the importation of foreign corn'. The debate was adjourned first to Thursday then to Friday, when it ended without a division, thanks to skilful use of parliamentary procedure. Next day the delegates met at Brown's Hotel to reaffirm their faith in their cause:

> The delegates are not discouraged by the result of the late debate; . . . they derive new determination, as they find new motives for exertion, in all that has occurred . . . they feel their various arguments are unanswered, their cause strengthened, their confidence in ultimate triumph unabated; and they pledge themselves to one another and to the nation, not to relax until the mighty grievance, under which the community is suffering, be removed. . . .
> Disassociating ourselves from all political parties, we hereby declare that we will use every exertion to obtain the return of those Members of Parliament alone who will support a repeal of the Corn Laws.

Meanwhile, Francis Place was pressing ahead with his attempt to establish a firmly-based Anti-Corn-Law Association in the capital, and on the Sunday after the Parliamentary debate, 7 April 1840, he wrote in optimistic terms to a sympathetic MP, Henry Warburton:

> We have made great progress in London. In three weeks from the time that we commenced operations we caused 407 petitions to be presented to the House of Commons with 87,000 real signatures appended to them, all voluntarily signed, and we shall have, I hope and expect, nearly as many more to present. In some factories where large numbers of workmen are employed, they have said 'we are Chartists but we will sign your petition'. . . . By means of a comparatively incomplete organization of a small portion of the great metropolis . . . Mr (Peter A.) Taylor obtained upwards of 100 petitions signed by 40,000 persons.

From the first, the Metropolitan Association prepared for a long-term campaign. A full-time secretary, H.S. Chapman, was appointed, at a salary of £8. 7s a week — more than Sidney Smith had been receiving in Manchester. £31. 19s was spent in fitting out an office in the Strand and £15. 3s. 4d on five months' rent. Smith himself left headquarters to work as a lecturer in London, but the report he sent to Manchester on 2 May 1840 from 2 Trinity Place, Charing Cross, painted a very different picture from that drawn by Francis Place:

I yesterday attended the meeting of the Committee of the London Metropolitan Association and I was . . . disappointed to find that Mr Place's representation to me of the disposition of the majority was altogether exaggerated and erroneous.

The state of the case is shortly this. The Committee consists of men of business who are most sincerely zealous in our cause. They see that the struggle must be a protracted one and that after Mr Villiers' motion is negatived . . . and the summer and autumn come on, a great apathy must succeed the present state of excitement. They have caused a minute finance enquiry to be made and discover that if they are to pay Mr Chapman's salary even the most reduced scale of expenditure will cost at least £30 per week. They know perfectly well that this sum cannot be realized after Mr Villiers' motion is decided and there is extreme anxiety to keep the Society in existence. . . .

I told the Association that as I had been mainly instrumental in calling them into existence I would not on any account permit them to die if I myself should attend at their office all day and night . . . I am determined that this Society *shall* go on.

Although the League always preferred to work by steady, unsensational methods, it planned one publicity stunt, the production in the House of Commons of a specimen of the inferior bread being eaten by British farm labourers. Even this idea was abandoned, however. 'Tell Mr J.B. Smith,' Sidney Smith wrote to Manchester on 4 May 1840, 'that I have seen Mr Hume and he states that he is strenuously advised not to show the black bread in the House.' The decision was not based on regard for parliamentary decorum, as Smith explained. 'He says his specimens have all got hard and useless. He wants fresh specimens when the question comes on — to be ready with, in case the enemy should talk about the finest peasantry in the world.'

That the League had been well advised not to provoke more hostility by such a demonstration was made clear when, on Tuesday 26 May 1840, Charles Villiers reintroduced his motion calling for a debate on the Corn Laws, following the submission already that year of petitions signed by 1,750,000 people. The result was even more discouraging than what had happened two months earlier, as Archibald Prentice indignantly recorded:

It became manifest, the moment he began to speak, that there was a fixed determination to give neither him nor the petitions a fair hearing. He was assailed from his outset with a volley of sounds, such as could have been heard in no other deliberative assembly in the world. The Speaker's calls to order were utterly disregarded and it was not till, losing all patience, he commanded the bar to be cleared and Members to take their seats that the enlightened advocate of free trade could be heard in the gallery. Again did the Babel-like confusion arise, and again had the Speaker occasion, most peremptorily, to assert his authority; but even this would have availed nothing, had not the time arrived when the *fruges consumere nati* ['those born to consume the fruits of the earth'] usually went to dine and then, with about a hundred auditors, Mr Villiers was allowed to proceed.

It was only a temporary respite for the diners returned 'heated with wine':

> Mr Warburton [a League supporter] was assailed in the middle of his speech by loud cries of 'Divide! Divide!' and when Mr Mark Philips, representing a constituency equal to the aggregate of fifty undisenfranchised but still corrupt boroughs, returning seventy-two members, rose to enforce the claims of the most important manufacturing community in Her Majesty's dominions [i.e. Manchester] he was greeted with deafening clamour. It was useless to carry on the discussion under such circumstances. The call for a division was acceded to and the numbers were found to be: against the motion 300, for it 177, majority 123.

Undiscouraged, the Metropolitan Association continued to collect signatures, for circulating a petition provided useful publicity. By 29 June 726 petitions had been returned, bearing more than 200,000 signatures, all collected since 24 February. 'Independent' petitions, drawn up on local initiative, added at least another 110,000 names. By 3 August, when Place's Business Committee issued its first Report, £269. 15s. 0d. had been spent on 'expenses incidental to petitions,' against only £244. 7s. 0d. devoted to 'Salaries and Wages'.

Overall the financial situation of the Metropolitan Association was far from healthy. Despite the earlier talk of thousands of supporters the number of subscribers listed in the Business Committee's Report, which covered the period to 29 June 1840, was only 240, their donations varying from the basic 5s to £50. Of the £862. 4s. 2d received, only £5. 11s. 7d was left. There were other signs, too, that all was not well. Like its parent body in Manchester the London Association had set up a 'Statistical Committee' to assemble economic data to support their case but it proved a failure. 'The Statistical Committee,' Place had written on 14 July 1840, shortly before the Business Committee Report appeared, '. . . have made a sad mess of their business. I am ashamed of them, but I have long been used to such things.' The only consolation, if such it was, was that in Manchester things were, at least so far as cash was concerned, not much better. Even the impressive new pavilion which had housed the enthusiastic crowds who had dined against the Corn Laws in January remained partly unpaid for. 'The League is in debt for the calico . . . to Mr Kenshaw and Mr Callender enormously', Sidney Smith, writing from London, reminded his colleagues, for a reason he soon made obvious: 'Paddy [probably the League's printer], Paulton [Smith's fellow lecturer] and myself are considerable creditors of the League and when these claims are paid off you will find that a large encroachment has been made upon the current funds.'

The end of the season's campaign was marked by a somewhat doleful exchange of letters between Francis Place and Richard Cobden, who had enquired about the situation in the capital. Place replied on 29 September 1840:

You ask me 'What are your plans in London?' My answer relates to the plans of the few men, my coadjuters, who attend the Business Committee.

First, we intended to organize the world of the metropolis, including a space on which dwells about two million . . . people. This went by from want of money. We will do it, if ever we have the means.

Second, an Association has been formed in the Eastern part of London. It includes four or five parishes. Some able men have congregated together, taken the lead, and will conduct it properly as a Branch Association. Two other such are forming, but they may per chance drop through from want of money to pay the expenses we incurred in forming them. . . . We could form similar associations in each of the boroughs, say five or six in each, if we had the means in money. . . . The expense when falling upon one body is very heavy; if it were divided among fifty or sixty sub-bodies it would be but a small sum for each. . . . But to organize the Branches would cost from £250 to £300 and we cannot raise £10 for the purpose. . . .

Third . . . there are many men in each borough who would come forward and act well, had we the means of forming them into associations. . . . It may seem strange that we should be unable to raise money to form such useful associations, but so it is, we have made very great efforts to procure more money but have wholly failed. We have not ten pounds in hand. . . .

Eighth, you ask: 'Cannot it be done in London with a few lords in it?' . . . No lord could be induced to attend. . . . A banquet here must be held at Drury Lane Playhouse, and we could not one quarter fill it. . . .

Ninth, in conclusion. To show you how poor and helpless we are I enclose you a list of the General Committee, every man of whom freely gave his name. . . . When we determined to call a meeting . . . we summoned every member by a special summons — yet only *one* attended and none sent an apology for absence.

Place's reluctance to take second place in any organization may have influenced his attitude, but the account he had submitted was essentially one of failure and Richard Cobden, in his answering letter of 5 October 1840, did not conceal his disappointment:

I am sorry to receive your last long letter which is certainly very much like a dying speech and confession. Is there no hope of sufficient help to keep this thing *nominally* alive? As to Manchester attempting to sustain an unreal show of opinion against the bread tax in London, I think you will agree with me, it would be impossible.

One member of the League's Business Committee remained cheerful and steadfast in adversity, Archibald Prentice, whose look back at what had been achieved during 1840 suggested a powerful organization only just getting into its stride:

During the year . . . no fewer than 763 petitions, with 175,840 signatures, had been sent to the Commons, and 22, with 18,003 signatures, to the Lords. An active correspondence had been opened with every borough where there was any probability of influencing the return of free-trade members; a million and a quarter of hand-bills and tracts had been distributed, and 20,000 of *The Anti-Corn-Law Almanack*; 330,000 copies of *The Anti-Corn-Law Circular* had been circulated; application had been made to the clergy, and to all the corporations and all the Poor-Law guardians in the kingdom, to join in the movement; and invitations to form Anti-Corn-Law Associations had been sent far and wide. . . . By the end of the year, arrangements had been made for a movement upon electoral districts . . . and it had been resolved to increase the publications of the League. The preparations were formidable, for . . . the opposition to be encountered was formidable. A nation had to be educated in the true principles of political economy, a nation had to be convinced of the folly and injustice of its past commercial policy, and 'stout hearts' set themselves determinedly to climb the 'steep hill'.

CHAPTER SEVEN

It Never Can Be Worse

'They told the labourers that it would be worse
for them, but we say that it never can be
worse.'
— Farm labourer giving evidence to Anti-
Corn-Law League enquiry, reported in the
Morning Chronicle, 30 March 1840

The foundation of the Anti-Corn-Law League coincided with an
upsurge of public interest in social reform. Many of those whom the
movement attracted were 'universal reformers', inclined to vote the
whole progressive ticket, which, though primarily concerned with
living conditions — Edwin Chadwick's great *Report on the Sanitary
Condition of the Labouring Population* was presented to Parliament
in July 1842 — also embraced many other causes. Temperance was
one and many stalwarts of the League fiercely campaigned against
the demon drink, notably Joseph Livesey, who had signed the first
teetotal pledge in 1832. Education was another and one of the first
investigations carried out by the Manchester Statistical Society,
founded in 1833, had revealed that in one working-class area of the
city only 41 per cent of children, 4,932 out of 12,117, were receiving
any education at all, even at a weekly Sunday school, though by
1840 the figure had risen to 66 per cent for the city as a whole, most
of the schools, however, being of a very poor standard. Securing
improvements in such fields, though attractive to many League
members, was not the League's business, but it was concerned to
publicize the true quality of working-class life to demonstrate that
protection had conspicuously failed to bring prosperity, comfort or
the hope of self-improvement to the poor. Above all, perhaps, they
lacked security. Behind the shoulders even of those in work lurked
the perpetual spectres of unemployment and the workhouse, which,
the League contended, only the benefits resulting from free trade
could finally exorcize.

Several typically thorough and unsensational studies of the
budgets and housing of ordinary families were commissioned by the
League, and much material was also collected by that industrious
archivist Francis Place. His papers include a press cutting,
apparently from Durham, which suggested that the amount a man
with a wife and four children needed to support his family had risen

from 12s. 3½d in 1834 to 16s in 1836. Only rent, tea, candles and
soap had remained stable in price. Everything else had gone up, with
the sharpest rise in goods produced by British farmers.

This was how an average, reasonably prosperous working-class
family spent its money in 1836:

	s	d
6 gallons of bread	7	6
4 lb of bacon	2	6
1 lb of butter	1	0
1 lb of cheese	0	7½
½ lb of lard	0	4½
½ lb of candles, ½ lb of soap	0	6
1 lb sugar	0	7
2 oz tea	0	6
Firing (i.e. wood and coal)	1	2
House rent	1	3
	16·	0

The effects of taxation on food prices were highlighted even more
strikingly in a contemporary pamphlet, *Oppression or the effects of
Monopoly on Family Expenditure*, quoted in the *Morning Chronicle*
of 18 August 1841, and based on twelve families in Southwark in
South East London. This was the budget of 'a poor widow with two
young children,' excluding rent:

	s	d		s	d
Six 4-lb loaves at 8d each	4	0	including	1	6 tax
1¼ lb of butter at 10d per lb	1	0½	"	0	3¾ tax
1 lb sugar	0	7	"	0	5½ tax
2 oz of tea at 5s per lb	0	7½	"	0	3¼ tax
6 lb of meat at 8d per lb	4	0	"	2	0 tax
7 pints of beer at 2d per pint	1	2	"	0	3½ tax
	11	5	including	4	10 tax

'The mistress of the house,' commented the author of the survey,
'will be astonished to find that however small and temperate her
friendly party, she cannot give a dinner at which Sir Robert Peel and
the Duke of Buckingham [i.e. the politicians who defended the taxes
on food] do not consume more than all the rest without in the least
contributing to the wit or wisdom of the entertainment.'

An important part of the repealers' case was that the very
agricultural labourer whom the Corn Laws were supposed to
protect was their principal victim. At the meeting of League

delegates at Brown's Hotel in March 1840 William Holman, a farm servant working near Taunton, gave evidence of his miserable lot — which was soon likely to become more miserable still for 'before he left home his master . . . told him that if he came up to London before the delegates he would get no employment in that neighbourhood after he went back'. The family of six struggled to live on Holman's 8s a week, though Mrs Holman did an occasional day's work, for which she was paid 8d. (A later edition of the same newspaper gave this figure as 18d, i.e. 1s. 6d, but the former seems more likely.) The Holmans' cottage contained only two rooms, but somehow a lodger was squeezed in and contributed half of the 2s-a-week rent. For coal and clothes the family relied on gifts, but, Holman confessed, 'I cannot go to church because I have not decent clothes . . . [I] have kept away from church three or four years past.' His greatest problem was boots — for though the children could go barefoot, boots were essential for work in the fields. Their cost, 11s, was paid by instalments over the two years a new pair lasted. The family furniture was described as 'scanty'. 'There are scores of families around us,' this representative of the 'agricultural interest' testified, 'with not a bed to lie upon. They use straw for that purpose; some have no other covering.'

The Holmans lived largely on potatoes, at the rate of 15d to 16d worth a week, buying them by the bag at 4s. Other essentials were salt, candles — 4 oz a week, which cannot have gone far in the dark, winter evenings — and 4 oz of soap, Holman explaining that this 'lasted because he never used it himself'. Their treats consisted of herrings, six a week among the six of them, 1 lb of bacon every two weeks, and an occasional quarter pound of cocoa, which cost 3d and lasted two weeks; at other times they used burnt bread, unsweetened, for they could never afford sugar, and tea was beyond their means. Poverty also denied the Holmans the very products resulting from their labour. They bought only around a pennyworth of skim milk a week, less than 1 lb of butter every two months and no cheese at all. He went to work at six o'clock, William Holman told his audience, and 'his girl brought him a drop of broth — water with leeks in it — in the morning with sometimes a bit of bread; but he was often obliged to make the broth alone serve, having no bread in the house'.

Bread dominated the Holmans' budget as it did that of every poor family. Of their 8s a week, almost half, 3s. 6d, went on bread. They ate six loaves, costing 7½d each, a week, 'made of what was called second flour,' each of which 'ought to be four pounds,' but was 'frequently as much as six ounces less in weight,' i.e. 3 lb 10 oz instead of 4 lb. 'After giving all, the children ask for more. We know nothing about the Corn Laws . . . [but] the labourers would rather have the bread cheap than dear.'

Another, more prosperous, Devon farm-worker, James Vickony of Great Torrington, about five miles from Bideford, who possessed a pig and could afford tea and cheese occasionally, gave similar testimony. 'We have,' he told the repealers, 'heard something about the Corn Laws lately. . . . The labourers wish that a change would take place, but some persuaded them against it. They told the labourers that it would be worse for them, but we say that it never can be worse.'

In March 1842 a League conference in London appointed a Statistical Commission to gather further details of the effect of the Corn Laws. Its investigators assembled four typical budgets, each for a married couple with four children. One desperately poor household, with earnings of 5s. 6d, could never afford butter, meat, cheese, beer, sugar or coffee, and was unable to make any provision at all for clothing, education or even rent: presumably they were in a free tied cottage. The 10s-a-week family managed 6d-a-week rent and even 5d-a-week on sugar and treacle, and 2d on 'tobacco, snuff and condiments'. The 15s. 6d family were relatively comfortable in their shilling-a-week cottage, with 9d a week set aside for clothing and 6d for a sick society, while at 26s. 6d life was almost luxurious, with 2s. 6d a week going on rent, 1s. 4d being put away for 'medicine and attendance' and 2s a week for clothing.

The figures convincingly demonstrated that taxes on food pressed most heavily on the worst-off. Expenditure on bread and flour as a proportion of total income increased as income declined. Thus the 5s. 6d-a-week family spent 1s. 9d of their meagre earnings on bread and flour, the 10s-a-week family 2s. 6d, the 15s. 6d-a-week family 3s. 6d and the 26s. 6d one 4s. The percentage of total expenditure paid in tax was also highest for those least able to bear it: 28 per cent of the desperately-poor man's 5s. 6d a week went to the Exchequer, compared to 25 per cent of the 10s-a-week family, 22 per cent for the one earning 15s. 6d and only 17 per cent for the man enjoying 26s. 6d. The same process also applied higher up the social scale, where relatively less bread was eaten, until the government's levy, crushing on the almost destitute, 'would be only a fraction of a penny upon the richest peer or commoner'.

The League also demonstrated that the claim that the Corn Laws enabled the landlord to house his labourers in decent comfort was false. This was the report on a village in the Wareham area of Dorset, around 1844, by one League investigator, Andrew Bisset:

What is this? A cottage built of wood and without a chimney, the smoke ascending through what appears a large hole in the roof. The chimney fell down, I learned on enquiry, sometime since, and had not been rebuilt. The thatch of the roof had been extended over the space where the chimney was; and the smoke, occasionally accompanied by sparks of fire, found its way through as it could. Soon after I came to another tenement in this village, which appeared to be undergoing some repairs. It was a cottage of two rooms, without a garden — rent 30s a year. The tenant of it was a labourer, with 7s a week and a wife and six children at home. The woman said she had lived there thirty years and could never get any repairs done, except a tile now and then.

The offending landlord in this case was a Cambridge college, but other tenants were just as badly treated by private landlords, including the other chief proprietor of the area, a nobleman. '"He's a marquis indeed!" was the observation I heard on the spot,' reported the League's researcher. '"He takes everything out of it and brings nothing into it. The Lord deliver us from such a marquis!"' Equally bad, as both landlord and pastor, was the local vicar, despite a living 'worth upwards of one thousand pounds a year'. 'We don't have much good from he,' one old woman told this visitor bluntly.

The plight of Corn-Law-protected rural England in the 1840s was epitomized by another home in the same area:

A man now pointed out a cottage worse than any [so far] described, saying he could drive a horse and cart through it. And in truth he scarcely exaggerated. . . . There were holes in the windows large enough to put both hands through; and holes in some parts of the walls large enough to put the whole body through. The roof was also full of holes. The occupants said the rain came in in a hundred places; that they could not lie in their beds dry. . . . The family in this cottage of which I now speak had no blankets. The children (there were seven of them), some in rags and almost naked, were cowering round the embers of a fire on the hearth within the large chimney — the only sheltered spot in the cottage. One poor little thing, a boy about two-years old, was playing among the embers. . . . His little brother had been burnt to death only a short time before, while engaged as he now was.

These children had recently lost their mother. . . . They were now under the care of their eldest sister, a girl about seventeen. Rather less than three weeks after this time, on visiting this village again, I was informed that this girl was dead and buried. She had gone to a gentleman's house at a little distance to beg, and, standing about two hours in the cold and the wet, she caught a cold, which from the state of the cottages, insufficient covering . . . and the want of necessaries, turned into a fever and carried her off in about ten days.

Such experiences, made known through the League's publications, lent to its campaign the quality of a crusade. The Corn Laws seemed to their opponents to have laid a blight upon the countryside, which left the farm labourer half-starved and crippled every kind of enterprise. Bisset regarded as typical an elderly man he encountered 'in a south-western county . . . in a strange long blue cloth dress coat, with enormous brass buttons, which had once been yellow, and top boots . . . his Sunday dress . . . at least a quarter of a century old':

He turned out to be a shoemaker. He said that for *ready* money he could make a pair of labourer's shoes for nine shillings and sixpence and get about two shillings and sixpence [profit] by the job. And even if in full work he could hardly make more than three pairs of such shoes in a week, which would bring him, if paid, but seven shillings and sixpence for his week's work. But he lost money, he said, by agricultural labourers not paying him. They promised to pay at the rate of one shilling a week, but could not.

The final irony was that food was actually dearer in the countryside:

The price of bread is always considerably higher in these places than in the neighbouring towns; a fact which is partly accounted for by the number of bad debts met with by those who sell bread and flour. One man said he could not get paid, and gave up the trade. He said he lost about fifty pounds before he shut up his shop. Another man said the people had got between two and three hundred pounds in his debt. In truth, the public in those parts of the kingdom could not and did not live on their wages; and the above is only one of the ways in which those wages were eked out so as to enable them to keep body and soul together in the most miserable manner.

The League did not merely critize the rural landlords. A number of its supporters tried to show that factory life could be pleasanter and in every respect richer than working on the land. Typical of such Christian-inspired manufacturers were the Gregs of Styal, a

Cheshire village about six miles from Stockport. The family business, Quarry Bank Mill, had been established in a tree-lined valley in 1783 using water-power to drive the still novel spinning jenny, but had expanded with the coming of steam and later diversified into weaving — i.e. manufacturing cloth and not merely making thread. Control of it now passed to Robert Hyde Greg and his brother, God-fearing non-conformist businessmen, 'enlightened' by the standards of the time: they made extensive use of child labour and indentured 'parish apprentices' but housed them decently, had them medically inspected and, after a twelve-hour working day, provided a compulsory school.

Robert Hyde Greg later described the transformation they had effected at Styal, after taking over a virtually rundown mill in 1832:

> We found nothing but . . . about fifty cottages; most of them well built and of a pretty good size, but in extremely bad repair and wanting many little accommodations, such as water, coal-sheds, cupboards, etc., which are so essential to cleanliness and comfort. . . . We endeavoured as far as possible to find such families as we knew to be respectable . . . and who we hoped, if they were made comfortable, would remain and settle upon the place; thus finding and making themselves a *home* and losing by degrees that restless and migratory spirit, which is one of the peculiar characteristics of the manufacturing population, and perhaps the greatest of all obstacles in the way of permanent improvement among them. Partly with this in view, and partly for the sake of giving them innocent recreation for their leisure hours, we took three fields lying in front of the cottages, between them and the mill, and broke them up for gardens which we divided with neat hedges and gave one to every house. . . . They are separated from each other by a neat thorn hedge. Beside these, they have most of them a little flower garden in front of their houses or behind them; and the houses themselves have been made as comfortable as their size and situation would allow.

The Styal houses consisted of 'a parlour and back kitchen and two bedrooms and a cistern and a yard,' which contained its own privy, the average number of occupants per house in 1841, 6.7, luxuriously little compared to most urban cottages. Wages were low. Only 10 per cent of employees earned more than 12s a week and 71 per cent received less than 9s, of which 1s a week went on rent. But, unlike the supposedly paternalistic rural squire, the Gregs provided for their workpeople not merely a Sunday school, staffed by older employees, but also a playing field equipped with 'quoits, trap and

cricket balls . . . hoops and swing'. They even arranged evening
parties with individual invitations for the elder girls and boys 'whose
manners and character mark them out as in some degree superior to
their fellows, or those who, we think, with a little notice and
encouragement, and the advantage of good society, may gradually
become civilized and polished'.

To a contemporary writer the Gregs' efforts resembled 'the
founding of a colony in a distant country,' and they helped to make
the family well-known and indirectly to benefit the League; as
already mentioned, when Robert Hyde Greg stood as a Whig and
Anti-Corn-Law candidate for Manchester in a by-election in 1839
he was elected to Parliament. He remained an important figure in
the movement throughout his life, a visible proof that the charge
levelled against the Manchester industrialists of condemning the
way the farm labourer was treated while exploiting their own
'hands' was false.

Almost as well known as the Gregs were the two Ashworth
brothers, particularly Henry, an active member of the Manchester
Statistical Society and later of the League, and a close associate, and
ultimately biographer of Richard Cobden. Like so many repealers,
Ashworth was a Quaker, and, in the opinion of one contemporary
commentator, was 'somewhat austere in appearance. Though a
friend for progressive changes he holds strictly to rule,' and 'has
everything defined and reduced to writing — the duties of the
master as well as those of the workmen'. The Ashworths owned two
factories near Bolton, both 'comparatively new and most
romantically situated,' at Turton 'in the bosom of a valley between
two wooded hills' and at Egerton 'in the centre of a more open
valley,' with the 'houses of the work-people . . . ranged on both
sides of the road'. The occupants, however, failed to live up to their
surroundings:

> Nothing can be more commodious than these cottages, in which
> the interior appearance invites to order and cleanliness. A cast-
> iron oven, which serves to bake bread as well as other provisions,
> is attached to the fireplace of every kitchen; the pantry is spacious
> enough to contain all sorts of provisions, and the upper story
> often contains four bedrooms. But the benevolent intention of
> the proprietor has, in this instance, been too much in advance of
> the habits of his work-people. They have not the sentiment of
> modesty sufficiently developed to separate their children of both
> sexes, during the night. There are never more than two chambers
> occupied and it is even a mark of attention to decency if they draw
> a curtain, or put a partition between themselves and their
> children.

The Ashworths would not, in contrast to most employers, take on married women, but did 'distribute some work, such as winding and repairing' for them to do at home, though 'a family cannot earn sufficient to be quite comfortable unless the children are also employed in earning wages'. Where this *was* the case, the resulting picture was one of domestic bliss:

> It is delightful to see the order which prevails in these households, furnished as they are with their chests of drawers, filled with linen and clothes, the polished furniture, and clean earthenware, with abundance of books — religious and historic . . . weekly periodicals and especially the *Anti-Corn-Law Circular*. The rent of each house is not more than £10 per annum; it costs £120 to build, and thus yields seven or eight per cent per annum. . . . Messrs Ashworth have bought an extensive plot of ground and have thus gained the power to exclude public houses from their villages. They attach much importance to the morality of the work-people and do not receive into their employ any notorious characters.

But, for all their efforts, some 'notorious characters' did penetrate this industrial Eden:

> Mr Henry Ashworth affirms that he has observed, from year to year, an improvement in their manners and habits. But, notwithstanding the severe discipline which reigns at Turton, in three years and a half, and in a single factory, there were twenty-four illegitimate births. Mr Ashworth remarks upon this that the seduction has not taken place within his own establishment, but that the seducers, with one exception, belong to the neighbouring establishments.

CHAPTER EIGHT

The Great Engine of Repeal

'Lecturing is truly the great engine of repeal.'
— Letter from Sidney Smith, 2 May 1840

The early-Victorian era was the golden age of the public speaker. The lecture was the classic means by which the ambitious sought self-improvement; *Self-Help* itself, published in 1857, derived from the lectures delivered by Samuel Smiles, an active member of the League, to the Leeds Mechanics Institute in 1845. The League had been founded on lectures, first at Bolton and then in Manchester, and the earliest act of the Manchester Anti-Corn-Law Association was to offer the star of those occasions, A.W. Paulton, a regular appointment as peripatetic speaker.

Paulton's career reflected the difficulty the League faced in finding someone intellectually qualified to do the League's case justice while also possessing the common touch. He had been destined for the Roman Catholic priesthood and sent to Stonyhurst, but lacked the necessary vocation and was apprenticed to a surgeon in his home town of Bolton, where he became interested in politics. Paulton seized every opportunity to speak in public, hence his appearance on the stage of the theatre there in July 1838, but opinions as to his merits varied. Samuel Smiles later recalled a 'very thinly-attended' meeting Paulton addressed at Leeds in December 1838 when 'the lecture was read with not much force'. But the usual complaint was that Paulton was too wild, and wandered away from the Corn Laws to harangue his audience about the need for electoral reform. 'He constantly says "my own individual opinion is that we never can carry this question without an extensive enlargement of the suffrage". . .', reported another lecturer, J.H. Shearman. 'It may get him a momentary cheer from the Chartists — but it hinders me from getting money.' C.J.S. Walker, Vice-President of the Manchester Association, also formed a poor opinion of Paulton when he heard him speak in London on 13 February 1839. The audience, Walker reported to Manchester next day, 'did not amount to one hundred persons, although the admission was free . . . I was sadly disappointed with the lecture. Paulton is in my opinion much too declamatory and abusive and asserts some things which will not bear the test of argument and searching examination. I am firmly convinced he will be of little service here.' Nevertheless Paulton was soon afterwards entrusted with the secretaryship of the infant League, and the editorship of its *Circular*, until called away to practise his old trade of orator.

Shortage of funds meant that the post of speaker often had to be combined with administrative duties. George Grieg, nominally full-time secretary of the Leeds Anti-Corn-Law Association at £200 a year, was loaned to League headquarters to work for them in Yorkshire, Northumberland and Durham. Formerly a private in the Blues, Grieg was a stimulating but outspoken speaker, who caused much offence to the more staid Anti-Corn-Law men by denouncing the land-owning aristocracy in a meeting at Barnsley, as a Chartist newspaper reported approvingly, as 'gluttons and debauchees . . . whose whole life is a routine of oppression, extravagance and luxury'.

Such incidents presented the League, as in Paulton's case, with a recurring embarrassment. Paulton managed eventually to tame his extremism sufficiently to stay with the League, while Grieg solved the problem by accepting a post with the National Temperance Society, where he could denounce publicans as fervently as he wished without upsetting his employers.

A third recruit was J.H. Shearman, formerly Secretary of the Voluntary Church Society in Birmingham. He was originally engaged to book halls and handle publicity, so that the lecturer accompanying him could appear on the platform with dignity undiminished. Though also used as a supporting speaker, Shearman came to resent his comparatively menial role and in October 1839 moved on elsewhere.

The speaker Shearman had accompanied, Sidney Smith, an ex-solicitor from Scotland, received the same as the other lecturers — £4 a lecture, less travelling expenses (though not the cost of publicity or the hire of the hall) — but was always regarded as socially a cut above them. He had been considered sufficient of a gentleman to be employed during 1839 as a fund-raiser among City businessmen and much of his later career with the League was spent in the capital, where he presented the case against the Corn Laws logically rather than emotionally. 'I believe McCulloch's *Dictionary* and Chalmer's *Political Economy* [i.e. John Ramsey MacCullough (or M'Cullough), *A Dictionary practical, theoretical and historical of Commerce and Commercial Navigation*, published 1832–9; and Thomas Chalmer, *On Political Economy in connection with the Moral State and Moral Prospects of Society*, Glasgow, 1832] are in my lodgings in Manchester,' he wrote from London in June 1840. 'I have been put about for the want of them here, as they are the authorities by which I can best refute opponents.'

Smith and Shearman began their double-act in the very stronghold of the enemy, the hunting shires of middle England and the rural eastern counties, where they soon discovered the true meaning of the 'traditional freedoms of Englishmen'. At Louth in Lincolnshire one leading magistrate denied them the use of any public hall, and when they held a meeting in the market place he had them brought before him and fined them for obstruction. At Huntingdon the initial reaction was one of indifference, as Shearman described:

We arrived here just after the news of the resignation of Ministers, and we took the theatre and commenced last night. [Lord Melbourne resigned on 7 May 1839 after being defeated in the House of Commons over its policy concerning Jamaica. The 'Bedchamber crisis' (see p. 30) followed. Peel refused to become Prime Minister unless the Whig Ladies of the Bedchamber were replaced by Tories, and on 10 May Melbourne agreed to remain in office.] It is one of those small, comfortable, genteel Tory places where empty skulls and full pockets are found. One of the most thinking people in the place said to us, 'My best customers are the most ignorant fellows in Christendom. . . .'.

There were very few people come — it was a wet and cold evening, but notwithstanding there were several tradesmen and from them and the working men we had plenty of applause. . . . When Mr Sidney Smith was showing up the tricks of Sir Robert there was a loud hissing and several people went away from the boxes and there was a loud cheering from the gallery. We are going on again tonight and then Mr Smith goes back to Peterborough while I do something here.

This first meeting seems to have alerted the protectionist lobby to the lecturers' presence for the next one proved very different. There was actually a reckless attempt to burn down the theatre while other opponents threw coppers down into the pit prompting a scramble which successfully disrupted the proceedings. Shearman set out to obtain revenge. 'As the Town Clerk was one of the chief disturbers there,' he wrote to Manchester next day from Cambridge, 'I have addressed a letter to the Secretary of State for the Home Department, calling his attention to the fact.' Lesser fry were made more directly aware of Shearman's displeasure:

How the Huntingdon Tories writhe under the fierce . . . cuts that we had the opportunity of giving them. I walked about the town . . . and found some of them in the shops and they almost shrank from me as if I were a fellow of infinite muscle and everlasting vengeance. I found one of them reading a paper and I said, 'I beg to thank you, Sir, for the *honour* of your distinguished *interruption* last night. . . . I hope I shall be permitted to die without being disgraced by your approbation. It would be as bad as the lion being noted into the Society of Jackasses. . . .' The apprentice behind the counter laughed outright and I said to the Master, 'Why, Sir, nothing could be better for us. The people now see that Corn Laws, brutality, rascality, violence, fraud, robbery, ignorance and incendiarism' (one of them tried to set the place on fire) 'go together.'

What had happened at Huntingdon proved but a mild introduction to what was now to befall in Cambridge. The name of either university town was enough to make visiting speakers apprehensive, but Cambridge was also the market town for a large agricultural area. On their first evening, as at Huntingdon, the two speakers were able to state their case without interruption, but word of their presence in the town then spread through the colleges and on the following evening the theatre was invaded by a cheerfully noisy mob of undergraduates, who enlivened the speeches 'with the sound of trumpets,' as Archibald Prentice learned, and 'other discordant noises'. The infuriated townsfolk swarmed into the box housing the most troublesome interrupter, 'the gownsmen rushed to the defence of their fellow student, a fierce battle ensued between "gown" and "town" and it required strenuous exertions on the part of the mayor and the police to put an end to the riot'.

This epic battle, during which, in Sidney Smith's words, 'festoons of academic caps and gowns torn from the enemy were waved from gallery to pit,' enabled the *Anti-Corn-Law Circular* to indulge in a weighty condemnation of the 'gang of unfledged ruffians in caps and gowns, who, after exhausting their obscene and blasphemous vocabulary, exhibited themselves in the character of prize-fighters. . .'. The incident demonstrated only too clearly 'the fearful want of discipline, and the utter destitution of moral and religious training at Cambridge'.

Shearman himself, despite his religious background, was by no means disposed to turn the other cheek. On Wednesday 15 May 1839, the morning after the riot, he did his best to ensure that justice was meted out to the offenders:

One of the rioters, a student, was brought before the magistrates and fined forty shillings and costs for breaking one of the inner doors and assaulting a policeman on Wednesday, and yesterday

(Thursday) his brother was fined the same for assaulting a policeman and breaking the outer doors. I applied to a solicitor who stands high here . . . and he pointed out that I had a clear case of action, or indictment, and advises me first to demand reparation of the brothers and their party which I did, . . . but in vain. This morning I have been to the Proctor . . . and he told me . . . he would lay the matter before the Vice Chancellor and let me know the result.

In the end, the university authorities took no action but Shearman's decision to commence legal proceedings caused great offence. 'My life is positively in danger,' he wrote dramatically on Monday 20 May, 'and I have found it necessary to issue warrants against certain of the students. I cannot leave until the case is disposed of.' Two days later, still stuck in Cambridge, he had equally depressing news to report:

I cannot get equity, justice or law here. I do not like being beat — nor, what is the same, not beating my opponents. Difficulties insuperable prevent my closing my accounts with them. The mayor and magistrates are old women and the theatre lessee and his party are rascally Tories. I am informed that there is an extensive combination forming to put Mr Smith down every- where in the districts of the agriculturists; and I am assured by many persons that his life would not be safe, if he were here again.

Shearman received little recognition or reward for his efforts. Instead of thanks, his first expenses claim was met with instructions to provide more detail in future and by the end of May 1839 both he and Smith were owed money; to meet their expenses during April and May, of nearly £100, only £75 was sent to them, plus their salaries. The lectures raised next to no money — only 25s — and those Associations which were founded proved short-lived. One, at Boston in Lincolnshire, met for the first and last time during Smith and Shearman's visit in April. They were next sent to Scotland from which none of the subscriptions promised had yet appeared, but the two men's exertions failed to persuade the Scots to loosen their purse-strings and Smith and Shearman had to write to Manchester for cash to meet their expenses. The experience did not increase their respect for their hosts. 'The Scots,' commented Paulton sharply, in one letter to Manchester, 'are a thrifty race — their religion and their purse-strings being about equally sacred in their eyes.' Shearman was even more critical, describing the Scots as 'a cold and cautious set of wretches'.

While Smith and Shearman had been quite literally collecting more kicks than ha'pence in East Anglia in the early summer, Paulton had been busy around Cheltenham and Gloucester with little more success, and during June, July and August 1839 the principal lecturing effort was directed at Southern England. The League's main spokesman here was James Acland, an experienced Radical organizer, who had won his spurs during the great Reform Bill battles of the early 1830s, when he had been active in both Bristol and Hull. Acland had received his post on the recommendation of the Liberal Party's chief legal agent; he had already been in jail for a breach of the electoral law, but this was regarded as a misfortune rather than a disgrace. He was to serve the League well, apart from one unfortunate weakness: he was forever in debt, perhaps in part because of the League's own unreliability as a paymaster. Like Paulton, his extremism alarmed some free traders brought up in a milder school. 'He talked,' reported Bowring to J.B. Smith on 3 January 1840 with horrified underlinings, 'of the *right* of the people to *eat* as the same as the right to *breathe* and held language which might easily be construed into a recommendation to *help themselves.*'

Acland was ultimately to prove the League's most successful lecturer, but the first reports he sent back to Manchester recorded only one disaster, private or professional, after another. His letter from the Crown Inn, Arundel, at the start of his tour of Sussex, on Tuesday 30 July 1839, gave a foretaste of others to come:

The post leaving at half past six I have just time to inform you of the position in which I find myself. I have just reached Arundel (on borrowed means) and entered this inn with something less than five shillings in my pocket and no remittance awaiting my arrival. My bills are out for a lecture this evening at this house but the landlord has just informed me that, having been threatened by several highly respectable farmers at his market dinner today with the loss of their custom should he allow the lecture to be delivered, he cannot permit it. . . . My printer informs me that he does not know an individual in the town favourable to repeal, or even to a consideration of the Corn Laws. . . . This is a strong reason for devoting more than ordinary attention to the agitation in question in this district. According to my view of the matter such warrens of fools as Petersfield and Arundel should be regularly invested. . . . But to this end there must be the sinews of war. The advocate of repeal must feel his personal independence. . . . I remain here until the morning in the hope of a remittance and propose getting away to Brighton in a contrary

event and there await the needful. But how to move hence and
thither without more cash, and where to get it, I do not know.

Next day Acland was still lamenting his lot: 'No remittance —
and I cannot but imagine some letter must have miscarried.'
Without 'the needful' he could not even settle his bill. ('How I am to
get away, I know not. There is not a single pawnbroker in the
town.') Eventually there was nothing for it but to abandon his
luggage as surety and set out on foot. 'Leaving bag and baggage at
Arundel,' he wrote from Brighton, twenty-one miles away, next
day, 'I have walked here in the hope of finding a remittance with
which to release my wardrobe, etc. But there is no letter at the post
office.' At last one was forthcoming, enabling him to reclaim his
clothes, but soon afterwards he was recalled to Manchester, the
League having decided to abandon this second lecturing campaign,
like the first, for lack of money.

During the autumn and winter of 1839 Acland, along with
Paulton, remained based in Manchester, being sent out to speak
whenever local supporters could raise the fee: £5 up to thirty miles
from Manchester, £7. 10s for thirty to a hundred miles, and £10,
over a hundred, plus local expenses. But money remained short and
Acland greeted the new year, on 8 January 1840, with his most
dismal missive yet, from Birmingham:

> I am in a dreadful state, rampant each night, couchant all day,
> leeched [Acland's handwriting here is barely legible but 'leeched'
> seems the likeliest reading] to fainting after each night's exertion
> to keep down inflammation without the means and, I must add,
> without the disposition to take care of myself at the expense of the
> cause. . . .
>   The straits to which I am driven you cannot well imagine. E.g.
> with 3s in pocket I dare not get a bit of mutton scrag for broth and
> am obliged to support the system on tea, that I may be able to pay
> for the fly [i.e. carriage] to the Public Office and back this
> evening.

Acland had, he pointed out, not received his usual fee 'because the
lectures were not gratuitous' but charging for admission had driven
away the potential audience since 'the receipts for the cause were
20s. 6d'. A week later, on 17 January 1840, Acland had a new
anxiety, about his home:

> I am worried in mind and sick at heart about house affairs. On
> Monday I shall owe two months' rent and the landlord wants us

out — and my wife's nurse writes me that they are aground for money and that Kirkby [the landlord] talks of making them go out tomorrow. Can you arrange with Mr Ballantyne to see K. as to let him know that although there are none but females at home so he must not think to play the brute with impunity, nor to act illegally? . . . Can you send £5 by Mr B. to provision the garrison?

Acland survived these domestic worries, as he had others, and by the spring was touring East Anglia, where Smith and Shearman had had such a rough reception a year before. In a letter, dated merely 'Wednesday night 1840' but almost certainly written on 6 May 1840 from 'four miles north of Woodbridge,' he recounted the most serious violence which he had yet faced:

On this evening at Woodbridge I had much impudent and blackguardly bullying to put up with for the two hours before Everitt [his fellow speaker, apparently a local man] made his appearance by my side on the outer steps of the Shire Hall. At the close . . . I took a show of hands of the question [of] agricultural protection, when not a hand was displayed against us. The score of ruffians had meanwhile retired to the Bull Inn (save two or three) and there they set upon me as soon as I got into the house, collaring and hustling and abusing me and ending by pitching my hat over the staircase and me after and upon it. I had previously announced my intention of leaving the town and had ordered my horse, happily so — for that saved me from the constructive disgrace of having been driven from the place. The reporter for the S. [presumably Suffolk] *Chronicle* was also assaulted by the same ruffians. But it is all for the best, if it stimulates you and the Council to agitate most where agitation is most needed.

Acland had even more need of such philosophical reflections at Saxmundham, which he visited soon afterwards, as the *Essex Mercury* described (the cutting, marked 'Thursday', is inserted into Place's papers under the date 18 May 1840. Acland's letters make clear, however, that the meeting took place on Thursday 7 May):

Immediately . . . that Mr Acland commenced every species of annoyance was put in practice. A hundred questions were asked at once. Loud questions to drown the lecturer's voice followed. Some farmers anxious to put questions fairly came in front of Mr Acland, but these solitary few were disturbed by full fifty others, who with a volubility and pertinacity unequalled, drowned the voices of the handful who desired fair play. . . .

The storm of words now rose and fell. For an instant a partial calm spread over the crowd. 'Hear him quietly to the end,' said some lover of fair play. 'Don't disturb the lecturer,' said another, 'because we shall think, if you do, that you cannot answer his arguments.' Appeals to reason, however, failed, a partial skirmish took place, when the rural police, who were in the process of military drill at Saxmundham, promptly intervened and separated the combatants. Mr Acland, taking advantage of a moment's lull, again entered upon his lecture, but at this juncture several persons attempted to dislodge the lecturer from his position by overturning a barrel upon which he stood. This was resisted and at length a fight took place. Mr Acland was now assaulted in person. He was struck, dragged forwards into the very centre of the crowd, and had not his friends and supporters fought hard for him, there is little doubt that his life would have been sacrificed. The rural police were now called out in earnest and after a struggle of no trifling nature, contrived to rescue Mr Acland, considerably bruised, from the hands of his assailants. He was conducted into the Angel Inn, the recent quarters of the rural police force, and, though against his own inclination, from thence to the Bell, where he was placed in a gig which was in waiting. He was then escorted by the police out of the town.

Acland was clearly the stuff of which heroes, if not martyrs, were made. He continued with his planned itinerary, happily with better results. 'Bungay on Friday night,' he reported from Norwich three days later, on 10 May 1840, 'and Beccles last night were triumphant without irrationalism.' As for his narrow escape at Saxmundham, this merely spurred him on to greater efforts:

I hold that the cause should be made to triumph everywhere and that the enemy should not be permitted to seem to triumph anywhere. Apply this to Saxmundham and you will understand my anxiety to return thither and give to the honest people there the knowledge compulsorily withheld from them on Thursday night.

By the following day, Sunday, as near to a day of rest as Acland allowed himself, he had worked out his tactics:

My plan is to rent a house in the High Street for the week, drive around the district of which that town is the centre, talk to the husbandmen, lecture from my window nightly (and, if necessary be a candidate for the county) until my address to my constituency shall have taught the Lynch Law farmers the lesson they so much need.

Acland attached his list of meetings for the coming week:

North Walsham	this evening
Aylsham	Tuesday
Mells	Wednesday
Fakenham	Thursday
Docking	Friday
East Dereham	Saturday
Swaffham	Sunday

He duly kept to this punishing schedule — though his concern over financial matters continued. As he wrote from Docking on the Friday evening:

I have lectured every night for three weeks and my days have been passed in the gig or thereabout. When you consider my expenses pray consider also the number of places agitated and the number of lectures delivered. It may be an expensive tour to the League; but it has been a most laborious and thankless task to me. All I care for is to make the effort an effective one and that the Council may say the expense was a good investment of capital.

From Swaffham, two days later, on Sunday 17 May 1840, he sent a detailed expenses claim, pointing out that 'The lectures of this week have only averaged £3. 10s each . . . excluding the new hat. The thing cannot . . . be done at less expense in the enemy's country. At all events it is very considerably less than it was in the south and west.' He was still determined to return to Saxmundham and set out his campaign plan in detail:

After dining with Messrs Marshall and Morse [two League supporters who had arranged for Acland to visit, in his own words, 'the dank localities of Norfolk' once his tour of Suffolk was complete] I shall drive towards East Suffolk, so that sleeping some twenty miles on the road I may reach Eye in the forenoon. Then I shall get a bold placard printed in the shape of an appeal to the inhabitants against the lynch-law of the farmers with a declaration that I re-enter the county with a determination that the half-starved labourer shall receive the important information relative to his social condition which his master would prevent by physical force. I shall be my own bill-sticker; purchase a paste-pot and brush and pasting my bills against gates, trees, walls, etc., throughout the infested district south of Bungay, north of Ipswich and east of Stowmarket. Halesworth, Framlingham, Woodbridge, Saxmundham, and Stowmarket will be the chief towns, adding thereto the bunches of villages which abound in that Tory Corn-Law quarter.

Headquarters in Manchester seem to have been more apprehensive about the coming counter-attack than Acland himself. Unlike Shearman, Acland disdained any revenge except to trounce his opponents: 'Pray put legal proceedings out of the question until I get my head broke. We must win by moral force. Three things are indispensable. They are one, money; two, plenty of it; three, immediately.' By happy timing, a remittance for £50 arrived soon afterwards, and the letter Acland sent on the following Thursday, 21 May 1840, came from within the enemy citadel in Saxmundham:

I have been driving about all day, calling at all the villages within six or seven miles, seeing the bills well posted and talking with the people. I think the steam is up; but in a couple of hours I shall know. I am told the police have orders to take me into custody as soon as I begin to speak; in which case I have arranged to have a blank letter posted for your information. . . . At all events you shall hear from me tomorrow. Meanwhile, be satisfied that row or no row, gaol or no gaol I shall neither play the coward nor the blackguard. I think there will be a *noise*, but no *fighting*.

A 'noise' there was from the gentry. Acland reported, on 25 May, that 'the head Tory magistrate of this district has forwarded my placard to the Lord Normanby [the Hon. Secretary] with a formal enquiry whether he can order my apprehension for seditious libel,' but the government's lawyers decided to leave well alone and the visit passed off uneventfully. The following week, at Halesworth market on Tuesday 26 May, Acland received a friendly reception from a crowd he estimated at 700 to 800. 'A man threw something at me and was thereupon removed by the police, who did ditto to another by whom an attempt was made to pull me down. The people were enthusiastic and repeal was unanimously voted.' It was the same story at Framlingham on the following evening, although 'heavy threats had been loudly uttered. I addressed 500 from a window in the Crown Inn, looking upon the market place. The mob put several gentlemen blackguards to the right-about and despite many interruptions from some half-score of desperate Tory farmers we won in a canter.'

One problem remained, however, just to show that times had not changed completely. From Ipswich on 12 June 1840 came a familiar plea: 'I must beg of you to transmit some of the indispensable. I go to Sudbury penniless. What a qualification!' Happily, some of the 'indispensable' was forthcoming and Acland was sent that autumn to Yorkshire. He was equally successful there, as an enthusiastic letter from a League member to J.B. Smith, on 16 November 1840, testified:

I write to thank you and the members of the Anti-Corn-Law League for your champion, the immortal Acland, who must be allowed by friend and foe to have done his work well, both at Sheffield and Doncaster. 'Adversity brings strange bedfellows together' was truly exemplified in the late discussion at the Doncaster Theatre, where pride and dignity could descend from their lofty pedestals . . . and mix with the common herd of man. The proud baronet and the doubtful character of a publican could be seen huddled together as chums on the same bench, mixed up with an incongruous crowd of Tory barons, shallow Whig sycophants, J. Walbanke Childers, the pretended Liberal MP and that impertinent grinning fool Henly Wright, MP for North Nottinghamshire. I assume your dignity never so far forgot its imaginary rank as it did on this occasion when Acland was telling these gentry that their estates were mortgaged for as much as they were worth and that they would be compelled to work, when they could no longer tax the bread-loaf to increase the rent-roll.

To counter the Chartist gibe that their lecturers knew nothing of how the working man lived, the League deliberately selected some with homely manners and uncouth accents. The Chartist *Northern Star* was infuriated when an operative from Leeds, Heyworth Hargreaves, was chosen to spread the free-trade message. 'The League having in vain despatched the more aristocratic lecturers, Messrs Paulton, Smith, etc.,' it declared on 4 July 1840, the League had now struck upon a new device, 'that of hiring an operative, in the hope that he could more persuasively appeal to the working people'. One such 'working man', taken on in April 1840, was a 'moral-force' Chartist, John Murray, who rated only £80 a year. Even more obviously proletarian was T.J. (or J.J.) Finnigan, also known as 'Finnegan' or 'Finigan', a barely literate Irishman who possessed both the gift of the gab and a cheerfully combative temperament. Finnigan had worked as a bailiff, sent in to distrain on goods for unpaid debts, and was well able to hold his own with hecklers. In 1842 he was to be accused of stirring up trouble during the 'Plug Plot' disturbances (mentioned later), but in 1840 he was more usually on the receiving end of violence. He was sent first to the West Country in the hope that the farm labourers would identify with him, but at Okehampton the mayor prevented him from speaking at all. Intimidation followed, as Cobden learned in a letter from a local supporter (included in the Place Papers) dated 31 March 1840:

> At Hatherleigh, our enemies not having a person able to answer him, hired a band of music and stationed them behind him and by their noise prevented him from being heard. The people got exasperated and threatened to smash their instruments; but finally Mr Finnigan moved to another place and the threats of the people had the effect of keeping the band at a distance. Mr Finnigan laid out the petition for signature at a person's house favourable to the cause and the people anxiously thronged in to sign. The farmers then burst into the house and frightened the labourers from signing, till the owners interfered and ordered the farmers out. They told him that he was doing a thing to ruin them; he retorted that they were ruined already and that he was living on their distress [i.e. as a bailiff] instead of following the trade he was brought up to — shoemaking.

The most gentlemanly of the League's lecturers, Sidney Smith, was meanwhile, as mentioned earlier, assisting Francis Place in London. He can seldom have been off the platform, for the Metropolitan Anti-Corn-Law Association organized no fewer than 154 lectures between 24 February and 29 June 1840 and Smith himself placed great value on them. 'Lecturing,' he wrote from the capital on 2 May 1840, 'is truly the great engine of repeal.' Francis Place found him almost *too* enthusiastic, complaining in a letter to Richard Cobden on 4 March 1840 of Smith's 'eagerness to "go a-lecturing". He, however, will have enough to do in his line to satisfy him,' Place continued. 'He will have to lecture six nights a week and sometimes in the daytime also. . . . We shall need more lecturers, not only for London, but for many places within some twenty miles of it.' That the lecturing campaign was attracting attention seems clear from a letter signed by 'W.P.', who wrote to a London newspaper from 'Princes Street, Hanover Square':

Mr Editor,
Amongst the other tricks resorted by the Anti-Corn-Law

agitators, is one which may have escaped your observation. A notice is put forward, informing the public that a discussion will take place upon the Corn Laws. The day arrives and two speakers are introduced, one as the advocate, the other the opponent of those laws. . . . The arguments employed by this pretended supporter of the Corn Laws have been so prepared as to leave an impression inimical rather than favourable to them, by causing their maintenance to rest principally upon the necessity of upholding the interests of the aristocracy and the wealthy classes; and by gentle indirect admissions of their hostility to trade generally, he leaves an easy triumph to his feigned adversary, who comes forward, of course, 'to vindicate the rights of justice, industry and the people in general against the iniquitous tax'.

Whether or not this charge was well-founded is uncertain; although it is the sort of tactic which the League might have adopted, there is no reference to it elsewhere. But the Metropolitan Association believed that in any case the lecturing programme had been well worthwhile. As recorded in the Place Papers, the 'general apathy' which the Association had 'found to exist among a large part of the middle class and . . . the absolute hostility of the working class' when it started work in February 1840, had, its first retrospective report asserted, by August 'been considerably moderated, though not wholly subdued,' thanks to 'the delivery of lectures in various parts of the metropolis and . . . the extensive circulation of the publications of the Association. . . . The lecturers . . . have generally been received with considerable enthusiasm and large petitions have resulted from each lecture.'

The Chartist working man John Murray, whom Cobden described as 'a safe and prudent man whom you may trust,' was now sent on an extensive tour of Ireland, while a new name, Walter Griffiths, who was bilingual in Welsh and English, was recruited to preach the free-trade gospel in Wales. His chief difficulty lay in securing a meeting place, but often the dissenting clergy offered the use of their chapels, sometimes preaching a supporting sermon in praise of free trade. Temperance, that other great proselytizing cause of the time, had as yet made little impact, even in Nonconformist Wales. 'Flint,' Griffiths reported ruefully in June, was 'in a state of drunkenness, and the people were very disorderly, which I understand is the case almost every Whitsuntide'; Griffiths' speech was greeted with 'disorderly' and ironic cheers. Occasionally he was reduced to speaking out of doors, as he described in a letter from Llanidloes in Powys on 6 September 1840:

Since my last from Newtown I have kept a meeting here. They would not let the public rooms for me for the same price as for other people, therefore I kept it in the open air last evening. The middle class here have great prejudice against any agitation at present, because the Chartists made so much riot. Some of the aristocrats prevented the bellman to proclaim the meeting but it was made public enough. The Chartists behaved themselves well. They all supported me quietly but at the same time they thought Chartism better.

CHAPTER NINE

Upset by Chartists

'[We] have not had a meeting where the public
were admitted which has not been upset by the
Chartists.'
— Member of the Anti-Corn-Law League
reported in the *Manchester Guardian*, 3
September 1842

While the opposition of the farming community was predictable,
that of the Chartists was harder to bear. In the past, extending the
franchise and seeking free trade had not been regarded as mutually
exclusive: the Peterloo meeting in 1819, called to demand
parliamentary reform, had also opposed the Corn Laws. After 1832,
however, attitudes changed. The more militant working men,
bitterly disappointed at still being denied the vote, had come to
regard all employers and middle-class radicals with hostility. The
People's Charter, formally launched at a meeting in Birmingham on
6 August 1838, a few weeks before the Manchester Anti-Corn-Law
Association was founded, set out a six-point programme which
made no reference to protection. Universal adult male suffrage,
payment of Members of Parliament, abolition of the property
qualification for MPs, equal electoral districts, vote by secret ballot
and annual Parliaments — once these essential reforms had been
achieved, all others, so the Chartists believed, would become
possible. But until the Charter had been obtained, every other
agitation was merely a distraction from the real struggle.

There was also a very real difference in the composition of the two
organizations. The League attracted middle-class people, especially
manufacturers and merchants, particularly those in prosperous and
expanding trades like cotton. The Chartists were strongest among
working men in declining occupations affected by mechanization,
such as hand-weaving, stocking-making and nail manufacture. Even
more divisive, while the League relied upon strictly constitutional
methods a sizeable section of the Chartists belonged to the
'physical-force' wing of the movement, whose attitude was
explained to a Chartist conference by a delegate from Stalybridge in
Cheshire: 'We will,' he declared, 'obtain our rights, peaceably if we
can, forcibly if we must. If we cannot obtain them by fair means, by
argument or reason, we will obtain them by other means, by the
pistol, the bullet, the pike and the bayonet.'

It was true, as the Chartists said, that some of those who expressed horror at such sentiments had not discouraged the riotous mobs whose threatening behaviour had won their betters, but not themselves, the right to vote. No factory-owner, however, could have been expected to sympathize with those Chartists who openly proclaimed, at meetings during 1841, that once they possessed the vote they would create work by 'limiting the use of machinery' and would seek to control 'the grasping capitalist in his selfishness after wealth'. Even the 'moral-force' Chartists were deeply suspicious of the League. 'Why do these liberal manufacturers bawl so lustily for a repeal of the Corn Laws?' demanded the placards at a Chartist meeting in Manchester on 19 March 1841. 'Because with the reduced price of corn they will be enabled to reduce the wages of the working man.' The most influential of the Chartist leaders, Feargus O'Connor, was hostile to the whole idea of foreign trade, and professed contempt for the League, referring to it as 'the Plague' and describing the free-traders as 'free-booters', whose true aim was to make the working class their slaves.

The reason why the more moderate of the Chartists distrusted the League was well put by one from Leicester in 1840:

> When we get the Charter we will repeal the Corn Laws and all the other bad laws. But if you give up your agitation for the Charter to help the free-traders, they will not help you to get the Charter. Don't be deceived by the middle classes again. You helped them to get their votes. . . . They said when they had . . . their votes, they would help you to get yours. But they and the rotten Whigs have never remembered you . . . now they want to get the Corn Laws repealed, not for your benefit, but for their own. 'Cheap Bread!' they cry. But they mean 'Low Wages'. Do not listen to their cant and humbug. Stick to your Charter.

The League was not quite as innocent of encouraging the Chartists as its leaders liked to pretend in public. 'The working classes are really those most interested in [i.e. have most to gain by] the repeal of the Corn Laws', wrote C.P. Villiers to J.B. Smith, in an undated letter, probably sent in August 1840. 'My great object in getting them to speak out is that I am convinced that until they do the aristocracy will never yield. . . . The *brickbat argument* is the only one that our nobles heed.' Cobden took the same view. The complete suffrage movement, he wrote a little later [i.e. December 1841], was useful as 'something in our rear to frighten the aristocracy'. Nor was he unsympathetic to the demand for the vote but, as he told Samuel Smiles on 3 August 1841, 'the suffrage-extension question is not at present a practical one. Nothing definite on the subject is before the electoral body. . . . Is not the agitation of the question a waste of power *now*? And will it not best be forwarded by sticking to the Corn Law?'

Samuel Smiles, though later regarded as the epitome of bourgeois complacency, did his best to achieve an understanding between the two movements in his adopted city of Leeds. He helped to arrange a 'conciliatory meeting', but the result, he acknowledged, was 'a failure. . . . The meeting was held in the large room of the Commercial Building and was full to overflowing. The Chartists were present in great numbers and the meeting was occasionally a scene of great uproar and confusion.'

Cobden found it puzzling that a textile town which contained two sympathetic newspapers, the *Leeds Mercury* and Smiles' *Leeds Times*, should have been so hostile to the cause. He attempted an analysis of the reasons in a long letter to Smiles on 21 October 1841:

> You had an orderly community, quite an example, at your public meetings, for intelligence and good behaviour. Manchester, on the contrary, had not for eight years been able to call a public meeting on any political question. The question now is — why does the cause stand so well in Manchester and why so adversely in Leeds? I can attribute it to no other reason than that it has been worked incessantly in the former place, *apart altogether from party politics*. . . . Two years and a half ago, we called a public meeting. The Chartist leaders attacked us on the platform at the head of their deluded followers. We were nearly the victims of physical force. I lost my hat, and all but had my head split open with the leg of a stool. In retaliation for this we deluged the town with short tracts printed for the purpose. We called meetings of each trade and held conferences with them at their own lodges. We found ready listeners and many secret allies, even amongst the Chartists. We resolutely abstained from discussing the Charter or any other party question. We stuck to our subject, and the right-minded amongst the working men gave us credit for being in earnest.

Writing again two weeks later, on 6 November 1841, Cobden reaffirmed his belief that the League and the Chartists could not work together:

> My opinion is every day strengthened that we must not seek official alliance with Chartists or any other party. The leaders of the Anti-Corn-Law party ought to take every opportunity of

avowing their sympathy as individuals for the suffrage men; but any formal coalition is unwise and unpracticable. Many of the Chartists as, for instance, O'Connor . . . have their own views upon [the] Corn Laws, which must prevent their joining us; and this ought to satisfy every honest man of their party that it would be quite impossible for the two bodies to coalesce. We must insist upon our right to carry on an independent agitation and if the hired knaves who interrupt our meetings persevere, we must harass them but in their own way. Our Manchester Operative Anti-Corn-Law men have declared the *lex talionis* [i.e. retaliation in kind] in force even to sticks and stones; and so formidable was the preparation for the last meeting that the Feargus [O'Connor] men did not venture even to lift their voices in opposition. Indeed, I am told that, since that evening, their committee have passed a resolution against further interference.

Relations between the Chartists and the Corn-Law repealers began in ill-feeling and continued in turbulence. The first clash came even before the League had been set up, in February 1839, when a Chartist National Convention assembled in London at the same time as the delegate conference of the local Anti-Corn-Law Associations. Unfortunately the Chartists found the room they had expected to use handed over instead to the Anti-Corn-Law delegates and had to move to inferior premises. The slight was not forgotten but was promptly avenged when, on 28 February 1839, the Association delegates from Manchester reported back to a meeting at the Corn Exchange. Archibald Prentice was present:

Several members had addressed the meeting when a person . . . demanded the right of speaking before a working man named Moore and, because the chairman decided in favour of Moore speaking, proposed to place in the chair one whom he called 'honest Pat Murphy', a potato-wheeler [presumably a market porter or itinerant potato vendor] in Shudehill, who, whatever his honesty might be, was not very clean, and very far from being sober. . . .

The scene that followed was unexampled in Manchester and almost baffled description. Upon the proposer calling out, 'Will you take the chair, Pat Murphy?' one drunken and very dirty fellow mounted the table, his clogs making deep indentations on its surface and, bruising the reporters' hands which were in his way, began to insult everybody who asked him to get off, and replied to one who asked him to desist: 'D--n they e'en, if theau spakes to me aw'll put me clogs i' they chops.'

Murphy was then 'pushed or dragged over the heads of the people, amidst great noise and confusion' and, having reached the platform, was greeted with cries of 'Take the chair', and 'Hand up the chair for Pat Murphy!', which drew an all-too-literal response, as Prentice described:

Some fellows here seized chairs which were in various parts of the room and threw them at the heads of the persons who stood on the stage. The consequence was that a scene of riot and confusion ensued, several gentlemen being severely hurt by the ruffians, who smashed the forms and glasses of the lamps. The respectable persons of the meeting, with the chairman, then quitted the room and left it in the possession of the ringleader who congratulated the meeting upon having done his bidding and his party . . . [and] passed a vote of thanks to the delegates to the National Convention by way of amendment to the original motion.

The lesson of this affair was not lost upon the League. 'It was seen,' commented Archibald Prentice, 'how easy it was for two or three hundred persons, out of a meeting of two thousand, by noise and clamour and resort to brute force, to drive away all the peaceably-inclined and respectable.' Future meetings were confined to members of the Association, admitted by ticket, and at the first of them, on the following Tuesday, 4 March 1839, at the Corn Exchange, Richard Cobden delivered a weighty indictment of those responsible for the recent outrage:

I must protest, in the name of the working classes of Manchester, against the conduct of men who will prevent all discussion upon this important question. . . . Working men of Manchester . . . these men will take possession of your meetings unless you check them in the bud. Nay more . . . even your quiet, happy and well-regulated firesides will not be safe, unless the strong arm of the law is brought to interfere between you and the wishes of those lawless men.

What had happened in Manchester was soon repeated elsewhere. Feargus O'Connor in the *Northern Star* openly advised his followers to try to convert Anti-Corn-Law meetings into pro-Charter demonstrations and whenever the League announced an open meeting placards were fly-posted exhorting working men to assemble in their 'countless thousands' to challenge the 'humbug clap-trap of the League'. Most unfairly, the League was often blamed for the resulting disorder. 'The middle class here,' Walter

Griffiths reported from Wales in September 1840, 'have great prejudice against any agitation at present because the Chartists made so much riot.' The policy of disruption cost the Chartists some powerful supporters, such as Francis Place, and also encouraged the formation of local Operative Anti-Corn-Law Associations, with their own officers and a very low subscription. One was founded in Manchester, with a 3d-a-quarter subscription, shortly after the February 1839 meeting which the Chartists had wrecked. A local informant in Carlisle wrote to the Home Office in January 1840 to confirm the foundation of a similar association, consisting of 'the working classes of the more respectable sort' there; and in Leicester, two months later, another attracted 'many of the better-paid and relatively more educated' workmen, including some 'former Chartists . . . ready to resume cooperation with the middle-classes'.

The Operative Associations also provided contingents of stewards to keep order at League meetings. Those in Manchester were known as the 'Irish lambs' and their leader, Michael Donohoe, as 'Big Mick'. Unleashing Big Mick and his cohorts was a far cry from the reasoned exposition of economic truths for which the League had been formed but there was probably no alternative. In March 1841, for example, the Chartists successfully took over a League meeting and replaced the mayor, who was in the chair, with one of their own faction. At another meeting, on 22 May 1841, 'we had,' wrote one observer, 'as pretty a row as ever I witnessed. Our associates and the Irish and other repealers of the Union and the Corn Laws mustered in full strength. . . . The Chartists were driven out of the hall four times. We regularly thrashed them and passed our own resolutions.'

This was merely a warming-up operation for the real clash which came ten days later, on Wednesday 2 June 1841, after nearly 3,400 local residents had signed an appeal to the mayor to call a meeting about the prevailing distress. When the mayor declined, they called on local trade and temperance societies to 'form a grand procession' to Stephenson Square, where Richard Cobden promised to preside. The Chartists meanwhile were determined to have a public showdown with their opponents and even — which further embittered feelings — accepted a cheque for £150 from the League's arch-enemy, the Duke of Buckingham, to finance their preparations. The encounter which followed was vividly described by one of Cobden's friends, who was up at six to visit the League's Headquarters and then called on one of the homes being used as an assembly point:

At this man's house I found a score of boys all ready for work.

These men were ostensibly 'flag-bearers', but from their being ornamented with good blackthorn sticks it was clear they understood the real meaning of their office, viz, A.C.L. police. I took these men with me to the square and we rather astonished the Chartists . . . by our appearance.

I got my horse and we went back to Kennedy's [home of a supporter in Cable Street] where our band assembled. After some preliminary preparations we marched up Oldham Road, down Livesey Street and George's Road, to the *Queen Anne* in Long Millgate. Here we took in tow the procession forming there and went all together to Stephenson Square. We got there at a quarter to ten. The place was nearly filled with people. . . . At half-past ten I went on the hustings. Almost immediately after, a body of Chartists from the country, carrying two banners, one of which had inscribed on it 'No New Poor Law' and the other 'Down with the Whigs', made their appearance and began to advance to the front, pushing our friends to the right and left. This was submitted to pretty quietly, but at last from the violent conduct of the parties, and from the view of the hustings being partly hidden by the flags, an attempt was made to pull them down. This was immediately resisted, and the Chartists showed their preparations for a row by drawing for short staves, with which they began to lay about them. Our Irish friends, made desperate at seeing this, and particularly by the brutal conduct of a fellow who nearly killed a poor man with a blow from an iron bar, rushed at the flags, tore them down, broke the shafts in pieces, and laid about them to such good effect as to drive the Chartists out of the square, leaving a kind of lane about four yards wide, next to the church. . . .

A procession was now formed at the front of which were Sir Thomas Potter . . . and a number of other gentlemen, on horseback. Near the front but on foot were . . . Richard Cobden . . . and other well-known friends of the Anti-Corn-Law cause. The long line of flags and banners, principally with devices and inscriptions on a pure white ground, produced a most imposing effect as they waved in the rays of brilliant sun. 'The total and immediate repeal of the Corn Laws' was the predominant inscription. . . . Among others were seen 'Down with the infamous bread tax,' 'No fixed duty,' 'No sliding scale,' 'God is with us,' 'Villiers, the friend of the people'. . . . Market Street presented one dense mass of spectators, loudly cheering as the procession passed, and the windows were crowded with ladies. On passing the rooms of the League, in Newall's Buildings, from the windows of which large banners were waving, each district division gave three hearty cheers. The various bodies congregated in St Ann's Square, where, after a few words from Sir Thomas Potter, the great multitude quietly dispersed.

The 'Irish lambs' proved their worth on other, later, occasions, as at a meeting in October 1841 when the Chartists followed their usual tactic of trying to convert an Anti-Corn-Law motion into a pro-Charter resolution:

> Mr Acland then spoke in support of the original motion, but was interrupted by a Chartist in the centre of the room. Upon this, a body of Irish . . . rose. A cry of 'Put him out' was raised and presently a forest of shillelaghs was seen flourishing in the air. The forms were upset and the sides of several of them torn off, and converted into short staves. In attempting to gain the door, several parties were overturned and lay struggling in heaps on the floor in different parts of the room; but . . . no person, as far as we could learn, received any serious damage. In a short time the Irish became almost the exclusive possessors of the room.

On a later occasion, at which the Chartist leader Feargus O'Connor was present, in March 1842, a pitched battle developed, described in Mr Jingle-like prose by one of those present:

> The result was a tremendous fight. All the furniture was smashed to atoms; forms, desks, chairs, gas pipes — were used as weapons and the result is something like as follows. 'The lion', the king of Chartism, F.O.'C knocked down three times; 'has,' he says, 'seven wounds, six he can tell the position of, the seventh was, I believe, inflicted as he was running away, which he did after fighting about two minutes.'
>
> Christopher Doyle [was] very much hurt. Bailey: confined to his bed. Murray: ditto. Four others (Chartists) seriously hurt. [The] Rev. Schofield: black eye, loose teeth, cut lips, contusions behind (got in following Feargus). Four of the 'lambs' are badly hurt, two with their skulls fractured. They, however, are used to it and will soon be well.*

In spite of such rebuffs the nuisance continued. A League supporter complained in the *Manchester Guardian* on 3 September 1842 that the repealers 'have not had a meeting where the public were admitted which has not been upset by the Chartists; the resolutions of the League being negatived and one in favour of the

---

*I have tried to preserve the flavour of the original but have repunctuated this passage to make it more intelligible.

Charter being substituted,' but by the end of the year the tactic of meeting force with force had triumphed and now, instead of the *Anti-Corn-Law Circular* protesting of 'outrages' at meetings, the Tory *Standard* was complaining of 'the wanton and cowardly brutality exercised by the Leaguers' upon those who dared to oppose their resolutions.

Events in other places followed a similar course, though the League was subject to constant provocation. In Huddersfield the Chartists pasted slips reading 'Poor' over the word 'Corn' on bills advertising a meeting to discuss repeal of the Corn Laws and, a local paper complained, 'a considerable number of people attended the Philosophical Hall under the illusion that such was the object of the meeting'. Whether disappointed not to hear an attack on the workhouse system or from a determination to 'kick up a row,' many in the audience, according to the same reporter, soon revealed themselves as 'utterly lost to all sense of decency, candour, honesty and fair dealing. The most ribald abuse of the speakers was indulged in and they were clamoured down by hooting, hissing, stamping on the floor and every other species of unmanly annoyance.' One speaker who stood his ground and declared 'I intend to remain until I am heard' was greeted with an unsympathetic cry of 'Oh, indeed. Well perhaps you had better brought your nightcap with you.' Much the same happened at Sheffield, where the antics of the 'physical-force' party frightened off some former supporters, including Ebenezer Elliott, who was to achieve national fame as 'the Corn-Law Rhymer'. In Leeds the Chartists' advocacy of violence lost them during 1840 the support of Samuel Smiles, whom they henceforward described contemptuously as 'the pigmy doctor' (he had originally qualified in medicine). A second defector was Edward (later Sir Edward) Baines, editor of the *Leeds Mercury*, who published a series of letters critical of Chartism, later reissued as a pamphlet, between November 1840 and January 1841. Thereafter the local Chartists dismissed those who shared his opinions as 'The Bainesocracy'.

In London, Francis Place told Richard Cobden in a letter of 29 September 1840, 'almost every working man who has ever thought upon the subject may be said to be a Chartist'. The extremists who would tolerate no cooperation with the League were few in numbers but, like other minorities, 'a formidable body' because they 'are banded together and the others are not'. He believed it should still be possible to hold public meetings for working men 'without permitting the out-and-outers to interrupt the proceedings,' but a further letter, of 2 March 1841, describing the events of the previous day, made it clear that he had been wrong:

In the evening we went to the Crown and Anchor Tavern. . . . It was a meeting of the Metropolitan Anti-Corn-Law Association and not one in fifty of the, say, two hundred and fifty Chartists who attended were members. . . . We, however, resolved to let them have their own way, their full swing as they pleased, that we might see them in their own light whatever they should say or do. . . .

'Their own light' was not slow in becoming visible:

I have seen many uproarious meetings, I have seen much ill-will, much bad feeling, much evil disposition, much malignity exhibited, much that was atrocious, but I never saw anything which would bear even a distant comparison with what I saw last night. I was very much vexed and very much ashamed of the people before me. There I sat thinking of the terrible evils of the French Revolution in its earlier periods and sure I am that if the men who composed by far the greater portion of the audience were not restrained by their fellow subjects, the policemen and the soldiers, all the horrors of the worst scenes of the French Revolution, all its monstrous cruelties and enormous evils of every kind would be outdone.

Before long, in London as in Manchester, the League was driven to meet force with force. There was, in every sense, a striking encounter between League and Chartists in the Mechanics Institute, Southampton Buildings, in Central London, the following autumn, as the *Morning Herald* reported on 1 December 1842. The chairman began by congratulating the audience 'upon the contrast which their orderly character presented to meetings of a similar nature called about eighteen months since,' but he had spoken too soon, for two mechanics, called Blackmore and Ridley, though ruled out of order, were soon on their feet trying to replace the official Anti-Corn-Law resolution by their own pro-Charter motion:

Blackmore rose to move his amendment. A cry of 'On the platform' was raised and he stepped on to it; but he had no sooner opened his address to his 'fellow countrymen' than he was assailed with tremendous cries of 'Turn him out!', 'Kick him out!', 'Throw him over!' and deafening shouts and yelling. . . .
    In the midst of the row Ridley, the other mechanic, jumped upon the platform, saying that he intended to second the amendment. This increased the uproar and the cries of 'Kick 'em out!', 'Pitch 'em over!', 'Knock 'em down!', became pretty

general among the Leaguers. The two last requests were very
soon complied with. Some half dozen of the more robust of the
Anti-Corn-Law men seized Blackmore by the neck and heels and
endeavoured to pitch him head first into the pit while at least eight
other Liberals laid hold of Ridley. A desperate struggle was made
by the two mechanics. Blackmore prevented his falling head first
into the pit by making a grip at the iron railing of the platform but
the Leaguers, by giving his knuckle some sharp knocks, made
him loose his hold and he fell into the area. . . . Ridley made a
more vigorous resistance. . . . This so exasperated the Leaguers
that they knocked him about without mercy and the reporter saw
one cowardly rascal while Ridley's arms were pinioned . . . walk
up to him and . . . deliberately strike him a heavy blow in the eye.
Numbers were at last victorious and Ridley was pitched into the
pit.

Although occasional violence continued, there were men on both
sides trying to arrange for the two movements to work in harmony.
Between September 1841 and June 1842, it later claimed, the
Metropolitan Young Men's Anti-Monopoly Association, a junior
branch of Place's organization, with 600 members, held nine
meetings 'exclusively devoted to explaining to the Chartists the
objects of the Anti-Monopoly agitation' resulting in 'that improved
feeling on the part of the Chartists towards the League which is now
visible'. At a Chartist meeting in December 1842 the delegate from
Finsbury moved a motion to the effect that 'While we remain
unaltered in our opinions respecting the Anti-Corn-Law League we
conceive it to be highly impolitic and unjust to oppose them in their
endeavours to repeal an obnoxious law.' He had, he explained, been
'authorized by his location to pass this motion . . . seeing that
many, if not all, of the League, were in favour of an extension of the
franchise'.

The conflict between League and Chartists was seen at its most
acute in Leicester, where, thanks to a declining trade, stocking-
making by hand, extremism flourished. The League had tried to
harness working-class discontent by appointing, in March 1840, a
Chartist framework knitter as chairman of a Working Men's Anti-
Corn-Law Association, but the attempt was a failure, due largely to
one dedicated near-revolutionary, Thomas Cooper. After being
brought up elsewhere, Cooper had returned to his native town in his
thirties as a reporter on the *Leicester Mercury*. The discovery of local
poverty converted him to Chartism and he became editor of a short-
lived Chartist weekly and, for the modest wage of 30s a week (often
unpaid), full-time secretary of the local Chartist Association.

Cooper's attitude was summed up as 'Manhood', i.e. the right to vote, 'even before bread,' and in his paper the *Midland Counties Illuminator* for 29 May 1841 he spelt out this doctrine:

> Operatives should parry every thrust of their opponents with that argument which even the least subtle among them find unanswerable at all times . . . 'Give us THE SUFFRAGE, and we will help you to abolish the Starvation Laws . . . but since you deny us the means of helping you, help yourselves!'

Like some other Radicals, Cooper detested the Whigs and he set out to hound and harry the Anti-Corn-Law League at every opportunity. What happened at a Repeal meeting on 1 June 1841, to which the city's two MPs had been invited, was all too typical. The two Chartist speakers were met on arrival by the Wigston band, who led a procession bearing placards denouncing the New Poor Law and having 'arrived in front of the Exchange a few minutes before the time set for the Whig meeting' proceeded to take it over:

> When a Unitarian minister arose and offered a resolution against the continuing duties on wheat, Cooper immediately objected and proposed an amendment denouncing the Whigs. . . . When a second resolution was proposed 'both the mover and seconder were compelled to do their business in dumb show, for not a syllable could be heard'. . . . At six o'clock, worn out by the unremitting opposition, the Whigs quitted their platform. Cooper called to the crowd to stand fast and . . . put forward his previous amendment as a resolution. . . . It was carried 'amidst enthusiastic acclamation'. An address to Queen Victoria 'praying her to dismiss her present evil advisers' was then proposed and carried with only two dissenting votes.

Although Cooper indignantly dismissed stories of receiving 'Tory gold' as 'a base lie,' he did not look too closely at the source of the donations he received. The band on this occasion had been paid with £10 provided by 'a certain Tory gentleman,' and Cooper also accepted £2. 10s to make up the wages of some of the workmen present, at 2s. 6d each. For himself he accepted £5 through a Conservative intermediary for an account of the meeting he sent to *The Times*, explaining blandly that 'contributions to *The Times*, if acceptable, are always repaid handsomely'.

As in other places, League supporters, exasperated beyond endurance by the wrecking of their meetings, sometimes responded in kind. One Monday night in February 1842, Cooper's appearance at a pro-League gathering in the Town Hall was the signal, according to the *Northern Star* of 19 February, for him to be 'seized by a false and malicious crew who laid hold, some of his legs, others of his arms; and one fiend-like being, gathering Mr Cooper's cloak in his grasp, pulled with all his might in such a manner that (the coat being fastened by a brass chain round the neck) the wearer was nearly throttled'. Cooper eventually shouted — probably with little exaggeration — 'Murder! They are killing me!', and a group of working men 'rushed to the rescue and with great exertion brought Mr C. upon the table, where he clung to the chains of the gas light for support,' until the mayor, who was presiding, 'put out his hand and pulled Mr C. beside him into the chair, thus placing him in safety'.

It is hard not to feel that Cooper and the Chartists often asked for what they got, but when, the next year, Cooper appeared in the dock alongside Feargus O'Connor, charged with a breach of the peace, he had the effrontery to read extracts from the League's *Anti-Corn-Law Circular* to justify his behaviour. If he and the other defendants had broken the law, he argued, 'they had erred . . . by following a precedent set them by the Anti-Corn-Law League'. He was sent to prison for two years, but had also harmed the League, for the judge described 'the passages which Cooper had read' as being 'of a very strong, inflammatory and wicked description'.

In spite of the many unhappy encounters between the League and the Chartists, many attempts were made — both locally and nationally — to produce a modified Charter which League supporters and the more moderate Chartists alike could support. A Midland Counties Charter, drawn up by League sympathizers, proposed universal suffrage for men over twenty-five who had been resident in the same place for a year, and other schemes involved granting the vote to the heads of each family. The Chartists rejected all such compromises. The *Northern Star*, on 30 May 1840, specifically warned its readers against 'walking into the Whig trap of household suffrage'. When Samuel Smiles founded, with others, a Parliamentary Reform Association in Leeds, the same paper dismissed it as 'the Fox and Geese Club'. The foolish 'geese' who joined it would in due course be eaten by their supposed friend.

On 17 November 1841 the League Council considered a proposal that it should officially support an extension of the franchise. It was agreed that 'it would be desirable to keep the League distinct from the question,' but 'at the same time . . . that it would be desirable to get as many individuals prominently engaged in Corn-Law agitation as possible to sign [the petition for a wider franchise] in order to conciliate the people'. This attempt to run with the hare while hunting with the hounds at first achieved some success. That year Joseph Sturge published an essay advocating *Reconciliation between the Middle and Lower Classes*, based on middle-class support for extending the franchise while rejecting other aspects of the Charter, from which emerged the Complete Suffrage Union.

The Chartist leaders remained unimpressed. In March 1842 the executive committee of the National Charter Association suggested to local societies that League members offering support should be coolly received:

> First, every Corn-Law Repealer or middle-class professor of Chartism, should make a public and unreserved declaration of attachment to the whole principle of the Charter. . . .
>
> Second, The Corn-Law party or middle-class agitators desiring to cooperate with us, should be called upon to agree to the unqualified right of speech for all our leaders at all political meetings and the full privilege of moving amendments to all motions, whenever it may appear . . . to be necessary.

Sturge was undeterred. More than a hundred delegates, including both 'moral-force' Chartists and leading members of the League, attended a meeting of the Complete Suffrage Union he organized in April 1842 in Birmingham. John Bright reported to Cobden afterwards, 'I never attended a more satisfactory conference. The best possible feeling prevailed and I think there is a great probability of real good being done.' The Chartists were less enthusiastic. Feargus O'Connor alleged, in Thomas Cooper's words, that 'the new movement was a dodge of the League' and considered 'Complete Suffrage was Complete Humbug.' O'Connor actually called a rival meeting in Birmingham to try and steal Sturge's thunder, and the Chartists virtually took over the Birmingham conference, which adopted all the points of the Charter. Sturge's unworldly, Quaker's faith in the reasonableness of all human beings had been proved misplaced. 'This new suffrage movement has damaged us much,' the organizer of the Manchester Operative Anti-Corn-Law Association wrote to Cobden that June. 'The Radicals who were with us before now have joined the Charter Association . . . and the poor, faithful, but ignorant and bigoted fellows who supported Corn-Law repeal . . . have been disgusted at what their poor brains consider a piece of cowardly conciliation and now give very lukewarm support.' Though O'Connor himself attended a second conference, in December 1842, the Chartist takeover was so blatant that Sturge and his supporters withdrew, until the Complete Suffrage Union finally collapsed in 1844.

The truth was, Cobden at least realized, that the aims of the two movements were totally different. 'Our business,' he told a meeting of the League in the autumn of 1842, 'is . . . to show the working men that the question of wages is a question depending altogether on principles apart from party politics. . . . If we had the Charter tomorrow the principles which govern the relations between masters and men would be precisely the same as they are now.'

CHAPTER TEN

Educating a Nation

'By the end of the year it had been resolved
greatly to increase the publications of the
League . . . for . . . a nation had to be educated
in the true principles of political economy.'
— Archibald Prentice, recalling December
1841

Public meetings, especially at election times, brought the League
useful publicity, but to undermine support for the Corn Laws in the
long term it looked to printed propaganda. A variety of
publications, known as 'tracts', accounted from the first for a major
part of its spending. Even during the first four months the publicity
budget of the Metropolitan Anti-Corn-Law Association had come
third only to its spending on petitions and on salaries, and the
215,000 copies of its publications circulated must have reached
substantially more people than the 152 lectures it had organized.
When the League raised special fighting funds much of the money
went on literature, or, as the League Council put it, 'a very large
portion of their resources has been expended in enlightening the
public mind'.

Although important from the beginning, the League's printed
publicity campaign was given even greater priority from around the
end of 1841 when it became recognized that a long-term change in
public opinion was required. A year later the ambitious project was
undertaken of attempting to 'send printed instruction into the house
of every voter throughout the kingdom,' for purposes Archibald
Prentice explained:

These silent missionaries, the tracts, would silently work their
way. They would speak truths to the sight, and truths that would
prevail. The lecturer's voice could not be heard in every village;
but the tracts, suited to every capacity, would reach every house
where an elector lived. Wherever £5 had been raised, and a
hundred bundles of tracts distributed amongst scattered voters,
there was an organization which would have a powerful effect in
every election contest. Everywhere were there organized Anti-
Corn-Law Associations — everywhere registered members of
the League. Even in the smallest boroughs the candidate would

find total repealers exercising their moral influence; and no county candidate could go into a village without finding men thoroughly qualified to discuss the question and determined to enunciate the doctrines of free trade, regardless of all local intimidation.

The operation was undertaken with the League's usual efficiency. A complete list of all the electors in every constituency was compiled and broken down into groups of fifty to a hundred, the maximum any one person could hope to cover in a day. Wherever possible, the ground was prepared by the League's paid lecturer for the area, the actual distribution being done by four or five paid assistants working under the supervision of a full-time League official, and as they also questioned everyone they visited on his politics, it was hoped to achieve a complete canvass of the whole country. Many League supporters, in return for their travelling expenses, gave their services free, and progress was rapid and substantial. By September 1843, 24 county constituencies and 187 borough ones had been covered completely, though some areas were suspiciously receptive. The organizer for the Cheltenham district, for example, was gratified to report that many local farmers had asked for extra packets of tracts, though it seems likely they merely wanted to waste the League's money. The basic package consisted of up to twelve different titles, the selection varying according to the area, and the campaign clearly had some effect. 'All say the tracts are producing a great change,' John Bright wrote to Richard Cobden in March 1843, while the information collected about the political loyalties of everyone on the electoral register gave the League an infinitely better picture of where its potential strength lay than any other party possessed.

The League's lists of pamphlets, leaflets, poems and posters covered scores of titles, many aimed at particular groups, notably farmers, and at middle-class readers. 'I must,' Cobden had written to Samuel Smiles in the late summer of 1841, 'reiterate my old song. The people are in nine cases out of ten profoundly ignorant of the nature and effects of the Bread Tax. . . . The fault lies in the apathy of the middle class. When the latter are fairly up, the working class instinctively fall into their places as the allies of the middle man.'

The paper war against the Corn Laws had begun long before the setting up of the League. Its real initiator, as mentioned earlier, was Colonel, later General, Thomas Perronet Thompson, whose classic *A Catechism on the Corn Laws, by a Member of the University of Cambridge*, first published in 1827, had by 1840 reached its twentieth edition. This 120-page volume was the Bible of the whole agitation movement, and in a 6d version, no doubt heavily subsidized, achieved a vast circulation. As one admirer wrote, 'to Colonel Thompson . . . belongs the credit of setting forth the truths which he has mastered in their clear, compact, familiar form, which . . . impressed the memories of the simplest reader'.

Perronet Thompson, as he was known, was at first sight an unlikely popularizer of economic facts. His father, a comfortably off banker and merchant, had been MP for the pre-1832 pocket borough of Midhurst, and Thompson himself had moved at fifteen from Hull Grammar School to Queen's College, Cambridge, and at nineteen, more surprisingly, to the deck of a fifty-gun man-of-war where he rapidly distinguished himself. In 1804, now twenty-one, he was elected a fellow of his old college, 'a sort of promotion,' as he commented, 'which has not often gone along with the rank and dignity of a midshipman,' but he spurned an academic career to join the 95th Rifles as a second lieutenant. He was captured during an attack on Buenos Aires, but soon released, and in 1808, still only twenty-five, was made first-ever governor of Sierra Leone, only to be recalled because of his liberal views on slavery. Thompson next served in the Peninsular War, with great distinction, but having 'exchanged' into another regiment in the hope of further fighting was court-martialled for 'rashly undertaking . . . with so small a detachment' a disastrous punitive expedition against Arab pirates in 1820. He survived the subsequent reprimand and moved steadily up the promotion ladder to the rank of lieutenant-colonel, so that it was as 'Colonel Thompson' that he was known throughout the Corn-Law period.

In 1829 Thompson bought the *Westminster Review*, to which he contributed more than a hundred articles. Politics was his favourite subject, but he was a versatile writer and his later works included *Geometry Without Axioms* and *Instructions to My Daughter for Playing on the Enharmonic Guitar*. An early advocate of Roman Catholic emancipation, and an even earlier one of House of Lords reform, Thompson made several attempts to enter Parliament and actually sat for Hull from 1835 to 1837, but though he fought three seats, making the Corn Law a major issue, he was out of the House during the time that the League was active. The *Catechism on the Corn Laws*, however, spoke for him. As one Victorian admirer remarked, 'the first half-dozen questions and answers take us at once into the middle of the controversy'. It begins as follows:

What is meant by Corn Laws?
Laws which enact that the labourer shall not exchange his produce for goods, except at certain shops — viz the shops of the

landowners; or not without paying a fine.
For whose benefits are these laws intended?
Manifestly of those who support them — the landowners.

The same robust approach marks the succeeding exchanges. When the anonymous interrogator asks, 'What is the answer to the proposition that the operatives are a lazy race and seldom go to work before Wednesday?', he is bluntly told: 'The landlords never go to work at all.' Only in response to the suggestion 'that the landlords are amiable and well conducted and their daughters handsome' does the colonel show any readiness to concede *some* good to his opponents. 'It may be true; but other men have handsome daughters to take care of too.'

So highly were Perronet Thompson's writings valued by the League that Cobden himself later edited a six-volume anthology of *Extracts* from his work which revealed, among much else, that he had a positively twentieth-century understanding of the importance of sex to a full and normal life:

> The time is not far off when the public will discover that the true criterion of the general happiness, the real measure of a home statesman's talent, is in the degree in which he provides for the honest gratification of the master passion, the tyrant instinct, which alone sustains the tragedy of life and prevents its comedy from being contemptible. . . . What a hateful world would this have been, if in addition to all the other ills of life, it had been really true that man was sent here only to work and nod at lovely women through the grate of preventive check. . . . Plenty of food leads to population and the power of populating is the measure, the gauge of public happiness.

Not every Anti-Corn-Law writer was a Perronet Thompson, but the League called upon an enormous variety of pens to advance its case, and especially to drive a wedge between the farmer and its real enemy, the aristocratic landowner. One device was to offer the handsome prizes of 20, 10 and 5 guineas for 'the best practical essays, each not to exceed sixteen pages octavo, demonstrating the injurious effects of the Corn Laws on Tenant Farmers and Farm Labourers and the advantages which those classes would derive from . . . total and immediate repeal'. The results delighted the League, which decided that all three finalists merited a first prize and issued the results as *Three Prize Essays on Agriculture and the Corn Laws* in a 4d pamphlet: 'Post free 10d, the trade supplied at half price.' The League's Chairman, George Wilson, in his introduction, cunningly mingled flattery with an appeal to the farmer's traditional reluctance to admit himself well-off:

> Although we have been constantly told that the Corn Law is maintained for your benefit . . . we ask you whether, since the passing of the famous Corn Law of 1815, with all your industry, intelligence and frugality, you have found farming to be a thriving business? On the contrary, how many moderate capitals have since that time been swept away for rent? How many small-holdings have been swallowed up by rich speculators. . . ? Cast your eyes around your various districts, tax the memories of your older neighbours and reckon the number of tenants that have been ruined and sold up for rent since the Corn Law of 1815! . . . We submit to you that the time is come when you ought to enquire whether the whole system of PROTECTION has not been contrived solely for short-sighted gain of the landlords.

These arguments proved sufficiently powerful and persuasive to provoke *A Reply*, price 1s, *to the Prize Essays of the Anti-Corn-Law League by a Lincolnshire Landowner*. 'Those who have read these publications will, we think,' asserted the author, 'come to the conclusion that these gentlemen have much to learn before they become authorities in political science.' As for the tenant-farmer who had written one of the essays, 'it is not difficult for anyone to see that Mr Hope is dissatisfied with his social position, and, finding it impossible to elevate himself above it, is endeavouring to depress those above him to his own level'.

Such ripostes, if read at all, merely gave more publicity to the original attack, and the League continued to concentrate its fire on this important target. One of the first publications of the Manchester Anti-Corn-Law Association had been an eight-page *Facts for Farmers*, and this was followed — as the League got into its stride — by *A Dialogue on the Corn Laws between a Gentleman and a Farmer* and *The Sliding Scale: or Sterling Facts for Farmers*, the latter priced at 1d: had not the Corn Laws left farmers too badly off to afford more expensive publications? Archibald Prentice contributed *An Address to Farmers, on the Way in which their Families are to be Provided For*, which explained how his family 'had farmed land on the same estate from the time of Queen Elizabeth' but how, as one of four brothers, he himself had been denied this opportunity. It was a common problem: in twenty families known to Prentice, only 4 out of 47 sons had become farmers and only 4 of the 32 daughters had become farmers' wives. 'The landowner had other means of providing for his sons; the Bar, the church, the army, the navy, the colonies, and government offices were all open to them. "But how," I asked, "are *you* the farmers of Great Britain and Ireland to find employment for *your* sons?".' The answer lay in commerce and industry, and in abolishing the Corn Laws to increase the prosperity of agriculture.

By 1842 the range of publications available to the League's supporters was enormous. *Monopoly or Machinery: Which is the Real Enemy of the Working Classes?*, *America and the Corn Laws* (by a citizen of Ohio), *Fallacies of the Protective System Exposed*, *Daily Bread, or Taxation without Representation Resisted*, and *The Moral and Religious Bearings of the Corn Laws* (by a clergyman) were but a few of the works on offer. Scores of speeches, particularly by Cobden, were reissued as pamphlets, while no League activist's home was complete without a copy of *The Corn-Law-Repealer's Handbook*, which gave statistics and quotations for instant use.

Literature was sold to local Associations at cost price, in the cheapest possible format. Charles Villiers' speech of March 1839, which had failed to move the House of Commons, did duty again, as Archibald Prentice noted, 'in two sheets octavo, containing as much matter as an ordinary shilling pamphlet, but . . . was charged to the various Associations at three-half-pence . . . Mr Poulett Thompson's speech, occupying sixteen pages octavo, was supplied at three-farthings.' The growing print-runs were an index of the League's expansion. 10,000 copies of the first 'tracts' were thought sufficient, but later editions ran to 50,000, and at the height of the campaign, to 500,000. Some publications were ceremonially burned by the League's opponents, but this was a counter-productive gesture, merely providing more publicity. By the end of 1841 the number of handbills and similar items distributed had already reached 1,250,000, and 20,000 copies of *The Anti-Corn-Law Almanack*, with appropriate quotations and facts on every page, hung in the homes of League members. No previous movement had conducted a propaganda campaign on anything approaching the same scale; but this was only the beginning, and as Prentice recorded, 'by the end of the year . . . it had been resolved greatly to increase the publications of the League . . . for . . . a nation had to be educated in the true principles of political economy, a nation had to be convinced of the folly and injustice of its past commercial policy'.

By October 1842 the League Council was contemplating spending, on all its propagandist activities, £1,000 a week, though announcing that 'more than five millions of tracts have been printed and circulated'. But there was no suggestion of any weakening of effort, and in November a new technique was started — that of binding copies of propagandist leaflets into the *Anti-Corn-Law Circular* so that subscribers could detach and distribute them to make new converts. 50,000 pamphlets were circulated in this way in October 1842, 60,000 in November, and 120,000 in December. By then, eight bales of pamphlets a night were, John Bright revealed, being despatched from Manchester. A report prepared by the Council in the autumn of 1843 confirmed that no fewer than 5,000,000 'tracts' had been distributed to electors door to door during the year, another 3,600,000 had been sent to 'the working classes and others' not yet on the register, and 426,000 had been bound with the League's regular periodicals, a total of more than 9,000,000 items, weighing in excess of a hundred tons. Inevitably, all this activity provoked a further response from the League's opponents, and Bright suggested that one such effort — a seventy-page article in the *Quarterly Review* — might be distributed with the League's literature 'that the people might read one and then the other'.

By 1842 the controversy had even spilled over into the pages of that year's edition — the seventh — of the *Encyclopaedia Britannica*, which under the new heading of 'Corn Laws and Corn Trade' argued in favour of a small fixed duty:

> Though advocates for the entire repeal of the restrictive system, and of all the regulations formed for the sake of protection, we are not of the number of those who propose throwing the ports open without any duty. We should do this if we were satisfied that the agriculturists were not more heavily taxed than the other classes. . . . Owing to the parochial and other burdens laid on the land, those occupying it are really subject to heavier burdens than most other classes. We should in this case reckon it safer to err on the side of too much protection, than of too little, and would not therefore object to fixed duty of 6s or 7s a quarter being laid on wheat and a proportional duty on other species of grain.

In one respect, and one alone, the League's propaganda was no better than that of the two other popular agitations being waged in this period, against the workhouse and the demon drink. The verse produced by Anti-Corn-Law poets was, without exception, appalling. Sir John Bowring, for example — though he had produced a series of anthologies with titles such as *Specimens of the Russian Poets*, *Specimens of the Polish Poets*, and *Poetry of the Magyars* — was no exception, as one specimen published by Archibald Prentice in the *Manchester Times* in 1841 demonstrated (though Prentice loyally asserted that it embodied 'in poetic form the feelings of millions at the close of this year of wretchedness'):

> '*Died of Starvation*' — *Coroners' Inquests*
> I met Famine on my way,
> Prowling for human prey,
> Clogged with filth and clad in rags,
> Ugliest of all ugly hags.
> Lo! a sceptre wreathed with snakes
> In her withered hands she shakes;
> And I heard the hag proclaim —
> 'Bread Tax is my sceptre's name!'

The Corn Laws made the reputation, though undeservedly, of one early-Victorian writer, Ebenezer Elliott, known to contemporaries as 'the Corn-Law Rhymer'; his *Corn-Law Rhymes* appeared frequently between 1831 and 1846 and were republished in his collected *Poetical Works*. Born in 1781, near Rotherham, the son of an unsuccessful iron-founder, Elliott's naturally solitary and gloomy temperament was encouraged by the failure of the family business which, with little reason, he blamed on the Corn Laws; the credit for his reviving fortunes, after he had moved to Sheffield, he attributed, with more justice, to a loan from his wife's relations. He abandoned the Chartists because of their refusal to cooperate in the great crusade. 'Our labour, our skill, our profits, our hopes, our lives, our children's souls are bread-taxed,' he declared, and indeed it was said of him that 'He scarcely spoke or wrote of anything besides the Corn Laws.' Elliott published his first *Corn-Law Rhymes* as early as 1831, and — together with his later *More Verse and Prose by the Corn-Law Rhymer* — they clearly struck some sort of chord in the public mind. In his day Elliott was praised by a Poet Laureate — admittedly only Robert Southey — compared to Crabbe, and 'discovered' and publicized by a much-acclaimed, though later obscure, Victorian novelist, Sir Edward Bulwer (later Lord) Lytton, who oddly enough was himself a dedicated opponent of the League throughout its career.

All too typical of Elliott's work is an incomplete fragment, inspired by a conversation with a stranger in a railway carriage. (The location was a reminder of how times were changing; a slightly earlier pro-temperance dialogue had been set in a stage-coach.)

> SCENE: *A wide plain, covered with skeletons and snow*
>   *Enter* PAYALL *and* ALLBELLY
> *Payall*: Heart of mud and brain of steel!

> What has thou been doing?
> *Allbelly*: Calming tumult, curing ruin —
>   Eating children, fathers, mothers,
>   Nieces, nephews, sisters, brothers;
>   Heaped thousands at a meal. . .
> *The plain is suddenly darkened, and a gigantic Shadow enters,*
>   *deepening the gloom.*
> *Shadow* (to Allbelly): Eternal Stink! Where are my children?

Although Elliott, a true Victorian, had thirteen children, they seem to have brought him little consolation; the common nineteenth-century interest in death he embraced with relish, as in this gloomy song designed to be sung to a traditional tune:

> Child is thy father dead?
>   Father is gone!
> Why did they tax his bread?
>   God's will be done! . . .
> Father, with panting breast,
>   Groan'd to be gone.
> Now he is with the blest —
> Mother says death is best!
> We have no place of rest —
>   Yes, ye have one!

If this verse, and others like it, accurately reflected the poet's approach to life, it must have been a disappointment to him to survive until the age of sixty-eight. After his death, in 1849, the working men of Sheffield, not perhaps great readers of verse, nevertheless subscribed £600 for a statue in his memory in the market-place — though it was later moved to a less prominent location.

Like its verse, the League's pictorial publicity was disappointing, except for the work which the League commissioned from Thomas Makepeace Thackeray, then a rising young journalist and illustrator (*Vanity Fair*, which was to make his name, did not appear until 1847). Thackeray was engaged to draw a number of cartoons directed among others at the future Lord Shaftesbury, then still Lord Ashley. Ashley's concentration on a single reform, protecting child factory workers, led Cobden to dismiss him, unfairly, as an 'aristocratic and canting simpleton'. Cobden's brief to Thackeray suggested a hard-hitting, not to say malicious, design for a woodcut:

A tall mill and high chimney in back — clock at 5 a.m. Two or three pale and starved children going to work with large bits of bread in their hands. Lord Ashley has taken the bread from the first child and has broken it in two, and whilst putting the larger share in his pocket and returning the smaller to the child, he lifts up his eyes and in a very sanctimonious tone says, 'I will never rest until the poor factory child is protected by a ten-hours bill from the tyranny of the merciless and grasping mill-owners.'

The caption revealed the reason for the League's hostility: 'The Landowner and the Factory Child', for conditions on the family estates had been the subject of much criticism, though the fault was Ashley's father's rather than his own. Cobden suggested that 'Mr Thackeray's next effort should be "the factory children and their protector". . . . We shall take care that every member of both Houses receives a copy. The clubs, too, must be strewn with these things.'

The League disdained no means of making its views and slogans known. There were Anti-Corn-Law tea-and-breakfast sets, bearing such messages as 'Give us this day our daily bread,' and the enthusiastic member could, for 1s, buy eighteen sheets of Anti-Corn-Law wafers, enclosed according to one admiring visitor to League headquarters, 'in a pretty cover,' and ready for sticking on to letters or envelopes. It was claimed in 1842 that 'several millions have been sold,' and each sheet contained thirty-five 'short mottoes, couplets and aphorisms of every class, grave and gay, serious and satirical, witty and unmeaning . . . sometimes taken from the Bible, sometimes from the works of celebrated writers and orators, sometimes from the speeches and publications of the Leaguers themselves':

Every man who would not welcome revolution should oppose the Corn Law, or it will revolutionize the kingdom. The landlords allow *bones* to be brought from foreign ports, but insist upon the *meat* and corn being left behind, to rot.

Who passed the Corn Law? The landlords. For what purpose? To keep up their high rents.

Another ingenious idea was to provide this diamond-shaped dissertation:

Thanks
for cheap
postage. May
we soon get cheap
bread. Free Communica-
tion with all parts of the
empire is good: but free
trade with all parts
of the world
will be still
better.

The cumulative effect of this prolonged and multifarious barrage of propaganda must have been substantial. 'All say the tracts are producing a great change,' John Bright told Cobden in March 1843, while Cobden himself, in the same year, professed quiet optimism. 'We have at the end of four years' agitation,' he wrote to a foreign friend, 'got a pretty strong hold of public opinion, and at the present moment the Free Trade Party is gaining ground more rapidly than at any former period.'

CHAPTER ELEVEN

Between Friends

'*The Circular* is the medium of communication
betwixt the League and its friends.'
— Letter from Sidney Smith, 2 May 1840

Although it attracted many sympathizers the real backbone of the
Anti-Corn-Law agitation lay in the paid-up members of the League,
who attended its meetings, distributed its publications, and above
all provided its income. As early as February 1839 the Finance
Committee of the Anti-Corn-Law Association had begun to assess
the amounts expected from the various local Associations. The
conference which that March converted the Association into the
League resolved that the League Council should collect £5,000 to
pay for its operations until December, but the local Associations
remained under no obligation to join the League or contribute to its
finances. Within a few months the League was seriously in debt and
kept going only thanks to the generosity of a few individuals. In
June 1840 Cobden wrote of 'knowing a certain number of real
friends upon whom we can rely permanently for an income
sufficient to enable us to keep alive the League'. By an unspecified
Monday in 1841, however, he was warning J.B. Smith that 'Up here
we are in a state of bankruptcy. But the officers of a ship should stick
to her while there is timber left. You and I are the commanders of the
League and we must do our duty now.' That same year, the League's
Chief Clerk, Joseph Hickin, told Cobden: 'We are still in an awful
situation here for want of money. . . . The present liabilities are at
least £1,400 and many of the claimants are becoming very
clamorous.' Once again, though, disaster was avoided, and from the
following year, 1842, onward the League's survival was never really
in doubt.

This transformation ultimately reflected a change of sentiment in
the country, but a major factor was the outstanding ability of the
men responsible for the League's day-to-day operations. The most
important, apart from Richard Cobden, was the League's chairman,
George Wilson. Born in Derbyshire in 1808, the son of a corn
merchant who in 1819 settled in Manchester, George Wilson
acquired his education at the Manchester commercial school and at
evening classes before setting up in business as a corn merchant and
later as a manufacturer of starch and gum. During the mid-1830s he

found his true vocation, as a political organizer, when he became secretary to the committee working to secure the incorporation of Manchester as a borough. In 1839, at the age of thirty, he became a member of the Anti-Corn-Law Association and, soon, with Cobden and 'Corn-Law' Smith, one of the three men who really ran it. His most striking and consistent service to the League was the masterly way in which he conducted meetings. One Manchester contemporary declared that he displayed 'the very genius of chairmanship, acquiring in that capacity a touch and virtuosity which have not been approached in the history of the platform,' and Cobden was well aware of the debt the League owed to him. 'You and I made the League and the League made others,' he wrote to Wilson in July 1846. At a meeting of the League Council Cobden paid his colleague further tribute:

> The services of Mr Wilson have not been on the surface like those of some of us. The practical details of the business of the League have been entirely under the care of Mr Wilson; and I will say, after seeing many public men, and knowing something of public business, that I never met with a man who possesses such instinctive sagacity in ascertaining the principles and motives which actuate men and such a comprehensive power of dealing with matters of business.

From its foundation in March 1839 Wilson regularly presided over the meetings of the League Council, and when, in 1841, J.B. Smith retired from the Presidency Wilson succeeded him. On 6 October 1842 he announced a major reorganization, which involved dividing up the country into twelve areas, each managed by a full-time secretary-lecturer. In each area active and reliable League members were designated 'registrars', responsible for collecting money and recruiting. The financial basis of the League was also strengthened by a then-novel device. Anyone joining a local Association automatically became also a member of the League on payment to the central office of a 1d registration fee, but anything else the Association raised it retained — and most Associations, as the League recommended, issued an elaborate membership card, for display on wall or mantelpiece.

The League's governing body was in theory its Council, consisting of all who had subscribed £50 or more, ultimately more than 500. For practical purposes, however, the League was run by a few Council members living near Manchester. The Council met each day for two to three hours, sometimes more than once, normally with 12 or more members present (though it once dropped to three); an exceptionally important agenda on occasion brought in 20 or 30 members. Inevitably the militants tended to do most of the work, notably Archibald Prentice, who attended 1,117 Council meetings, a total exceeded only by George Wilson's 1,361, though six other members attended more than 250. Other Council members often dropped in at the League offices to keep in touch with what was happening.

While Wilson was presiding over the Council meetings, the actual administration rested primarily upon Joseph Hickin, who had been chief organizer of the Radicals in Walsall, Staffordshire. In 1841 he moved to Manchester to become Chief Clerk in the League office, where he introduced more effective methods of controlling expenditure and handling correspondence. Hickin felt a deep loyalty to the League's ideals, and on one occasion discretely warned Cobden when a Council meeting consisting only of Prentice and two fellow militants had instigated a dangerous change of policy; the offending decision was duly reversed at a later meeting.

The administrative machine which Hickin operated and George Wilson directed was far more effective than that of most comparable bodies of the period. Before the League's appearance, commercial organization had barely emerged from its pre-Industrial Revolution state. The start of a national postage system and the League's establishment were intimately bound up together. Like Francis Place, Richard Cobden had been an active campaigner for a cheap and reliable postal service and in May 1838 had given evidence about it on behalf of the Manchester Chamber of Commerce to a Parliamentary select committee. At that time, he estimated, four out of five letters between London and Manchester were being delivered by private means, the state having priced itself out of the market. He had invited Rowland Hill, the real author of the 'penny post', to lecture in Manchester, and the League was one of the first beneficiaries when, in 1839, the chaotic old system with charges levied on the recipient was replaced by a standard 4d pre-paid rate. The penny post finally came into operation on 10 January 1840, immediately multiplying the volume of letters handled by three, and increasing the League's own correspondence a hundredfold. Cobden told Rowland Hill in 1843 that the whole agitation was 'the spawn of your penny postage' and without the new postal service and the railways, the League could never have made the impact it did.

The League had a vast postbag and all letters on arrival were routed through a central registry and assigned to one of four appropriate departments: Publications, Electoral Organization, Finance or the Secretariat. Each department at headquarters was supervised by a chief clerk, earning £200 a year; the juniors received from £1. 7s to £1. 10s a week. Some of the more senior officials were experts in electoral law, but the League also retained a firm of solicitors as legal advisers and engaged others as necessary in individual constituencies. By 1843 it also employed no fewer than 300 people, full-time or part-time, in packing and distributing its publications in Manchester alone.

In maintaining its mailing and subscription list the League pioneered the use of a card-index system, with cards colour-coded, and identified by letters and numbers, to indicate the member's area and usual subscription. According to one employee, this revealed 'at a glance the value of the cards sent out . . . the names and residences of the parties to whom sent, the amounts and deficiencies of those returned, and so on'. Financial control, at a time when many organizations suffered from defaulting treasurers, was strict. One major item of expenditure, postage, was controlled by having all outgoing mail handled by a central office. The League also employed a resident accountant in its cashier's office and the accounts were audited annually by an outside firm, but in any case the quality and integrity of its staff were high.

General administration was in the hands of the League Secretariat, which — in contrast to the casual way in which government business was then transacted — worked out a regular office routine. Papers needing to be considered by the Council had to arrive before 10 a.m., publications matters were considered at noon on Thursday, accounts approved at 3 p.m. that day, and so on, ensuring the most economical use of the time of the busy businessmen who managed the League's affairs.

Proof of the soundness of the League's administration was provided by the ease with which it managed to expand its activities from 1842 onwards. By now the original accommodation had proved insufficient and additional rooms were rented in Newall's Buildings, including a former picture gallery for the largest meetings. The offices had become so famous that they were on the itinerary of foreign visitors. Among the latter was a German, J.G. Kohl, who later included in a book a handsome tribute to the efficiency of the League's operations:

> I was astonished to observe how the Leaguers, all private persons, mostly merchants, manufacturers and men of letters, conducted political business, like statesmen and ministers. . . . Whilst I was in the committee room immense numbers of letters were brought in, opened, read and answered, without a moment's delay. . . . Some brought news of the movements of eminent Leaguers or of their opponents. . . . Others contained pecuniary contributions

from well-wishers . . . for each of whom the President immediately dictated an appropriate letter of thanks. Other letters related anecdotes, showing the progress of the cause and the gradual defection of the farmers. . . . The League has now, by means of local Associations . . . extended its operation and influence over the whole country and attained an astonishing national importance. Its festivals, Anti-Corn-Law bazaars, Anti-Corn-Law banquets and others of like nature, appear like great national anniversaries.

. . . All the publications of the League are not only written but printed, bound and published at the League Rooms in Market Street, Manchester. I went through the various rooms where these operations were carried on, until I came at last to the great League Depot, where books, pamphlets, letters, newspapers, speeches, reports, tracts and wafers were all piled in neat packets of every possible size and appearance, like the packets of muslin and calico in the great warehouses of Manchester. Beyond this was a refreshment room, in which tea was offered us by several ladies. . . .

Meetings of the Executive Committee might stretch over the whole day, and its members also travelled a great deal to speak all over the country — but even more striking was the work done by unpaid volunteers. 'Never, perhaps,' wrote Archibald Prentice, 'had there been any association where so large a portion of the labour to be performed was without other remuneration than the consciousness of discharging a duty. Occasionally circumstances arose that required instant attention and instant work and, on these emergencies, it was not uncommon to see thirty or forty persons, for weeks together, coming at five or six o'clock in the morning, and labouring until midnight as closely and earnestly as if their own existence depended upon the swiftness of their pens.'

From the moment that the League began to make a national impact, there was discussion, if not dissension, about the location of its headquarters. It seemed sensible that a national campaign, aimed at influencing opinion in Parliament, should be directed from London, but the 'capital' of the free-trade movement was Manchester, where its leaders and most active members had their homes. Nor were League supporters in London enthusiastic about a move south, fearing the loss of their own independence. Nothing, Francis Place warned Sidney Smith, could be more inexpedient, in his view, than bringing the *Anti-Corn-Law Circular* to London: 'The expense and loss will be enormous.' Smith duly relayed this opinion to Manchester, on 1 May 1840.

It was not until the first conference in the Free Trade Hall early in 1843, already described, that the decision to move the League's headquarters was finally reached. The actual changeover took place that spring, and was by no means popular among those involved — the Manchester men were no doubt as reluctant to be uprooted as people usually are in such circumstances, while those working in London resented the sudden influx of strangers. 'The League office,' complained one Londoner, the propagandist writer W.J. Fox, 'is become perfectly horrible since the main body of the Goths and Vandals came down from Manchester; it is worse than living in a factory.'

In fact, the move proved more apparent than real. The Council remained in Manchester and its Chief Clerk, Hickin, and his immediate colleagues soon returned there. The impressive offices opened at 67 Fleet Street were used largely for a temporary and local campaign to raise funds, and the arrival of the newcomers does seem to have stimulated the London contingent to fresh exertions. A door-to-door collection on a large scale was organized and a series of mass meetings held, the Theatre Royal, Drury Lane, for example, being hired for five nights in March and April 1843 for £300 — a transaction which gained valuable publicity in the Liberal press.

The move to London also involved the transfer of the editorial offices of its members' newsletter. The *Anti-Corn-Law Circular* had been launched as a fortnightly publication, intended primarily for members, in April 1839, and claimed a circulation of 15,000, though many copies were given away. It suffered from a small and cramped format, but as Sidney Smith explained, in a letter to Manchester on 2 May 1840: 'the *Circular* is the medium of communication between the League and its friends'. On 21 April 1841 the name was altered to the *Anti-Bread-Tax Circular*, but the change failed to reverse a serious decline in sales, and on 25 April 1842 the League's printer reported to Cobden that 'the *Circular* is down to 2,400, out of which 700 are gratuitous, reducing the actual sale to 1,700'. Bravely, the frequency of publication was increased and from 1 December 1842 the *Circular* became a weekly, until on 30 September 1843 it was replaced by the *League*, a three-column sixteen-page periodical, measuring 13½ by 8½ inches, closely packed with text. By now the original intention had given way to a desire to reach outsiders, especially farmers, for reports of meetings were mingled with a column giving up-to-the-minute crop prices, and such items as a report of a local farmer 'at the meeting of the Stow-on-the-Wold and Chipping Norton Agricultural Association . . . being congratulated on his successful prize for stock'.

The *League* had some success in attracting advertisements, the final three pages of the issue just quoted, for example, consisting of classified advertisements. 'Frampton's Pill of Health,' the keen League member was assured, should prove efficacious 'for correcting all disorders of the stomach and bowels', as indeed it should have done at 1s. 1½d a box. In spite of advertising, the commitment to provide a free copy to everyone subscribing more than £1 a year proved a constant financial strain, costing the League £500 a year. Like the League itself, the *Circular* had in one respect started life at a fortunate time, for the newspaper stamp duty had been reduced in 1837 from 3d to 1d. The excise authorities having ruled in 1839 that the *Circular* was a newspaper, it became liable to this duty, but also qualified for free carriage through the mails.

In addition to the *Circular* and the *League*, a four-page paper, the *Free Trader*, edited by Sidney Smith and priced 1d, was issued for a time, but it was poor, rambling stuff, consisting of turgid or would-be facetious comment on contemporary events. Much more effective, at least as journalism, was a 'fringe' publication, the *Struggle*, whose founder, editor and virtually sole contributor, Joseph Livesey, came from a far humbler background than any of the League's great men.* Livesey, orphaned at the age of seven, had taught himself to read and write and worked as a handloom weaver from the age of ten, until setting up in business as a cheese merchant. In 1831, aged thirty-seven, he had first begun to campaign actively against the Corn Laws and he later became first Secretary of the Preston Anti-Corn-Law Association. In December 1841, aided by experience with temperance publications, his chief interest, he launched the *Struggle*, an illustrated four-page paper, about half the size of *Punch*, which had recently been founded, but priced at ½d; the *League*, when started two years later, cost 3d.

Although the *Struggle* appeared every week, it was numbered not dated, and each issue was self-contained and could be used as a pamphlet, being small enough to be enclosed in an ordinary letter through the penny post. An editorial on the first page of the first edition struck the keynote for all 235 issues:

> The character of this paper is indicated by its title — the *Struggle*. Good and evil, truth and error, are constantly struggling against each other. . . . Though this paper will at present *struggle* for Cheap Bread, it may occasionally step aside to contend with other evils. It has no connection with any association and no person is responsible for its contents but myself.

*Joseph Livesey's life is described in detail in my book, *The Waterdrinkers*, pp.38-41.

Livesey expressly disclaimed any 'pretensions to literary attainments' but his paper, with its brief paragraphs, pithy anecdotes and vigorous language, was by far the most readable of all the publications associated with the League. 'After the name of Cobbett. . . ,' testified Richard Cobden of Livesey, 'I know of no writer who has had the happy art of putting questions of a difficult and complex character in a more simple and lucid form,' while John Bright commented that the paper 'told the story of cruelty and wickedness of the Corn Law in pictures and language that could not be misunderstood'. The *Struggle* had at its peak a weekly circulation of 12,000 to 15,000 so that nearly 3,000,000 copies were printed during its 4½-year life, making it, as Livesey's biographer pointed out, 'the most popular journal the free-trade movement ever had'. What marked it out, apart from its simple language, was its emphasis on human-interest stories which translated general statements about poverty into concrete examples. This item in issue No. 2 was typical:

A poor woman came to visit her relations in Preston. She went to nine houses, and none of them could afford her a meal's meat; the last place she called at was in Albert Street, where the man pawned his shirt for 6d, with which four pennyworth of bread, one pennyworth of butter and one pennyworth of tea were purchased for the party.

When the Duke of Norfolk advised people who were starving to take a pinch of curry powder to quieten their clamorous stomachs, Livesey was quick to publicize and deride the suggestion; when that traditional butt of the League's hostility, Lord Ashley, advocated baths as a means of improving one's appetite, Livesey carried a cartoon showing a poor man replying 'God bless me, my lord . . . I have got the appetite; what I want is the food.' To wild predictions of agricultural disaster if protection were lifted, Livesey replied with robust common sense:

People talk as if some great convulsion would happen to the land if the Corn Law was repealed. The land, happy in its resources, would be entirely unconscious of the change. Cows would give quite as much milk; the same quantity of potatoes would come off an acre; and the corn fields would not yield one ear less than at present. There would be no difference; green fields would still be green; and English hens would not lay one egg less if French eggs came in duty free. There would be this advantage, that as horse keep and man keep would be much cheaper the land would be cultivated at less expense.

Livesey's advocacy was also valuable in helping to rebut the often-made suggestion that the League's agitation was, to quote his biographer, 'a class movement in the interests of the manufacturers' and on the question of Chartism, though in favour of extending the franchise, he was entirely at one with the League:

> In plain truth, next to the air we breathe, our first want is *food*, and the *first* act of every legislature should be to secure *an abundant supply to every human being*. . . . The nation should listen to nothing else till *this* be done. The people should set their minds upon it and determine to have it. The *dinner agitation* should be the first, and every other question regarded as of inferior moment.

In spite of its constant appeals to high moral principle, the League was not above commissioning writers to make its case while pretending to be independent. The most successful was Alexander Somerville, best perhaps described as a professional working man. The son of a Scottish carter and the grandson on his mother's side of a farm labourer, Somerville had worked as a 6s-a-week cowherd and sawyer before, in 1832, enlisting in the Scots Greys, who were about to be used against pro-Reform-Bill rioters. For organizing a protest within his regiment, Somerville received the savage punishment of a hundred lashes, which proved the making of him. A natural barrack-room lawyer, he secured a court of inquiry into his condemnation, which converted him into a popular hero, and £300 was raised to resettle him in civilian life. After serving as a mercenary in Spain, Somerville succeeded in supporting himself as a journalist. His letters to the *Morning Chronicle* caught Cobden's eye and, in 1842, when Somerville was thirty-one, he was offered work by the League as a roving investigator, collecting information about rural poverty. His identity, as an already-notorious Radical, was kept dark, his articles being signed *The Whistler at the Plough*, and he was referred to in correspondence by a code name, Reuben. He proved a sore trial to his employers for he had a weakness for the bottle and disappeared for days at a time while indulging it, or sleeping it off. Later in life, Somerville became destitute, blaming his downfall on his agents and publishers. His admirers raised enough to ship him off to Canada, but it proved the same old story, and he died ingloriously in a shed in Toronto, in 1885, at the age of seventy-four.

Another publicist covertly engaged to present the League's case was William John Fox, the self-educated son of an unsuccessful Suffolk farmer. After working as an errand boy and a clerk, Fox found his route out of poverty via a nonconformist training college and a post as a unitarian minister. Fox became famous as a preacher and orator — Francis Place described him as 'the bravest of us all' and Archibald Prentice, after hearing him speak at Drury Lane and Covent Garden, wrote of 'a beauty of elocution which Macready on the same boards might have envied'. He also became a highly effective journalist, and worked at various times for the *Sunday Times*, the *Morning Chronicle* and the *Daily News*; but like Somerville, he had his private difficulties, in Fox's case a separation from his wife and his advocacy, when the subject was still barely mentionable, of easier divorce. When on form, Fox was considered unrivalled in the combined appeal to sentiment and piety which the Victorians so much admired. 'I take it,' Cobden wrote caustically, 'that we may have Fox's pen and tongue by paying for them,' and this indeed proved the case, Fox obligingly, and very competently, turning out any special appeal or denunciation that was required for £20 a time. Fox, to be fair to him, did have a deep commitment to social justice, and having been elected as MP for Oldham in 1847 he added to his reputation in Parliament. Shrewder and more sober than Somerville, he made good use of an annuity settled upon him by a wealthy supporter and died at the age of seventy-eight, in 1864, one of those 'great Victorians' since wholly forgotten.

The League also recruited a much-respected academic, Dr W. Cooke Taylor, to find historical justification for its championship of free trade — evidence which, not surprisingly, was duly forthcoming. 'I find it an invariable rule,' he wrote to Cobden, 'that free and equitable trade always was a bond of peace and that the spirit of monopoly . . . became the frequent source of war.' Later the good doctor wrote a supposedly objective travel book, *Notes on a Tour in the Manufacturing Districts*, which the League also secretly financed.

The League's collective conscience seems to have been untroubled by such deceptions or the even more dubious practice of secretly subsidizing newspapers which promised to carry laudatory reports or articles about its activities. In the summer of 1839 it began to pay £125 a quarter to the *Sun* newspaper (no connection with today's daily of the same name) for this purpose and, lower down the journalistic scale, the *Penny Satirist* was also rewarded for carrying Anti-Corn-Law articles and cartoons. A slightly subtler method was a promise to buy in bulk any paper which carried a favourable leading article, and during 1842 no fewer than eight weekly papers provided 3,000 copies of appropriate issues, which were later given away on trains and in shops and inns, in addition to the 130,000 copies a week sold in the normal way.

The League's most remarkable publishing achievement was the launching as a propaganda organ of the *Economist*, which still flourishes today of course, though now independently. The *Economist* was never formally owned by the League, but was founded in 1843 by a dedicated League supporter, James Wilson, avowedly to support it, and the League Council undertook, that August, to buy 20,000 copies for distribution to leading opponents. The magazine was careful to avoid any direct connection with the League or the Liberals, but it seems likely that at least once a substantial donation was forthcoming in its early years to keep the *Economist* afloat, though it later proved well able to survive unaided.

CHAPTER TWELVE

Millions of Signatures

> 'Petitions have been presented to the legislature
> with millions of signatures praying for the
> redress of the great wrong under which the
> country groans.'
> — Address issued by the Council of the Anti-
> Corn-Law League, 13 October 1842

The petition to Parliament as a means of advertising a national grievance had a long and honourable history even before the Anti-Corn-Law League came on the scene. Few organizations, however, can have used it so enthusiastically. The Manchester Association had hardly been founded before it was supplying printed petition forms to others elsewhere, and it became regular practice to pave the way for Charles Villiers' annual motion in Parliament with a barrage of such documents, the first in 1839 having 1,250,000 signatures, and the second, in May 1840, some 250,000. The bombardment continued, until the clerks responsible must have groaned at the very name of the Corn Laws. Up to 2 March alone, in the 1842 session, 2,758 petitions calling for repeal were presented, bearing 1,469,476 signatures; the figures on the other side, pleading for the Corn Laws to remain, were by contrast merely 123 and 71,279 respectively. The League Council did not exaggerate when, in October 1842, it issued a progress report which asserted that 'petitions have been presented to the legislature with millions of signatures, praying for the redress of the great wrong under which the country groans'.

Typical were the terms of one of the earliest petitions, submitted even before the Anti-Corn-Law Association had been formally launched:

PETITION
TO THE
HOUSE OF COMMONS
PRAYING FOR THE
TOTAL AND IMMEDIATE
REPEAL OF THE CORN LAWS

To the Honourable the Commons of Great Britain and Ireland in Parliament assembled

The humble Petition of the Inhabitants of the Borough of Manchester, assembled at a Public Meeting duly convened by the municipal authorities of the said borough.

HUMBLY SHEWETH,

That a free exchange of the products of industry for the corn and food of other countries is the natural and inherent right of the people of every nation — a right clearly recognized by the Creator himself, in awarding to various climes the different productions of the earth for the common benefit of all His creatures.

That the Corn Law violates the sacred principles of religion and morality, by interposing a barrier between the bounties of divine Providence and the wants of the industrious millions of this country; thus depriving them of the means of independent subsistence and subjecting them to the evils of disease, demoralization and premature death. That, at the present time, the baneful influences of the Corn Law are exerting themselves with peculiar severity upon the middle and working classes of the community; injuring the banker by the derangement of the currency; oppressing the merchant and dealer by the excessive rate of interest; annihilating the profits of the capitalist; and that, unless repealed, this destructive law will, by banishing our manufactures to other countries, and throwing upon the soil the entire burden of supporting a destitute and unemployed population, involve the landowners, with every other class, in one common ruin,

Therefore, your petitioners most humbly pray your Right Honourable House, that the Corn Laws be entirely and immediately abolished.

Such statements, however little attention Parliament paid to them, had a useful propaganda value, and other versions were soon in circulation, though few as crisp and to the point as the 'Family Petition' which Joseph Livesey submitted in 1843, and also published in the *Struggle*:

The Petition of Joseph Livesey (and family) cheese factor, Preston, in the County of Lancaster,

Humbly Sheweth

That they regard the Corn and Provision Laws of this country as unjust, cruel, impolitic, deceitful, and impious, and fast tending in their influence to ruin the whole country.

They, therefore, humbly beg your Honourable House IMMEDIATELY to REPEAL the same. . . .

The names of all eleven Liveseys followed, including young Joseph and Jane, perhaps the youngest signatories to such a document, though Children's Petitions had already enjoyed something of a vogue. The *Northern Star* had protested on 25 January 1840 that the teachers at Sunday schools in Bradford, Keighley and Macclesfield had not merely organized petitions among their pupils but had added the names of those too young or unlettered to do so. Nor was similar pressure on adults unknown. According to the same, hostile source, the workpeople in one factory in Huddersfield had complained that the petition 'was in the counting house and we had to sign'. The *Anti-Corn-Law Circular*, however, insisted that such demonstrations of feeling were spontaneous, claiming, for example, that nearly every adult male in Rochdale had signed an Anti-Corn-Law petition as had the majority of those approached not merely in Manchester, Barnsley and Rossendale, but also in Kirkcaldy in far-off Fife. Manufacturers were certainly asked to circulate petitions and Cobden was told, in a letter of 24 March 1840, that 'almost every mill in Stalybridge, Ashton and Dukinfield agreed to take sheets for signature yesterday and I hope we shall induce the manufacturers in the other adjoining towns to do the same'.

In November 1841, shortly before the reassembly of Parliament, a delegate meeting in Manchester, attended by 120 people, unanimously voted in favour of 'petitioning the House of Commons for the total and immediate repeal of the Corn Law, from, if possible, every town, village, congregation and workshop'. Though such a petition never materialized, the desire to secure every possible signature to every possible petition led at least once to the League overreaching itself. Few areas were less enthusiastic about repeal than the rural districts of Yorkshire, and there was, therefore, a good deal of surprise when the *Doncaster Gazette* reported that in the small town of Epworth, sixteen miles away, more than a tenth of the 2,000 residents — which meant at least one in five of the men — had signed a petition presented to the House of Commons on 9 May 1843. So sceptical were the League's opponents that a counter-petition from Epworth followed, alleging that the previous one was a forgery. A Select Committee, which included Charles Villiers, was appointed to investigate the charge and soon established that there had been 'an extensive forgery of names' and that only 13 of the 214 signatures had been proved to have been either the signatures of the parties themselves or written with their consent. The culprit — or hero, according to how you regarded him — was one Samuel Potts, who being, as he modestly admitted, 'light and . . . very clever at walking,' had covered the whole sixteen miles from Doncaster in three hours; an indication of the stamina required of the League's helpers in rural areas. Epworth was distinctly off the beaten track as no coach-routes passed through it, and, stretching over an area three miles long, was almost virgin soil for the League — indeed, as one long-standing local resident testified, 'we have had nothing but vestry meetings and such as that unless a person comes to lecture on scientific subjects'. Potts' usual technique, it transpired, had been to assure those he approached that 'One, two or three gentlemen in the market-place already have signed,' but his tactics with a farm worker had been different. This time he claimed to have been sent by 'a Doncaster gentleman' and not merely wrote down the name of the man approached, who had refused to sign, but also that of his neighbours. 'He wrote again; he then rips up the paper and out of the yard,' added the witness. . . . 'The man went away and I never seed him no more.'

Even more damning was the evidence given by a framework knitter, in London to present a petition about the problems of his own trade, who had fallen into conversation with Potts while staying at the same no doubt modest inn, the 'Magpie and Horseshoe' near Westminster Bridge. The result showed the unwisdom of confiding in casual acquaintances. 'My impression was,' this witness explained, 'that he opened his mind to me in consequence of considering that I was just placed in his situation' so that 'he laughed, and says, "By God we shall all have to go over the water together!"' — i.e. be transported for forgery. Potts had, he explained, been commissioned to get up a petition in the surrounding towns and villages, Epworth being only one of thirteen assigned to him:

> He then proceeded to say that he found it very difficult to obtain signatures and that, consequently, he had recourse to this method; that when he got outside a town, or in different places, where no one could observe him, he wrote some names that were in the villages where he had been; and other names which had occurred to him; and by this means he filled up the sheets; and that, in the case of the Epworth petition, the signatures so obtained were more than two-thirds.

Potts claimed to have collected more than 200 signatures in less than twenty-four hours, although many of those concerned were at work in the fields, and his defence to the charge of forging signatures was that most men in the area could not write. But he had obviously overreached himself, and the ensuing official enquiry rapidly revealed the scale of the deception. 'I never saw one person that told me they had signed it,' testified a local farmer, while one man whose name had been used had not merely refused Potts' request but had told that 'I should consider it like taking a knife and cutting my own throat'.

The League's answer to the Epworth revelations was that Potts had been recommended by 'a highly respectable man' and been most carefully briefed, as the person responsible, a Doncaster grocer, described:

> I said to him, 'Now, Potts, you are going out into a neighbourhood or a district where you will be looked upon as a poacher in the agriculturists' preserve . . . our wish is that you shall use the utmost care in preventing any improper signatures being allowed on the petition. Take care that no boys sign under twenty years of age; allow no person to sign for a suppositious friend who is not present, for a pretended friend who happened not to be present; and especially, take care that you do not allow the petition to go out of your sight, lest anybody should tamper with it. . . . It will not make the least difference to your wage, whether you bring five names to the petition or 500'; and I added that we would rather have five *bona fide* names to the petition than 500 that any cavil could be made about. The man admitted these general instructions before four very respectable men.

The Epworth affair does not seem to have done the League any lasting harm, but similar malpractices were to bring them further trouble three years later when a petition from Cheltenham was also challenged. This time it appeared that five signatures had been 'transcribed from genuine signatures which were on another sheet,' and that 'twenty-four names . . . were written by one and the same person . . . with the sanction . . . of the persons named'. This time, the Select Committee concluded, the League had 'acted irregularly' but without 'fraudulent intention', and it hoped such experiences would not 'bring into discredit that mode of giving expression to the sentiments of the subjects of the realm'.

In addition to its long-term aim of securing the signature of every adult male in the country the League also welcomed petitions signed by the representatives of a particular trade or profession, and the clergy were a natural target for such efforts. In June 1841 the citizens of Manchester were confronted by the imposing sight of a massed array of respectable-looking gentlemen in clerical collars at a tea-party in the Corn Exchange, held nominally to welcome to the League's full-time service an official of the British India Society, George Thompson, who had been loaned to the League, while remaining on the Society's pay-roll. A little naively, since they had been specially invited, Thompson began his speech by remarking on 'the unprecedented number of the ministers of religion here with us':

> Are they *with us* in the full import of the word? Not merely with their bodies, but their souls, their sympathies and their best efforts? . . . They would not have been so with us, I am certain, without first considering deeply, conscientiously, and prayer-fully the merits of this great question. . . . Their presence assures us that our cause has claims which may not be despised; that there are obligations resting on us which will urge us on in the work upon which we have entered; not upon the narrow grounds of political expediency, or temporary necessity, but upon the high and impregnable foundations of immutable truth and justice.

God, in other words, was clearly on the League's side, and, just to establish this beyond doubt, seven of the subsequent fifteen speakers were clergy or missionaries. A circular from George Thompson to local clergy followed, designed to found a specifically clerical Anti-Corn-Law lobby, and a preliminary meeting of twenty-eight ministers decided to call a national conference. The response to the invitations to this event indicated very clearly where the League was likely to garner support. Of five hundred Wesleyan Methodists currently meeting in Manchester only one responded to the invitation, plus a solitary Anglican, and two ministers of the Church of Scotland. The reason, Archibald Prentice concluded, was that the system of paying their clergy partly from commuted tithes related to the price of corn, gave 'to incumbents in those two establishments a direct interest in sustaining high prices,' while the Wesleyan Methodists, he believed, were still under the thumb of the same leaders who had been hostile to Parliamentary reform. These major exceptions apart, however, there was an encouraging response to the invitations sent out to nearly every minister in the country, for 1,500 replied, of whom only 6 expressed outright opposition to repeal, and in the end nearly 700 assembled in the Town Hall, Manchester, on Tuesday 17 August 1841, all of them being found accommodation in the houses of League members. Those attending had had to pay their own travelling expenses unless financed by local sympathizers, and almost all came in a personal capacity, not as spokesmen for their congregations. The conference was, in theory, organized by nonconformist ministers resident in the Manchester area, but they leaned heavily on the League's full-time officials, who selected and briefed the witnesses to be heard and no doubt helped to draft the resolutions that were debated and — it need hardly be said — passed. Those attending faced a gruelling four-hour session in the morning, followed by another five hours in the evening, and the conference once again demonstrated the League's efficiency, as one admiring Congregationalist recorded:

> The meeting was managed with amazing tact, skill, energy and power. I do not think on any other subject, or in any other place, such a meeting could be obtained. This arose partly from the unbounded liberality of the Anti-Corn-Law League, who furnished clerks, messengers, door-keepers, assistants of all kinds, printing . . . etc. . . . partly from the power, and energy, and untiring perseverance of the secretaries and committees. . . . There were many of the Manchester ministers who devoted themselves to preparing measures, and several others who were scarcely ever in the hall, but sitting in the committee rooms from seven in the morning until ten in the evening.

This observer recognized clearly enough, however, that the results were a foregone conclusion:

> The thing never came to a *Conference* at all. . . . There was no discussion. The Committee took care to provide resolutions which were moved and seconded. . . . The room being crowded with spectators checked discussion. Besides the feeling was so general in favour of the extreme view . . . that no person on the other side would have had any chance. As an effort of generalship, nothing could have been more complete.

Good generals, of course, won their battles and the League must have been well pleased with the results of the conference, which from the first ran smoothly along the intended lines. One early speaker, extensively quoted by Archibald Prentice, struck a keynote which was constantly to be echoed in the succeeding days:

> The doctrine and practice of free trade was in harmony with the essential principle and the benevolent design of the gospel. In answer to the objection that it was not befitting in ministers of religion to give opinions or advice on politics, he entered his determined protest. What are politics, he demanded, but the knowledge and practice of the claims of right and the obligations of duty to men as members of society? Is not this knowledge and practice an essential party of morality? . . . Our object is to teach the politics which follow from piety, the politics of equitable

benevolence, the politics of the gospel and the politics of Jesus Christ our Lord and Saviour.

The climax came with the appearance of Richard Cobden, who read an address from the Executive Council thanking those present and reminding them of their special influence not merely on earth, but also, it seemed, in Heaven:

> We beg respectfully to tender you our earnest and grateful thanks for the zealous and truly Christian services which you have rendered to the cause of humanity, and to express our acknowledgements for the sanction which your dignified proceedings have given to your past labours, and from which we shall derive increased encouragement and a new stimulus to our future efforts.
> The religious world will regard the acts of your conference as a noble illustration of the true spirit of a Christian ministry, whose benign influence can never be more consistently exerted than when vindicating the cause of the poor and the destitute. . . . We rely on the moral weight of your example; we trust much to the efficacy of your pulpit exhortations; we feel that to your supplications at the throne of the Most High, the poor and wretched may yet look with humble hope. . . .

The meeting ended by agreeing to support a petition which hinted that Honourable Members who neglected their duty might ultimately have more than their constituents to reckon with:

> Your petitioners therefore, convinced of the sinfulness of these laws, which violate the paramount law of God . . . implore your honourable house, as you fear that God who is the friend and avenger of the poor, as you love that country whose interests are committed into your hand, to take into your early and serious consideration the Provision Laws, and especially the Corn Laws, which have wrought this enormous amount of evil and misery, for the purpose of devising such means as . . . may seem meet for their abolition.

The conference of clergy had, it was believed, far-reaching effects. 'For several weeks after these gatherings,' reported Archibald Prentice, 'accounts reached the League from towns and villages in all parts of the kingdom, at which ministers who had been present at the conference had given a history of its proceedings and exhorted their hearers to put their hands to the good work.' A

'National Day of Humiliation', which the conference had agreed to call on Monday 6 September, when God was to be asked to 'remove the distress which at this time afflicts the poor . . . to endow our senators . . . with wisdom', was not widely observed and appears to have achieved little; but other conferences of nonconformist clergy passed even more extreme resolutions, like this one, carried by a meeting of the Congregationalist ministers of Caernarvonshire in August 1841:

> That the present Corn Laws are impolitic in principle, unjust in operation and cruel in effect; they are condemned throughout the sacred volume; they are opposed to the benignity of the Creator and they are at variance with the very spirit of Christianity.
>   That it is the sacred duty of every Christian sect, denomination, and creed to use every means and every influence within their power towards having such unjust and un-Christian laws removed from among the statutes of this great nation.

A further conference, of forty ministers from various denominations, held at Caernarvon for three days from 30 November 1841, agreed 'that the existing Corn Law was a public evil and essentially adverse to the plainest injunctions of Holy Writ,' and drew up an address to the Queen to appraise her of these facts. On 11 January 1842 a convocation of sympathetic Scottish nonconformist ministers, each accompanied by two laymen, was held in Edinburgh. This time, the ministers of the Established Kirk of Scotland were not invited, but the response of their dissenting brethren from 'the Secession, Relief, Independent and Baptist Churches' was all that could have been hoped. Of 494 replying to the 670 circulars sent out, '459 . . . expressed decided opinions in favour of the total repeal of the Corn and Provision Laws . . . about 12 were in favour of a small fixed duty, or gradual abolition; and the remaining 33 did not answer the question . . . 431 stated that their congregations were nearly unanimous in approving of total abolition. . . .'

Many congregations now found themselves treated to sermons attacking the Corn Laws, ministers being kept up-to-date with a regular supply of publications. Everywhere, however, the Anglican priesthood remained aloof, causing Cobden in May 1842, in a letter to John Bright, to utter what was clearly a cry from the heart. 'The Church clergy are almost to a man guilty of causing the present distress by upholding the Corn Laws, they having themselves an interest in the high price of bread.'

The emphasis placed on securing support among the clergy

made against it to its advantage and that spring launched its most determined campaign yet in London. Exeter Hall in the Strand, the traditional arena for radical and reforming oratory, was denied it, but it was able to hire the Drury Lane Theatre. 'Never, in the palmiest days of the legitimate drama,' claimed Archibald Prentice, 'had pit, boxes and gallery been so filled' as at the opening meeting on Wednesday 15 March 1843; another, equally successful, was held on 22 March, prompting Prentice to reflect that he had witnessed 'the greatest assembly that could be brought together under one roof in the great metropolis of the world'. Prentice himself, and that other stalwart of the League Old Guard, Abraham Paulton, decided 'while the more prominent members of the League were occupying the Board of Old Drury' to try and attract an audience to the Sadler's Wells Theatre, which seated 2,400, and were, gratified to find 'the place . . . completely filled'. George Wilson, arriving to support this League 'second eleven', at first assumed from 'the tumult within . . . that the Chartists of Finsbury had overpowered us,' but it was merely the audience showing its enthusiasm. Wilson was in the chair at the League's final meeting of the series, in Drury Lane, on 12 April 1843, when, carried away by his surroundings, another of the League's founding fathers delivered a rousing peroration in verse:

How oft on this illustrious stage
The words of fire from Shakespeare's page
Your passions rouse, your souls engage.
Here truth shall make
A still more eloquent appeal
To all who think — to all who feel.
The public woe, the public weal
Are now at stake. . .
Say! Will your burst the ignoble thrall,
Answer, ye men of England, all;
Ay, answer now!

The answer given by the men of England in the House of Commons proved, alas, very different from that forthcoming at Drury Lane. On 9 May 1843 Charles Villiers brought forward his usual motion calling for an enquiry into the Corn Laws, opening a debate which lasted four days. At midnight on the last day one of the League's supporters moved the adjournment, believing they would not get a fair hearing at that hour or have their speeches reported in next day's newspapers. The scene which followed was compared, by the following day's *Sun*, to a menagerie at feeding-time:

The wild beasts on both sides . . . were all in the fiercest stage of excitement — yelling, braying, roaring, each vieing with the other in the manifestation of impatience and irritability . . . an uproar . . . such as has not been witnessed since the night of the memorable division on the Reform Bill. There was cock-crowing in the highest perfection, the bleat of the calf, the bray of the ass, the hiss of the goose, together with divers supplemental sounds, to which Mr Cobden did not more than strict and impartial justice, when he described them as being 'the most extraordinary and inhuman noises' that he had ever heard. . . .

When the tempest was at its height, the leaders, Sir R. Peel and Lord J. Russell, left the House; and, thus freed from all restraint, the belligerents became fiercer than ever; the blood of both parties was fairly up; for nearly two hours, declamation roared while reason slept; and during the vociferous display, the voice of the Speaker was little more regarded than a whisper amidst a storm. . . . Worn out at length by the violence of their exertions, and despairing of victory, the majority yielded.

It was a rare victory for the repeal party and it was followed, on Monday 16 May 1843 when the debate was finally concluded, by the customary defeat, by a majority of 256: 125 to 381. The League's support was, however, creeping up; a year before it could muster only 90 votes, and Cobden's speech in the closing stages came in for praise on all sides; even the Tory *Morning Post* described him as 'the hero of the night':

The parliamentary representatives of the industrial interests of the British Empire quailed before the founder and leader of the Anti-Corn-Law League. They winced under his sarcasms. They listened in speechless terror to his denunciations. No man among them dared to grapple with the arch enemy of English industry. No man among them attempted to refute the miserable fallacies of which Mr Cobden's speech was made up. . . . Melancholy was it to witness, on Monday, the landowners of England, the representatives by blood of the Norman chivalry, the representatives, by election, of the industrial interests of the Empire, shrinking under the blows aimed at them by a Manchester money-grubber; by a man whose importance is derived from the action of a system, destructive in its nature of all the wholesome influences that connect together the various orders of society.

Other papers were more unstinting, and less patronizing, in their praise. *The Times* acknowledged that 'Mr Cobden's speech was clever and pointed. . . . The debate is over; the question is settled; but for how long?' The *Spectator* drew attention to the division within the ranks of Cobden's supporters, with some favouring 'Peel free-trade', and others a small fixed duty. 'The doom of the Corn Laws,' it suggested, 'is to be learned in these indications.' The *Morning Chronicle* saw in Gladstone's promotion to be President of the Board of Trade a sign of things to come. 'Of course the country gentlemen will dislike it. . . . And the appointment, therefore, is the best possible evidence of the very little account which Sir Robert makes of his supporters and of his determination to follow his own course, in spite of their discontent.' There was, the *Globe* suggested, little to choose between 'the Tories . . . standing on the shibboleth of the two words, "Sliding scale"' and . . . 'the Whigs . . . standing on two words, "fixed duty"'.

On 12 June the House of Commons again rejected a proposal for an enquiry, by 145 to 244, a majority of 99, but by now the main argument was being conducted in the country. Cobden and Bright, appearing separately or together, had on the whole attentive audiences, sometimes addressing crowds of thousands, including farmers who had ridden in from thirty or more miles away. The contrast with what had happened two or three years before, often in the same towns, was remarkable. At Colchester, for example, in rural Essex, the League's opponents inserted advertisements in the local newspapers calling upon farmers to attend, the meeting was held during the afternoon, when few labourers could be present, the chairman made no bones about his support for protection and a prominent local landowner moved a wrecking amendment to the customary Anti-Corn-Law resolution, but, in a crowd of six thousand, secured only twenty-seven votes. It was a triumph for the speakers, Cobden and Villiers. John Bright, supported by Archibald Prentice, was meanwhile having an equal success in the rural areas of Scotland and Northumberland, in spite of a thinly-veiled invitation to violence in the *Newcastle Journal*. 'Bright, the Anti-Corn-Law agitator,' it warned its readers, 'is expected to visit the wool-fair which will be held at Alnwick shortly, in order to scatter the seeds of disaffection in that quarter. Should he make his appearance, which is not improbable (for the person has impudence for anything of this sort) it is to be hoped there may be found SOME STALWART YEOMAN ready to treat the disaffected vagabond as he deserves.' 'Notwithstanding the appeal to the physical force of the "stalwart yeoman",' Prentice was able to report, 'we had an enthusiastic reception and a most satisfactory meeting.' John Bright went on to Newcastle and Sunderland, where the mayor took the

chair, before travelling south to join Cobden at Winchester, where a
resolution condemning the Corn Laws was enthusiastically carried.
Archibald Prentice, arriving at Lanark by the coach from Edinburgh
on 12 July 1843, found himself welcomed by a deputation from his
native parish of Covington, seven miles away. They stayed to hear
him address an audience of 'respectable farmers', one of whom,
according to a local reporter, was later heard to declare 'He made
everything very plain, and . . . proved that the Corn Law did us nae
guid.'

The League's most successful campaigning season so far reached
its climax with, as mentioned earlier, a by-election at Durham,
which carried John Bright into the House, on 25 July 1843, by 488
to 410: the seat had been won by a protectionist Tory only three
months earlier. Bright's success, as a Quaker in an intensely
Anglican cathedral city, was seen on all sides as deeply significant.
'Free trade,' he wrote to a friend, 'was the only watchword, the only
motto on our banners. We had no music, no flags, no delusions, but
we entirely converted the constituency in a week.' To a man of
Bright's convictions, entry on to the wider London stage was not a
matter for personal display, but he was anxious to make a decent
showing. 'I want thee,' he wrote to his sister, 'to make up in a parcel
my new coat and best great coat and send them off immediately by
first train . . . as I must be decently attired when I enter the House.'
Bright still seemed nervous when he delivered his maiden speech, on
a motion advocating further reduction in tariffs, on 7 August, but
had not had time to make much impact before the House adjourned
on 24 August 1843.

Anticipating a renewal of the previous summer's troubles the
government had taken powers to train and arm ten thousand
Chelsea Pensioners as a peace-keeping militia — a move which the
pacifist Bright opposed. In the event the next few weeks passed off
quietly while the League concentrated on a new appeal for a fighting
fund of £100,000, double the amount raised in the previous year. In
place of Drury Lane for five nights, the great theatre in Covent
Garden was to be hired for fifty nights, at a total rent of £3,000. The
League's newspaper was to be sent free to everyone contributing £1
a year, at a cost of £10,000, and the small, fortnightly, *Anti-Bread-
Tax Circular* was to be replaced from Saturday 30 September 1843
by a full-size weekly, the *League*; a massive speaking programme
was also to be undertaken. Most of the fighting fund was to be
devoted, however, to specifically electoral purposes (described
later). The appeal was officially launched at Covent Garden on 28
September 1843, the theatre being packed out with 5,000 to 6,000
people, when Cobden, according to the *Morning Advertiser*, was

'received with, if possible, greater applause than ever,' while Bright was soon 'displaying more than his wonted eloquence and power'.

A later meeting, on 12 October, was even more successful. 'Crowded,' wrote Archibald Prentice, 'is a weak word to express the condition of the house. Stage, pit, boxes and galleries were crammed and every entrance, public and private, was besieged by crowds of eager applicants for admission, but for whom no room could possibly be found, although an additional gallery had been reopened for the occasion.' The League's three leading MPs, Villiers, Cobden and Bright, were all present, and the occasion turned into a massive demonstration of support for the free-trade candidate in a by-election about to be held in the City of London. The League was able to announce the timely conversion to its cause of a number of wealthy businessmen. The best-known was a millionaire, Samuel Jones Loyd, though he seems to have been careful with his money, for his donation amounted only to £50. His example was more important, however, than his cash and the result of the by-election, on 27 October 1843, continued the gathering momentum of success, for the free-trade candidate won by 201 votes after a hard-fought poll in a constituency with an enormous electorate: 6,535 people voted for him against 6,334 for his rival.

In these early months of 1843 the League's leading speakers were constantly 'on the road,' or more commonly, in the railway carriage, though both Cobden and Bright had to decline nine out of ten of the invitations they received. Once at least John Bright travelled all night, to keep a speaking engagement in Doncaster, though sleeping-cars on trains were still unknown. Most of the effort was directed towards towns in farming areas, like Worcester, Canterbury and Berwick-on-Tweed. Everywhere the response was enthusiastic and sometimes extraordinary, as at Kendal in Westmorland, a small, remote town in the Lake District, where five thousand people poured in from miles around. The fund-raising effort, by contrast, was concentrated in known centres of support, being launched at the Town Hall, Manchester. Archibald Prentice had to discourage one man from giving £1,000 'because,' as he explained, 'we wanted twenty subscribers of £500 each and could not expect to have so many if he began with so large a sum'. Grudgingly, the would-be donor agreed to keep his second £500 in reserve — but 'threw to the chairman a bundle of bank notes with the words "There's my £500 for the League!" and sat down'. 'I have,' wrote Archibald Prentice, 'heard Brougham, Canning, and all our best orators but never heard a speech that produced the effect of Mr Chadwick's,' and £12,500 was subscribed in the next hour-and-a-half. Other places, in relation to their size, proved almost as generous, and the whole campaign totally vindicated the League's boldness in setting so high a target; its cash-in-hand when the £100,000 appeal was launched had stood at £2,476. 10s. 3d.

The seal was set on the Anti-Corn-Law campaign as an idea whose hour had come by a leading article, in *The Times* on 18 November 1843, which was henceforward to be constantly quoted:

> The League is a great fact. It would be foolish, nay rash, to deny its importance. It is a great fact that there should have been created in the homesteads of our manufacturers a confederacy devoted to the agitation of one political question, persevering at it year after year, shrinking from no trouble, dismayed by no danger, making light to every obstacle. It demonstrates the hardy strength of purpose — the indomitable will — by which Englishmen, working together for a great object, are armed and animated. . . . These are facts important and worthy of consideration. No moralist can disregard them; no politician can sneer at them; no statesman can undervalue them. . . . A new power has arisen in the state.

Other newspapers with varying degrees of enthusiasm, followed suit. The high Tory *Morning Post* contrasted the 'violent and selfish men . . . of great activity and great perseverance,' who led the League, with their feebler opponents 'who were more likely to give up the battle upon a fair excuse, than to fight it out from a sense of duty'. The *Morning Herald*, in attacking the League, also paid implicit tribute to its success:

> That confederacy *is* powerful . . . and its ultimate success is certain, unless vigour and unanimity be re-infused into the Conservative Party [lower case initial capitals, i.e. 'conservative party', are used in the original but reference to the political party seems to be intended]. Flushed with triumphs at London and Kendal, the League now assails Salisbury, threatens to invade every vacated borough and has an organized correspondence in every town and village. . . . Two or three years ago, Acland and Smith were its itinerant orators; this year Cobden and Bright are its travelling agents. Then the former were kicked out of agricultural towns, now the latter address large audiences therein without interruption and we fear, with applause; then the landowners were, comparatively speaking, active, now they are quite supine; then there were few men of wealth or respectability, without the circle of its satellite towns, subscribers to its funds, now our Jones Loyds contribute to its rent; then it raised

£50,000, now it is demanding £100,000; and those who were then ashamed are now proud of their membership. We last year warned the farmers that . . . they were playing into Mr Cobden's hands; and we now repeat the advice we then gave them: that in union to support the present Corn Law and the present ministry alone is their safety. . . . In expressing dissatisfaction with ministers, farmers are lessening the power of their only friends. . . . In Mr Cobden's triumph there is ruin to the Conservative Party.

Other press comment was even more critical of Peel and his colleagues, the *Yorkshire Gazette* predicted that unless the Tories reacted more vigorously, 'the time may come when resistance will be in vain and we shall see British industry laid prostrate by the machinations of selfish and avaricious manufacturers'. 'What are the Conservatives doing?' demanded the *Gloucestershire Chronicle* even more bluntly. 'Nothing. The contrast between the two parties is most striking. The Conservatives seem steeped in criminal apathy. . . . That the operations of the League are magnified on paper . . . is like enough; but there is no longer room for doubt that they are a most formidable and mischievous body.'

Such comments were read with delight in Manchester, and the *League* was surely justified, in its own editorial of 30 December 1843, in looking back on the departing year with satisfaction. In twelve months, it pointed out, everything had changed. Rich men supported the League instead of opposing it; 'the numerous', i.e. working, 'classes' now offered the League 'general and hearty co-operation'. The 'Chartist traitors', once so troublesome, were now silent. Anti-Corn-Law meetings, in populous places, were not merely secure from interruption, they were sure of enthusiasm. Particularly striking had been the progress in London:

In the metropolis the League, as a distinct and organized body, scarcely showed its face till the present year. It chiefly appeared as merged in the annual Anti-Corn-Law Conference. The series of meetings at the great theatres is wholly unprecedented. They are an event in the record of demonstrations of public opinion.

Above all in Parliament, the decisive theatre, the half-way house of a sliding scale now hardly had a friend.

Hopefully, then, shall we enter on the new year. Hopefully; and yet with saddened feelings that justice, however certain in the end, is still delayed. For, as the old proverb has it, 'While the grass is growing, the steed starves.' Every month of delay is the prolongation of indescribable wretchedness. We begin another year of multiplying bankruptcies and blighted hopes; of terrible suffering and terrible crimes; of overflowing workhouses and blazing barns. Rest the responsibility where it may, it is an awful one. The greater be our exertions. . . . The League has wintered and summered it, ever making progress. And now for one great effort more, to vindicate the rights of industry, lessen the burdens of poverty, and secure the just recompense of honest labour.

CHAPTER EIGHTEEN

Appeal to the Constituencies

'The Council of the League now turns from
Parliament to those who make the Parliament;
it appeals to the Constituencies.'
— Anti-Corn-Law League pamphlet, March
1844

The League entered 1844 in a condition in which many a man might
wish to greet a new year: in excellent health, with spirits high and a
sound bank balance. The country's supposedly richest
businessman, Jones Loyd, had already given his donation; now, on
New Year's Day itself, its wealthiest nobleman, the Marquis of
Westminster, sent a cheque for £500 with an encouraging letter. 'I
venture to express a hope that you will not relax your endeavours,'
wrote His Lordship, in courteous, but unnecessary, exhortation.

The League's plan of campaign for the coming year had been set
out in the address to the nation which the League Council had issued
the previous autumn. This stressed that henceforward the emphasis
would be on trying to secure every possible pro-repeal vote in
Parliament, and added a strictly practical summary of tactics:

1. Copies will be obtained of the registration lists of all boroughs
    and counties throughout the kingdom and the collection
    lodged at the Metropolitan Office of the League . . . to be
    consulted as occasion may require. . .
2. An extensive correspondence, by means of the post, and of
    stamped publications, will be kept up with electors, in all
    districts. . .
3. Every borough in the kingdom shall be visited by deputations
    of the League, and meetings held, which the electors will be
    specially invited to attend.
4. Prompt measures will be taken to ascertain the opinions of
    each elector in every borough. . .
5. Every constituency, whose representatives have not hitherto
    supported Mr Villiers' motion . . . will be invited to
    memorialize its members to vote for such motion when next
    brought forward.
6. Whenever a vacancy occurs in the representation of any
    borough, the electors will be recommended to put a free-

trade candidate in nomination; and the League pledges itself
to give such candidate every possible support. . .

7. In the event of any borough being unable to procure a suitable
    candidate, the League pledges itself to bring forward can-
    didates, so as to afford every elector an opportunity of
    recording his vote in favour of free trade until the question be
    decided.

The effort already made to reach electors had been prodigious.
During 1843, five million copies of publications had been issued to
them — compared to 3,600,000 distributed to the far larger number
of people without the vote — and 24 counties, containing 237,000
electors, and 187 boroughs, with a further 260,000, had been
systematically circularized. The results were not, however, very
evident in the House of Commons, which, as the League pointed
out, had been elected in 1841, since when, it believed, a massive shift
in opinion had occurred. The Corn Laws were not mentioned in the
Queen's Speech at the opening of Parliament on 1 February 1844,
though in the subsequent debate Peel himself professed himself
satisfied with the results of the 1842 Act. 'The government,' he
insisted, 'have never contemplated and do not contemplate any
alteration to the existing law.'

More encouraging was the evidence that the agricultural
community was now taking the challenge to the Corn Laws very
seriously. On 18 February 1844, the Agricultural Protection Society
came formally into existence, its governing body demonstrating the
justice of the League's gibes at the aristocratic nature of the
opposition to it: the seven senior posts were filled by six dukes and
an earl. These noblemen now *Addressed to the Industrious Classes of
the United Kingdom* — who were expected to pay 1s for the
privilege — a statement of *Reasons* for its formation, namely to
'disabuse the public mind of misstatements actively circulated on the
subject of protection to industry and to maintain at least the
protection it at present enjoys to British agriculture'.

The resolutions passed at the inaugural meeting included one very
similar to that adopted by the League: 'Party politics shall not be
introduced into the proceedings of the Society.' But it went on to
add — as the League had not done — that 'The Society shall on no
account interfere in any election for a Member to serve in
Parliament.' Its principal purpose, again like that of the League, was
to co-ordinate the work of similar local associations, such as the
Yorkshire Protection Society, formed at almost the same time. At its
first meeting, in York on 22 February 1844, its chairman, the Earl of
Harewood, struck from the first an apologetic note:

No man could be more sorry that I am to have to preside at a meeting of this kind. But, gentlemen, we are compelled to assemble for our own defence. We are driven to it, and by whom? By a party of the manufacturing community whose trade has been supported in bad times by the very people whom they are now attempting to ruin. . . . No man who has his proper senses about him can for a moment suppose that, should the Anti-Corn-Law League carry their object, the agricultural districts would not suffer in the most calamitous way.

The whole agitation, suggested another speaker, was spurious, and commanded little public support:

I do not believe in the progress of the League. Progressed they have in travelling about the country and raising large subscriptions — they who gave next to nothing to their own workmen when they were starving. . . . They have not progressed a point on the intelligence and conviction and moral feelings of the people generally. . . . Do we not see the same names — always the same — leading the proceedings of the League? The same half-dozen travelling orators, the same dozen stars in Covent Garden. The League owes its existence, it owes all its present energy and vitality to one set of people, to the mill-owners in and about Manchester. Without them it would die tomorrow.

Although the League in the propaganda battle still made most of the running, it did not have things all its own way, and at least one, anonymous, pamphlet accused its leaders of having purely selfish motives:

We always find that when these manufacturers wish to raise a clamour about anything, for their own interests, they endeavour to identify themselves with their poor, miserably oppressed slaves and they use the word 'we', meaning of course the master — the overseer — and the poor little half-famished children, whose death knell is the factory bell. When was this word, 'we', ever heard in connection with a fair division of the profits of machinery? . . .

This Corn Law question is not a dispute as to whether the people should have cheap bread or not, but an attack on the part of the great manufacturers — the Cotton Lords . . . against the ancient aristocracy and gentry of this country, and through them the humblest tiller of that soil.

The challenge such attacks — and Peel's recent declaration — posed to the League was rapidly taken up. A new series of mass meetings at the Covent Garden Theatre began during February, and on Tuesday 12 March 1844 Cobden moved in the House of Commons for an inquiry into the effects of protection on tenant-farmers and farm labourers. His speech, thorough and restrained, was a masterly performance which earned praise even from the government spokesman, W.E. Gladstone, to whom the *League* paid a back-handed tribute: 'The President of the Board of Trade is an able man; but it requires great ability indeed to speak against one's own convictions, especially when there is a feeling of conscience and honour in the breast of the individual.' When the House divided at 1 a.m. Cobden's motion, according to the *League*, was supported by '153 friends of justice and fair play' but 'opposed by 244 fearful monopolists,' a majority of 91. But the number of League supporters was creeping up, and on Tuesday 25 June 1844 Villiers once again introduced his motion, in terms which admirably summarized the League's case:

That it appears by a recent census that the people of this country are rapidly increasing in number. [The 1841 census showed a total population, including Ireland, of 26,751,000, compared to 24,135,000 in 1831.]

That it is in evidence before this House that a large proportion of Her Majesty's subjects are insufficiently provided with the first necessaries of life.

That, nevertheless, a Corn Law is in force which restricts the supply of food and thereby lessens its abundance.

That any such restriction having for its object to impede the free purchase of an article upon which depends the subsistence of the community is indefensible in principle, injurious in operation, and ought to be abolished.

That it is therefore expedient that the Act 5 and 6 Vic., c.14, shall be repealed forthwith.

Peel's reply was half-hearted — 'A sudden withdrawal of protection. . . ,' he argued 'would cause great confusion and embarrassment' — while John Bright, who followed him, was on rousing form:

Good harvests will not always be granted us; and when the unfortunate seasons come round again, then again will come disaster and distress. Must we wait for justice till events compel you to grant it? Why not abolish restriction now, whilst we have a respite? You may shuffle and evade the question, you may use sophistry, you may deny our facts and disregard our arguments, but . . . I am convinced that, whatever may be the feelings of confidence now entertained by the right. hon. baronet, whenever bad harvests may again occur, he will either abolish this law or his government will be overthrown . . . I do not wish this law to be repealed in times of excitement, nor do I wish its destruction to be achieved as a great party victory; I would rather it were forever abolished by the unanimous verdict of the honest and intelligent classes of the country.

The motion was lost by 206 votes — 330 to 124 — but, as so often, the moral victory lay with the League. Those voting for repeal had not changed much, from the 92 votes of 1842 and the 125 of 1843, but the opposition had dropped, from 395, to 381, to 330, and the hostile majority even more sharply, from 303 to 256, and now to 206. MPs were not altering their allegiance, but fewer were willing to stand up and be counted in the Corn Laws' defence. If the process continued ultimate victory was inevitable, but the League was not prepared to wait for the slow erosion of opposition. Its response to the latest defeat was that of Peel to the 1832 Reform Act: 'The battle must be fought in the registration courts.'

The Victorians, for all their high moral principles, took a distinctly accommodating view of electoral law. There *were* honest elections, but public voting and tiny electorates hardly encouraged them. The Liberals, with fewer 'pocket boroughs' in their gift, were as culpable as the Tories and employed agents who specialized in this shady political half-world. The profession had its own conventions. Sometimes one agent would agree beforehand with the other not to challenge the result or would persuade an unsuccessful candidate not to attempt to unseat his rival if this was likely to prove expensive. To prevent, by bribery or subterfuge, known opponents from voting was considered enterprising rather than discreditable. It was, however, considered bad form to accept a higher bribe from the Tories after accepting a lower one from the Whigs, or vice versa, and some electors only took money from the side for which they had always intended to vote. The amounts were also fixed by custom. £10 was usually considered a reasonable incentive, or even a mere sovereign, but £20 was traditional in some places, while tickets entitling the holder to free food and drink at some specified hostelry were commonplace. The actual dispenser of funds was usually brought in from outside and had no direct contact with the local organizers. He might work through a subcontractor, who 'sweated the bribe,' i.e. undertook to deliver, say, thirty votes for £150 and pocketed a third of this for himself, while the sub-agents, who contacted the actual voters, might also levy a commission of ten per cent. Some party loyalists solicited bribes specifically to provide evidence for challenging the result if their opponent won, but this was regarded as not playing the game. It was legitimate, however, to follow a rival agent about in the hope of catching him redhanded, and a conviction for bribery, which could earn up to twelve months' imprisonment, was accepted philosophically. One such unfortunate, in 1839, was given £200 compensation by the Conservatives; in another case, at Cambridge in 1841, where the Liberals were literally the guilty party, the agent's defence was financed from party funds and he received £100 on completing his year in jail. The man who had employed him, James Coppock, was the most famous agent of the century, a solicitor with a robustly man-of-the-world view about the law. 'The crime of bribery,' he declared, 'is in the detection . . . not in the commission.' The job of professionals like Coppock was to get the Liberal elected whether he supported the League or not. He had visited the famous by-election at Walsall in 1841 and rightly predicted that if the Tory won he was bound to be unseated for malpractice. Whenever the League was, as at Walsall, not challenging an 'official' Liberal, Coppock was prepared to offer it advice, to the embarrassment of its more high-minded members. 'The Council seems to be of the opinion,' complained Cobden in a letter of 23 April 1845, referring to Coppock and the Party's chief legal agent, Joseph Parkes, 'that we ought not to consult *them*. I am on the contrary sorry that I did not consult them about the state of the little rotten boroughs before we committed ourselves to the ridiculous pledge of 1843,' i.e. the undertaking to oppose any Liberal who was not a repealer.

The League, when it came to fighting elections, was on its own but it soon proved as well able to master the electoral arts as it had those of propaganda. In March 1844 the opening shot was fired in this new stage of its campaign with the issuing of a detailed pamphlet of *Directions to be Observed by All Persons Engaged in the Registration of Electors for Cities and Boroughs*, soon followed by another, *Practical Instructions for the Annual Registration of Voters in Counties*. The preamble to the 'Cities and Boroughs' pamphlet, by far the more hopeful area from the League's point of view, set out the reasons for the new initiative with crisp directness:

The National Anti-Corn-Law League, established to obtain the abolition of the Corn and Provision Laws, has, during the six years of its existence laboured incessantly to inform the public mind on this momentous question. During that period, *millions* of the people have petitioned the Parliament for the repeal of these laws, and have petitioned in vain. The House of Commons has refused even inquiry into their pernicious effects.

The Council of the League now turns from Parliament to those who make the Parliament; it appeals to the Constituencies. To give effect to that appeal, the number of friends of Commercial Freedom in the electoral body must be greatly increased. This can only be done by a more searching and close attention to the Registration. Every Free Trader should put his hand to this work. . . .

The Law offered a variety of loopholes which might enable one to add known supporters to the electoral register or disqualify known opponents. The basic qualification for voting since 1832 had been to be a 'ten-pound occupier', i.e. to live in a house, worth, including the surrounding land, at least £10 a year to rent, but 'A mere lodger. . . ,' warned the pamphlet, would not qualify unless he had 'the exclusive use of his room and the key to the door of it'. An even richer source of potential argument lay in the 'Ancient Rights' of pre-1832 voters, who were 'qualified on the 7 June 1832' and still living in the same premises. If, however, 'the voter's name was omitted from the register for two years successively,' even by accident, the right to vote was lost. To disqualify a voter all that was required was for an objector, by 25 August in the same year, to submit a formal complaint to the Town Clerk — in a form set out in the League pamphlet — with a copy to the unfortunate voter.

The League helpfully listed possible reasons for making such an objection, but warned that challenging a vote was troublesome, if the voter did not let it go by default, for it had to be done in person at the Revising Barrister's Court, held in the autumn in each constituency. Like bribery, though the *Directions* did not say so, it was also a game which two could play. Over-zealous objections by one party one year could lead to a counter-offensive by the other the next, until virtually a whole town might be disenfranchized.

The more positive section of the *Directions* ensured that the League claimed the vote for every potential supporter who might be entitled to it. They revealed, for instance, that a servant might be entitled to a vote, if he occupied a house of the required value, even though the rent was paid by his landlord, while 'a cow-house or stable, of sufficient value, will give a qualification'. The League was later, as will be seen, to go much further in making use of this aspect of the law.

If the situation in borough constituencies was complicated enough, that in the counties was far more bewildering. The largest categories of voters were freeholders for life, 'possessed of a freehold estate for life of the yearly value of £10,' or else 'freeholders of inheritance,' occupying an estate worth £2 a year upwards but which they would bequeath to their heirs. There were special provisions for 'lessees', 'assignees', and 'sub-lessees', and a number of pitfalls which the ingenious could exploit. For example, anyone describing as freehold a property leased for less than a thousand years could lose his vote, though a 'property held under a lease for lives, without any mention of years, must be described as freehold'. The League also listed in its *Practical Instructions* for the *Annual Registration of Voters in Counties*, the numerous categories who were automatically disqualified for 'personal incapacity': 'Women; persons under twenty-one years of age; Peers; . . . Aliens, . . . persons of unsound mind, such as Idiots, Lunatics; persons convicted of Felony, Bribery, Perjury or Petit Larceny' and so on, down, a little unexpectedly, to 'all persons in the employ of the Post Office . . . and all persons in the Thames and Metropolitan Police. . .'. As in the boroughs, there might also be, somewhere in the county, 'parish clerks, sextons, schoolmasters . . . dissenting ministers,' unaware of their right to vote, provided always that they had an income of £2 a year directly chargeable to land, and were appointed 'for life' or 'during good behaviour,' qualifications which offered a whole new and rich field of potential controversy.

The League had come late to the business of claiming new votes, and challenging old ones, but its leaders had, claimed George Wilson, at the final major meeting of the 1844 season at the Covent Garden Theatre on Wednesday 7 August, 'proceeded like men of business' to tackle the subject:

> We selected 140 boroughs upon which, we thought, with reasonable exertions, an impression might be made. We selected for our visiting agents to such boroughs men fully acquainted with the subject of registration in all its parts . . . and they had reported to the Council of the League the result of their enquiries. In some instances they found the registration had been totally neglected — in many partially attended to, whilst in others it had been entirely in the hands of legal agents — or rather in the hands and power of victorious bribers. . . . They then formed committees where none existed, and exacted a pledge from the free traders in many boroughs that the subject should be fully attended to hereafter; and although the work is a very great one, and it cannot be brought to perfection in a single day, yet I believe now that the first stimulus, the first great impulse, has been given.

The first test of these new tactics was in a by-election that August at Dudley, in the Black Country, an 'iron town' dominated by a single employer. The result was a disappointment. The free-trade candidate collected only 175 votes against his opponent's 388, a defeat attributed by the *Morning Chronicle* to the effects of public voting. The Tory candidate, challenged on the hustings to promise that no one who voted against him would be victimized, stayed silent, amid shouts from the crowd of 'Let us vote as we like.'

During the winter the registration campaign went ahead vigorously, with results soon evident for all to see. George Wilson was able to report, to a mass meeting in the Free Trade Hall in Manchester on 24 October 1844, that they had managed to get struck off the register no fewer than 878 of 7,571 of the voters of South Lancashire who had voted for the anti-League candidate at the last election. Although their opponents had retorted by getting 422 of the 6,973 who had cast their votes for the free-trade candidate disqualified the net result favoured the League; 'we are striking off,' Wilson commented, 'more than two to their one'. In all the other places studied — Bolton, Oldham, Ormskirk, Rochdale, even Manchester itself — it had been the same story. Even if the League made no further converts, Wilson told his audience, the revision of the registers by itself should give them an extra 500 votes in North Lancashire, and enable them to win South Lancashire, plus 21 of the 24 borough seats in the county, leaving 'the monopolists . . . 5 out of the whole 26 members for the entire county'. Cobden, who followed Wilson, had no doubt of these figures' significance:

> Quiet as have ['has' in original] been those statistical tables that you have heard by our chairman I venture to say that they will strike more terror into the ranks of the monopolists than the loudest demonstration or the most brilliant declamation with which we have ever tried to interest you.

As for the county constituencies elsewhere, 'our landlords', Cobden suggested, had created 'a rod in pickle' for themselves in retaining the 40s freehold as the basic voting qualification:

> With the vast diffusion of wealth among the middle classes . . . and among a large portion, I am happy to say, in this district, of the superior class of operatives, too, that forty-shilling franchise is become merely nominal, and is within the reach of every man who has the spirit to acquire it. . . . Every county where there is a large town population as in Lancashire, the West Riding of Yorkshire, South Staffordshire, North Cheshire, Middlesex,

Surrey, Kent and many other counties . . . in fact every other county bordering upon the sea coast or having manufactures in it — may be won, and easily won if the people can be roused to a systematic effort to qualify themselves for the vote.

Cobden went on to suggest that fathers should deliberately buy or rent franchises of the necessary value for their sons:

There is no investment so secure as the freehold of the earth and it is the only investment that gives a vote along with the property. . . . Sometimes a parent, wishing to teach a son to be economical and saving, gives him a set of nest-eggs in a savings' bank [many small Savings Banks were set up after 1815 under management committees of local dignitaries. The state-run, nationally administered, Post Office Savings Bank was not established until 1861]. I say to such a parent, 'Make your son, at twenty-one, a freeholder . . . for you make him thereby an independent freeman and put it in his power to defend himself and his children from political oppression.'

In the next few months similar advice was given at other meetings in Rochdale, Huddersfield, Leeds and Halifax. Some League members, however, clearly felt uneasy about this new development and Cobden did his best to reassure them in that familiar haunt of League activity, Covent Garden Theatre, on Wednesday 12 December 1844:

Many people say 'This is something not quite legitimate; you cannot go on manufacturing these votes.' We reply, 'The law and the constitution prescribe it and we have no alternative.' It may be a very bad system, that men should be required to have £40 or £50 laid out on the surface of the earth, in order that they should be represented; but the law prescribes that plan, and there is no other. And we say, 'Do not violate the law. Conform to it its spirit and in fact, and do so by thousands and tens of thousands if you can.'

The doubters were convinced, or at any rate inactive, and the new electoral register, displayed on every church door, soon proved incomparably superior to the untrustworthy lists used in the past. Many of the new names on it belonged to 40s freeholders who had obtained the right to vote through the League's intervention. Often they hardly knew what property they owned but had let their name be used to purchase a house they had no intention of occupying. The

League and other publications regularly advertised suitable property and all a would-be purchaser needed to do was to fill in a form and hand the money to a League official. The amounts involved were by no means prohibitive: in North Lancashire a mere £30–£35 would suffice and even in East Surrey one needed only £55–£60. By buying a house, dividing it up, and renting it to a number of people simultaneously, a single property could yield a large number of votes. One desirable residence in Brighton was bought on the League's behalf for £900 by a solicitor, who remained the nominal owner. It was then let, at £50 a year, and sub-divided into eighteen separate establishments with a minimum £2 rent, thus giving the League 20 votes (including those of purchaser and principal tenant) — and the owner a respectable 5½ per cent return on his money. For an expenditure of £56 a head another 17 to 20 votes were created in a similar way for a single house in Hounslow. There were offices in both Manchester and London specializing in this work in potentially winnable constituencies which kept thirty solicitors busy, full or part-time, but the main effort was made in the North. John Bright told a meeting at Covent Garden in February 1845 that already their 'friends in Lancashire, Cheshire and Yorkshire [had] invested a sum of not less than £250,000 in the purchase of county qualifications'. As Cobden reminded a meeting, the last time Villiers had presented his famous motion he had not 'a single county voter' from England or Wales. 'We are,' promised Cobden, 'going to try if we cannot get him a few.' By 15 January 1845, at the usual pre-opening of Parliament meeting at Covent Garden, George Wilson was able to report that forty 'thorough business meetings' for this purpose had already been held in Lancashire and Yorkshire which, along with Middlesex, were 'counties . . . such as any man might well be proud of becoming a freeholder of. It never can be long the destiny of these counties to be held in the thralldom of an aristocracy.'

A later speaker, W.J. Fox, who wrote in the *League* under the pseudonym 'A Norwich Weaver Boy', went even further, arguing that the whole registration scheme, far from being morally dubious, was an instrument of social improvement:

In this plan there is a moral good beyond, perhaps, what in the original conception was thought of. It tends to act upon the character of the entire labouring population of the country — the working classes, the more toilsome section of the middle classes; it holds out to them a hope, promise and incitement of the most desirable and elevating description. It says to them 'Become proprietors of a portion, however small, of this our England;

have a stake in the country; be something here'. . . . It gives them a tangible bond of connection with society; a feeling of independence and honest pride. . . . Obtaining it, I think we shall be on the high road towards a better choice of legislators. . . .

On 22 January 1845 the League Council reported to the annual meeting at the Free Trade Hall that 160 boroughs in England and Wales had already been visited and the returns showed 'an undoubted gain in 112 of the boroughs,' sufficient 'in many of these . . . to ensure the return of free traders . . . in the event of an election'. As for the counties, the Council would claim 'a large addition to our ranks . . . in Middlesex, North Lancashire and several other populous counties, while, 'within the last three months, a sufficient number of persons have purchased freehold qualifications in North Cheshire, South Lancashire and the West Riding of York to secure to those important constituencies a free-trade majority'.

Another, more grandiose, scheme later that year came to nothing. In October 1845 Cobden wrote to George Wilson to report a plan he had discussed with Bright to buy a whole estate in Buckinghamshire 'with a view to create say 1000 county votes,' although publicly the League would say that it sought to 'establish a model farm with a model lease, model offices and model cottages with gardens, to prove our faith in our principles than the soil is as capable of as great a profitable development as manufactures'. The announcement would, Cobden predicted, 'strike everybody and create a great deal of talk. . . . The money in £60 shares might be raised in a fortnight but not a word must be said about the votes. . .'. The League went as far as asking a sympathetic farmer to try to find a suitable property costing £60,000 to £80,000, but presumably he failed for nothing more was heard of the proposal.

No less important than creating favourable votes was securing the disqualification of hostile electors and here the League was assisted by a change in the law, which made it, after 1843, legitimate to send a copy of an objection to the voter concerned by post. Provided the postmaster stamped a duplicate notice, proof of posting was regarded as proof of delivery, and in the three days before the final day for posting objection to the 1845 register, 24 August, and especially on that day itself, the League's officials posted no fewer than 23,000 objections to voters in seven counties. The deliberate intention was to swamp the post office with more letters than it could handle, and to ensure, with many places receiving only a weekly delivery, that most would arrive too late for the recipient to challenge them. The postmaster at Manchester did protest but Acland, in charge of the operation, replied blandly that he was behaving 'in conformity with the Act of Parliament,' although many of the objections, a subsequent enquiry found, were 'directed against persons of undoubted qualification, men of large property in houses and land . . . and other persons of that description'. By now the League was challenging known Tory votes on the flimsiest grounds. Somewhat cheekily, even the Prime Minister's vote at Tamworth was objected to, though he largely owned the place, while those of his Law Officers were also disputed. These great men were not disenfranchized but often the League succeeded beyond its wildest expectations. Many electors on receiving the copies of objections to their votes assumed they were thereby disqualified, while others failed to attend at the revising barrister's hearing 'by remoteness of residence, illness, business' or 'unwillingness to lose their time'. The whole procedure had, at the very least, considerable nuisance value, and the Conservative majority in the Commons was so alarmed that it set up a Select Committee to examine 'the alleged facilities afforded to vexatious and fraudulent objections and fraudulent claims by the present system of registration of County Voters'. The resulting hearings and subsequent Report, published in 1846, gave national publicity to the League's tactics. Copies of the *League* were introduced in evidence. The issue of 13 December 1845 had reported, the Committee learned, that 'in North Warwickshire over which the monopolists have sung their songs in triumph . . . our clear gain . . . on the registration is 106 votes or 2 per cent. . . . We then threw a shell into Buckinghamshire'. During 1845 alone, it emerged, £15,500 had been spent on the registration campaign, but George Wilson, giving evidence on 30 April 1846, was unrepentant. 'In making these objections,' he acknowledged, 'we knew there were a great many to whom we objected who probably had good votes, but their description upon the register was so vague and indefinite that we felt it to be desirable that they should be asked to comply with all the law required.' As for those who had lost their vote through not challenging an objection, 'I believe the greater proportion of those who were struck off . . . had no vote. . .'. 'I think,' he added piously, 'we are entitled to some thanks from those desirous of purifying the register.' Whatever the League's motives, its work had been carried out on a massive scale. In the fourteen county constituencies, about a third of the whole country, where the League had concentrated their efforts nearly 11 per cent of all the voters on the register — 13,323 out of 123,114 — had been objected to, 7,050 of those challenged had lost their votes and most of the remainder had only survived by having their 'description' — i.e.

particulars such as address — amended. In some counties not a single objection had been ruled to be unsound, and the total in the whole 13,000 scrutinized was only 1,549. Allowing for changes made in the Court of Common Pleas, to which those affected could appeal, 88 per cent of all the League's objections had finally been upheld in some form. In 53 per cent of cases the vote had been expunged from the register and in the rest the elector's particulars had been amended to meet the legal requirements.

George Wilson was quite candid about what had been done. The League would, he agreed, 'give every facility for the acquisition of votes. . .'. 'I believe,' he told one of his questioners, 'if you or anyone else go to one of our agents with the desire of procuring a vote and leave him £60 for that purpose he will get you a vote,' but of the corporate purchasing of votes, which would have been corrupt, there was no evidence whatever. 'If one sixpence was spent for the purchasing of votes. . . ,' testified Wilson, 'I should know of it as certainly as if it was a man's private account.' The League emerged from the enquiry with honour untarnished and its reputation for efficiency enhanced.

CHAPTER NINETEEN

The Cooperation of the Ladies

'We have obtained the cooperation of the ladies.'
— Richard Cobden MP, 25 August 1842

'It was found that mothers, wives and daughters took a deep interest in the question which so much engrossed the attention of sons, husbands and brothers. . . . Thousands of female hearts beat indignantly at the thought that food should not be had where it could be had, while millions were in a state bordering upon starvation. Were the frigid rules of artificial society to exclude women from an agitation widely to diffuse the benefits of "plenty and cheapness"?' Thus Archibald Prentice, explaining, almost apologetically, why women played a larger rôle in the work of the League than in any previous political organization. Here, too, the League was a pioneer, and Prentice, looking back, was sure he had been right in enlisting women's help. 'I never had the smallest doubt,' he wrote, 'of its perfect propriety and its perfect consistency with the softer characteristics of female virtue.'

Other contemporaries were less open-minded than Prentice, notably a French historian of the League, M. Frederick Bastiat:

I doubt not that the reader is surprised, and perhaps scandalized, to see woman appearing in these stormy debates. Woman seems to lose her grace in risking herself in the scientific melée, bristling with the barbarous words 'tariffs', 'salaries', 'profits', 'monopolies'. What is there in common between dry dissertations and that etherial being, that angel of the soft affections, that poetical and devoted nature, whose destiny it is solely to love and to please, to sympathize and to console? But if woman does become alarmed at the dull syllogism and cold statistics, she is gifted with a marvellous sagacity . . . she has comprehended that alms-giving is not the only form of charity. . . . We are willing to feed those who are hungry, to clothe those who are cold, but we applaud efforts which have for their object the removal of the barriers which interpose between clothing and nakedness, between subsistence and starvation.

Bastiat went on, however, to describe women's role in distinctly patronizing, if heavily gallant, terms:

Is not the part which the English ladies have taken in the work of
the League in perfect harmony with the mission of woman in
society? There are fêtes, soirées, given to the free-traders; éclat,
warmth and life are communicated by their presence to those
great oratorical jousts in which the condition of the masses is
discussed; a magnificent prize is held out to the most eloquent
orator, or to the most indefatigable defender of liberty.

What could he mean, his cynical French readers may have
wondered. But enlightenment was soon forthcoming. The
'magnificent prize', it appeared, was nothing more substantial than
feminine approval, a traditional and acceptable reward, for,
explained Bastiat, it was 'woman . . . who forbids by a tear, and
commands by a smile'. The League could in fact hardly have
functioned at all if the wives of its leading members had not tolerated
their husbands' almost constant absences, and the heavy demands
the free-trade campaign made on their time and money. Sometimes
they were even more generous than their spouses. One collector for
a League appeal who called on the businessman Robert Ashton and
'found him sitting with his lady' was gratified to be told 'I gave you
£100 last year and shall give you £200 now,' but his wife demurred.
'Give him £500, Robert,' was the quiet suggestion of the lady; and
Mr Ashton, who 'is worthy of such a wife, at once assented'. League
daughters, too, were to the fore, especially at social occasions,
though Prentice does not record any romances which resulted.

Women's formal involvement in the League's work began in
October 1840 with a large-scale tea party in the Corn Exchange,
Manchester, attended by 850 people of both sexes. The 65 tables
were each presided over by a woman, 13 of them spinsters,
including Prentice's daughter Mary. 'This,' commented her father,
'was the commencement of a cooperation, in which the ladies
rendered effectual service.' They began to make a less traditional
contribution in November 1841 when the annual delegate meeting
in Manchester carried unanimously a resolution 'That memorials
from the females of the United Kingdom be presented to the Queen,
praying Her Majesty to exercise her royal prerogative in favour of
the total repeal of the corn and provision laws'. A meeting in the.
Corn Exchange early in December was treated to a powerful speech
justifying this dubious constitutional procedure from George
Thompson, a famous orator expelled from the United States for his
attacks on slavery:

She is a woman, she is a wife, she is a mother; tell her the nation
which has just rejoiced in the birth of a son she has given to be the

sovereign of these realms [the future Edward VII, born three weeks earlier on 9 November 1841], contains millions of husbands, wives and children, who know not where to obtain tomorrow's bread. Implore her, as she desires to save her country from distraction, to gladden homes that are desolate to bring upon her the blessings of the perishing, and to rule over a happy and contented people — to exercise all the influence the constitution gives her in favour of that great measure which we have advocated tonight. . . . Let millions of women urge their united appeal to a woman's heart. If any should tell you, you are unfeminine in that which you do, tell them it would be still more unlike women to slumber in inactivity when mothers and their little ones are perishing for bread. . . . Hunger waits not! Death waits not! . . . Be up and doing. This is the time: the hour is striking. To your work then — your proper work; the work of women — of Englishwomen — of English Christian women.

Those who responded to this stirring appeal soon faced more than accusations of being unfeminine. 'The unmanly attempt,' Archibald Prentice observed, 'was made to cast foul slander on their characters; and was persevered in on the part of one influential journal until the proprietor was told . . . that unless he gave orders to his underlings to desist, he would be made personally responsible for their clumnies.' He gave no further details, and before long the League ladies had silenced the doubters by their evident efficiency, though the petition to the Queen, predictably, produced only a formal response.

Meanwhile, in September 1841, a committee had been formed to consider how women could best assist the League and had settled on the idea of a nationally-advertised bazaar of a very ambitious kind, a kind of Great Exhibition — though this still lay ten years ahead — in miniature. In Prentice's words, 'thousands of fair fingers were instantly at work' and the original committee of 85 women, based in Manchester, with Mrs Cobden as president, swelled to 360, distributed throughout the country, where each formed the centre of a network of local contributors. The intended venue, the Manchester Town Hall, soon proved too small and the Theatre Royal was hired instead.

Within this impressive setting no effort was spared to promote the free-trade message. Stall No. 10, for example, as the *Manchester Times* described, was heaped with Anti-Corn-Law pincushions, embroidered with 'Let me come free,' around a sheaf of corn, and 'Freely give and freely will I grind' around a windmill. The whole function provided a suitable object for a day out of which even the

Bright family, who had been brought up to regard bright clothes and music as unacceptably frivolous, could approve — as John's sister, Priscilla, described in a letter from Rochdale:

> The factory people all went yesterday to the Free Trade Bazaar, my brother paying for a cheap train to conduct them to Manchester. There were 700 of them and George Wilson let them go in free. They assembled on the moor just below these gates; the women and girls went first in twos and threes, then followed a band of music and the men and boys brought up the rear. It was really a beautiful sight. They were all so well-dressed and in such high spirits . . . I wished Lord Ashley and his followers could have seen them [a reference to the future Lord Shaftesbury's attacks on the Lancashire manufacturers for allegedly ill-treating their child workers]. I cannot help thinking music may be useful in bringing about a moral and intellectual regeneration of the working class; but I did not quite like the band yesterday, it felt to me like doing a good action with a great noise.

In the ten days it was open, from Monday 31 January 1842, the bazaar raised, including cash donations and an auction of unsold goods, almost £10,000, of which nearly £1,400 came from admission charges: 2s. 6d the first day, 1s. 6d later. Henceforward the place of women in the movement was assured, provoking a sour comment from the *Quarterly Review*. 'It has,' it observed, 'ever been a frequent device of revolutionary agitators to bring women forward as a screen and safeguard to their own operations.' Female involvement could, however, be interpreted in a very different way and Cobden cited it, in his speech of 25 August 1842 already quoted, as proof of the League's pacific nature. 'We have,' he told the Manchester Association on that occasion, 'obtained the cooperation of the ladies.' That November the sympathetic *Leeds Mercury* remarked on 'the enthusiastic spirit manifested by the assembly of both sexes' at one meeting and, in describing a soirée held in the following month, referred to 'the important sanction of the ladies'. The League Council had suggested in October 1842, after launching its £50,000 appeal, that local committees should include members of both sexes, with a specially handsome card supplied to lady collectors; but to *The Times* it still seemed remarkable a year later that women should listen to speeches on economic policy: 'Maids and matrons,' it noted, in its much-quoted leader of 18 November 1843, 'flock to theatres as though it were but a new "translation from the French".'

The registration campaign which dominated 1844 hardly affected the League's female members, but they came into their own in the following year. The idea of following up the success of the Manchester bazaar of January 1842 with another in London, on a more truly national scale, began to be raised during the second half of 1844, and on 30 December the membership was informed of what was proposed by George Wilson:

The Council of the League, at the earnest entreaty of a number of ladies, have determined upon holding a Bazaar in the Theatre Royal, Covent Garden, London, during the month of May, 1845, in aid of the £100,000 fund now in course of collection. . . . In accepting the co-operation so nobly proferred, the Council cannot omit to record their grateful acknowledgements to those ladies by whose exertions alone the Bazaar held in Manchester, in the early part of the year 1842, was begun, carried on, and brought to a most triumphant conclusion, giving an impulse to the public mind on the subject of the Corn Laws, of greater and more permanent value than the pecuniary results of that undertaking, unprecedently large as they were. . . . The first particular . . . will be the formation of a Ladies Local Committee in each town. . . . Each town should, if practicable, endeavour to furnish a stall entirely: and . . . it is respectfully suggested that . . . the contributions from each town . . . consist in a great degree of articles for the manufacture of which it may be celebrated. . . . The following classification specifies the articles most suitable for such an occasion:
  1. Articles usually contributed to Bazaars.
  2. Articles of Manufacture British and Foreign.
  3. Models of Mechanism & C.
  4. Designs, Architectural and Fancy.
  5. Specimens of Coins, Minerals, Birds, Insects, etc.
  6. Books and other publications from Authors, with Autograph.
  7. Autograph Letters from Celebrated Men and Women of the present and former times.
  8. Portraits, Pictures and Illustrated Works.
  9. Philosophical Instruments.
  10. Music.
  11. Original Poetry and Tales.
  12. Pecuniary Contributions. . . .

Along with this highly practical document went one specially designed to strike a responsive chord among any readers who resented the inferior position society had assigned them:

TO THE WOMEN OF GREAT BRITAIN

LADIES. By a majority of the other sex you are excluded from direct interference in political matters. On the wisdom or justice of this exclusion I make no comment. . . . By this same majority and by universal consent you are invited to interpose in matters of charity. . . . To a good work of this description you are invited . . . by the Council of the Anti-Corn-Law League. The peculiar reason why *you* should respond to that invitation may be given in one word — the Corn Laws are INHUMAN.

Who of you has not sympathized with the poor sempstresses of London, stitching through fifteen hours a day for 3s per week. . . ? A difference of one sixth, that is 6d a week, is taken by the Corn Laws out of the sempstresses's wages of 3s. It is the worth of one day, every week, of that eye-blinding and heart-bleeding work. Is not this inhumanity? . . .

The proposed Bazaar . . . affords a most unquestionable mode in which your aid may be as efficient as it will be welcome. . . . What *mere* charity can be compared with the great and sacred cause of justice, which you are thus invited to advance? . . . How much you achieved towards the abolition of the slave trade! And how much you may achieve towards the abolition of the starvation trade.

At the usual new year's meeting in the Free Trade Hall, Manchester, on 8 January 1845, Cobden stressed the moral nature of the campaign. It was, he proclaimed, 'not a mere contest for a few more pigs, a few more sheep or a little more corn. . . . No the triumph of free trade [was] the triumph of pacific principles between all the nations of the earth'. A week later, the customary pre-opening of Parliament meeting at Covent Garden on 15 January heard of the progress of the registration movement, already described, and at the annual general meeting of the League in Manchester on 22 January George Wilson described the huge scale of the League's other activities. Its offices in London and Manchester had, he said, received nearly 26,000 letters in 1844, and despatched almost 300,000. Two million copies of publications had been distributed, plus 1,340,000 copies of the *League* newspaper, and lecturers had visited 36 of the 40 English counties. £83,000 of the £100,000 appeal fund of 1843 had already been raised and the amount only fell short of the target because the great bazaar had not yet been held.

Preparations for the event dominated the next few months. A meeting in the Manchester Free Trade Hall on 5 March, attended by more than six thousand people, learned, as Archibald Prentice recorded, 'that . . . thirty towns [had already] promised to supply a stall each and seventy others [had] promised . . . to furnish a portion'.

By 11 March, when a major planning meeting was held at Newall's Buildings, it was clear that 'bazaar' was a misnomer and this became even more obvious when, on 10 April 1845, George Wilson spoke to the final preliminary meeting in Covent Garden in London:

> We want to see assembled in this theatre our friends from all parts of the kingdom, in order that they may converse together; that they may confer together; that they may become known to each other; that they may derive from such meetings and from what they will see here a new impetus and carry to the extremities of the country a redoubled resolution to assist us in prompting the great object which we have in view.

From the moment it opened, on Tuesday 8 May 1845, the 'bazaar' was an enormous success, and even normally hostile newspapers like the *Morning Herald* could not withhold their praise:

> Notwithstanding the very unfavourable state of the weather, and the high price of the tickets of admission, the attendance at the doors was very numerous and the stair, saloons and lobbies — even the body of the house itself — was soon full to overflowing. The arrangements to prevent confusion, however, appeared to be very excellent and to be well carried out by the stewards. . . . The public were only admitted through the chief entrance in Bow Street, from whence they ascended . . . up the grand staircase to the Shakespeare saloon, now fitted up with tapestry, carpets, shawls, etc. . . . in this place also is a magnificent mirror, one such as giants only should survey themselves in, also an interesting stall of chemical preparations; and a box from Darlaston ['Darlestone' in original], in Staffordshire, containing coal and iron, the latter in its various stages from the rudest order to the most polished and tempered metal. . . . In the box lobby on the left is a stall for Miller's glass works, containing many remarkable curiosities, and also the apparatus at work by which they are produced, and glass thread is woven into soft and beautiful fabrics. Passing on to the centre of the lobby we find two boxes are removed and come suddenly upon a scene so novel and romantic, so incongruous and grotesque, that for a moment we could fancy ourselves transported to the east and about to deal with Turks and Mussulmans. Certainly, in its palmiest days no

visitor to Covent Garden ever witnessed on its stage a more complete transformation. The whole area of the pit and stage is boarded over, and transformed into a Norman Gothic Hall with an arched roof, gaily decorated, and supported on each side by rows of ornamental pillars. The sides are covered with imitation panelling, with grotesque ornaments and devices and numerous free-trade mottoes. At the extreme end is a large Gothic window so prepared and lit up as to resemble stained glass; there are also similar windows at the sides, and from the roof are suspended rows of illuminated lamps, which cast a rich but subdued light over the hall, and add very much to the beauty of the spectacle.

All these wonders, however, merely provided an introduction to the bazaar itself to which ultimately forty-six provincial towns had contributed stalls of their own, plus twelve districts of London:

> Descending a few steps we find ourselves in the body of the hall, which is 150 feet long by 50 feet wide, and is occupied by four rows of stalls, each about a yard in width, but divided into various lengths. . . . Upon the stage . . . and in the refreshment room there are additional stalls. The length of the counter is said to be 900 feet. . . . We find the boxes on each side converted into stalls, the one being allotted to Northampton and the other to Dunstable and respectively filled with the staple commodities of these places — shoes and bonnets. Upon entering the hall we saw the stalls on the right allotted to Rochdale, Halifax, Leeds and Bradford. . . . They contained chiefly fancy articles of needlework, toys of various descriptions, carpets, shawls, materials of various kinds for ladies' dresses, and curiosities, among which may be mentioned a piece of muslin, printed by the late Sir Robert Peel [father of the Prime Minister] and a pen-and-ink portrait of the Queen, the lines of which, instead of being blank, are written words, and comprise the whole contents of a book which is attached to, and descriptive of it. This singular specimen of ingenuity is to be raffled for at 2s. 6d a head and, strange to say, we saw several Quaker ladies pressing forward to have their names set down as gamblers for it.

Besides pressing the Prime Minister into unwitting fund-raising service, the League had also exploited its great ally, the penny post. At the 'Post Office' in the Theatre the visitor was encouraged to 'knock and inquire if they had a letter for him, and upon his supplying them with his name and address,' the *Morning Herald* discovered, 'he is himself in due time, supplied with a packet (not pre-paid) which, on receiving, he finds filled with League tracts and other free-trade publications. The scheme was so successful that the arrival of a "foreign mail" was soon notified and of course it brought with it a despatch for every applicant and at the foreign rate of postage.'

Probably the most successful feature of all was the display of manufactured goods from 'Sheffield, Colebrookdale and the Potteries' assembled in 'the lower saloon,' which anticipated — the propagandist element apart — the collection which was to be assembled under Prince Albert's inspiration six years later:

> Here are instruments and tools of every description . . . from the revolving saw, which cuts through steel bars or gnarled oaks as easily as a knife divides a twig, to scissors, needles and other things appurtenant to a ladies workbox . . . among which we may particularly mention a large pair of shears, on which were exhibited excellent full-length portraits of Mr Bright and Mr Cobden. The exhibition from Colebrookdale . . . consisted chiefly of ornamental iron works, in some of which our native artists appeared to have attained perfection. There were vases, fountains, bronzes, ornamental gates, fire-screens (on which were painted striking portraits of Messrs Cobden, Bright and Villiers).

The final proof of the League's ingenuity in propagating its message came in the refreshment room:

> Next to the creams and ices vended there, the chief object of attraction is a huge plum cake — a cake the idea of which would, we think, have occurred in a dream only to some imaginative schoolboy — so vast is its expanse, so ponderous its size, so rich its ingredients, so delicious its fragrance. It is a Bury Simnel and measures, we should think, some five feet in diameter, weighs 280 lbs, and bears upon its broad surface, a sheet of iced sugar so large as to have inscribed upon it nearly all the maxims which embody the religion of the League, and so sweet and richly ornamented as to almost induce the visitor to swallow them. We hear that it is to be cut up and distributed on the last day of the exhibition.

From the very first day the organizers were aware that they had a massive hit on their hands. The *Morning Herald* man had complained that 'the place was much too small both for the exhibition of the goods and for the accommodation of visitors,' but an uncomfortably crowded hall was better than an embarrassingly empty one. The bazaar's success was reflected in the daily *Bazaar Gazette*, an eight-page pamphlet priced at 1d, which warned about 'complaints having been made that some articles were too highly priced' and drew attention to publicity-worthy exhibits, such as 'a coffin for the Corn Laws' — presumably the gift of some undertaker supporter — 'with a proper mortuary plate, a blank being left for the date of the death'. Destined no doubt for some already over-filled drawing room was 'a Free Trade sofa cushion, richly embroidered with ears of wheat in heavy gold and most tastefully formed and fringed,' which rapidly fetched ten guineas. In similar vein were the 'series of card medallions, each containing a lock of hair of some celebrated leader of the League . . . the Free Trade waistcoats, decorated with Free Trade devices . . . the Free Trade pocket handkerchiefs' — a particularly popular line, rapidly sold out — and 'three large autograph books, superbly bound, each containing from sixty to seventy autographs,' valued at thirty guineas each but raffled separately at 10s a ticket. There were similar draws throughout the three weeks the bazaar lasted, to sustain interest and to clear space for new goods. 'Contributions continue to flow in,' the *Gazette* reported almost complainingly in Issue 15. 'So unchecked is the stream that notwithstanding the vast amount of goods already sold the stalls appear as rich as on the first day of opening.'

The *Gazette* also included a selection of the puns and word puzzles always dear to the Victorians:

> My first is a horse of great worth on the road,
> My second of tigers and bears the abode;
> Unite them together, the name you will view
> Of an honest free-trader and patriot true.

The hidden syllables spelt out the name of Cobden, and his chief lieutenant was similarly honoured in the initial letters of an acrostic poem, while the Free-Trade Alphabet, on sale at one of the three stalls allotted to Manchester, also paid tribute to the movement's heroes from 'A is the Ashworth, of Free Trade renown. . .' to 'W the Wilson, of endless exertion. . .'.

A Rhythmical Notice describing the bazaar, of which signed copies were on sale, proved a popular souvenir, and Harriet Martineau contributed a specially-written ninety-four-page story called *Dawn Island*, about a remote Pacific community, given to wars and to sacrificing their first-born babies, until the arrival of a ship manned by white men introduces them simultaneously to the ideas of free trade, peace, and a respect for human life. It was, like the *Poor Law Tales* she had written earlier to popularize the workhouse, sorry stuff. A more convincing demonstration of the value of unrestricted commerce was provided by the exhibits listed in the *Bazaar Gazette*, which revealed on page after page the delights which both the British and foreign home might enjoy in the future — from 'Fryer's Improved Patent, Single Double and Treble Washing and Wringing Machines,' to 'Budding's Machine for Cutting Grass Plots,' which, the potential purchaser was assured, 'leaves a more even and uniform surface than can be produced by the most skilful mower . . . [or] with a scythe'. The exhibition was considered sufficiently valuable for 'the senior students of the government school of design,' who had previously been to the far larger Paris Exhibition, to be sent to it, where 'they spent a long time . . . minutely examining the castings from Colebrookdale'.

The 'Lost and Found' section of the *Gazette* also gave its own insight into the arts and crafts of the time, for the visitors had managed to shed 'A gold purse tassel . . . a black silk parasol . . . a small purple plaid shawl . . . a white veil . . . a Lady's Boa . . . and a small gold tube belonging to an Ear Trumpet'.

The most serious problem which the organizers faced was that of overcrowding, as Issue No. 8 of the *Gazette*, published after the first week's operations, revealed:

> In the afternoon of Wednesday the ladies attending the stalls sent a strong representation to the Council of the League declaring that they were unable to bear the pressure of the overwhelming crowd, which had filled every inch of available space in the body of the hall and effectually put an end to all facilities for buying and selling. At the same time those in charge of the doors sent in the most anxious reports of the fearful amount of pressure from without, declaring that there was peril to life and limb in its continuance.

The answer was found in raising the price of admission from a shilling to half-a-crown and in extending the opening hours until 10 o'clock in the evening; previously it had closed at nine, after opening at noon. It soon became a popular evening attraction. 'At nine o'clock. . .', issue No. 15 of the *Gazette* noted, 'the pressure was so great that it was feared there would be a necessity for closing the doors.' With about 1,500 people being admitted per hour, for an average stay of two hours, there was bound to be congestion, since the total that Covent Garden Theatre could comfortably accommodate was about 2,000 at a time.

That the bazaar, by far the most ambitious event of its kind any political movement had so far organized, was both a publicity and a financial success was never in doubt. Less certain was its long-term effects. The *Morning Chronicle* suggested that while it might not 'make even as many as a hundred actual and immediate converts to Free Trade . . . it will put many thousands on the way to conversion,' but its chief value was probably in boosting the morale of existing supporters and in demonstrating their numbers and influence:

> The Free Trade Bazaar . . . is not a mere spectacle, though merely as a spectacle, it is unsurpassed in beauty, attractiveness and interest by any that our metropolis affords. It is a greath social and political fact. It marks the breadth, depth and force of public conviction on a question of profound social and political importance. It is by far the most decisive sign that the history of the Free Trade movement has yet shown, not only of the resources, zeal and sound judgement of the extraordinary association under whose auspices it is presented to the world, but of the extent and thoroughness with which Free Trade principles have leavened the public mind. . . .

Several commentators remarked on the major role that women had played. The *League* itself acclaimed 'those ladies who, for seventeen days, had devoted their time, their toil and, we fear, their health, with unwearied assiduity, to advance the great cause of humanity and justice. . . . They were not conscious of the capacities they possessed until they found them developed in action by the force of circumstances.' The *Patriot* spoke of the 'ingenious . . . and beautiful' contribution made by 'our fair friends,' while the *Illuminated Magazine* was even more impressed:

> Women have made presents of their jewels, toys and trinkets, as well as their time; and we have no doubt that had such a proposal been made, and a free-trade use found for it, thousands of women would have been found to sheer away the hair from their heads, as is recorded to have been done in one of the sieges of old to furnish cordage for the engines of death.

Financially the bazaar achieved even more than had been hoped, raising £25,046. 0s. 11d, while a large quantity of unsold goods remained to stock the stalls of a similar function in Manchester planned for later in the year. But it was in its propagandist value that its real importance lay. The most succinct statement of what it had achieved appeared in the final issue of the *Bazaar Gazette* on 27 May 1845:

LOST: the cause of the monopolists. It is of no use to anyone, being quite worn out and in a deplorable condition from the rough manner in which it has been treated.

CHAPTER TWENTY

The Time is Come

'The Queen thinks the time is come when a removal of the restrictions upon the importation of food cannot be successfully resisted.'
— Queen Victoria to Sir Robert Peel, c. 28 November 1845

During the opening months of 1845 the parliamentary fight had continued as usual. Early in the new session came the annual ritual of the Budget, during which Peel reduced the duty on sugar and abolished altogether the duty on 430 minor items like dyes and drugs. The Corn Laws remained, and when Cobden, on 7 March 1845, moved for a Select Committee on the alleged agricultural distress the motion was lost by 213 votes to 121, a majority of 92.

On 26 May, with the town still flocking to the bazaar, Lord John Russell moved a series of resolutions recommending measures to 'improve the condition of the labouring classes,' among them a reconsideration of the Corn Laws, but his resolutions were rejected by 182 votes to 104, a majority of 78. Two weeks later Charles Villiers' annual resolution was even more decisively voted down by 132 votes, with 122 ayes and 254 nos. The League consoled itself by pointing out that since 1842 the ratio of 'pro-repeal' to 'pro-Corn-Law' votes had risen from 4:17 to 4:8, but its strongest card remained the poverty in rural areas, and it was during the winter of 1844–45 that the two-man survey of living conditions already quoted was carried out, being published soon afterwards.

As the harvest season of 1845 approached, there were signs of stirring in the countryside. More than a thousand people, mainly labourers and their families, assembled at Upavon in Wiltshire 'under a fine old tree on the green' to protest at their lot, though many local employers had threatened to dismiss any of their men who attended. The meeting's chairman, a former farm-boy, took this warning as his text, comparing the farmers to the carters he had known in childhood, who 'would give the boys the whip and threaten that they would give it them again if they told their parents. . . . You will never be better as long as you are kept down in this way,' he declared, 'But if you come forward boldly and tell your case, you can't make it worse.'

At Covent Garden, a few days later, on 18 June 1845, a very different audience heard George Wilson, Richard Cobden and John Bright deliver the familiar plea for abolition. 'They had narrowed it down to one little word — "When?",' said Cobden. It was, he argued, madness for the government to contemplate repeal only 'should Divine providence think fit to punish us with a bad harvest,' for then corn would be scarce everywhere and 'Where was the supply to come from?'

As the 1845 session of Parliament drew towards its close the weather stayed mainly fair, but in one of its last debates, on 5 August, Lord John Russell once again denounced 'the misery of an uncertain law with respect to corn,' based on continuing 'doubt whether the next fortnight will bring us a harvest tolerably good or miserably deficient'. 'The state of trade,' commented Archibald Prentice, 'fluctuated with the rise and fall of the barometer,' and with it the price of wheat, which reached £2. 17s in the middle of August, but had fallen to £2. 14s by the middle of September.

Harriet Martineau, in her history of the period published four years later, recalled the changing seasons with the keen eye of the professional writer:

> Meantime, it had begun to rain. It began to rain, after a cold and late spring, at the beginning of the summer; and it seemed as if it was never going to leave off again. In some parts of the country the sun was scarcely seen from the month of May till the next spring. Those who first marked the soft perseverance of the soft falling rain, thought of the budding and blossoming promised in scripture, where the snow and rain are shown forth as illustration of the fertilizing influences of Providence. . . . Then, as the fall went on with less softness and more chill, and fewer intermissions, men began to fear for the harvest, and to calculate that much dry foreign wheat would be necessary to mix with our own damp and unripened grain. Then arose the fear that our own inferior grain would not keep . . . and, in the midst of this, it became clear that throughout Europe, with a few local exceptions, the harvest would prove a deficient one.

In the event it was not the high price of corn in England but the virtual disappearance of the potato in Ireland which brought about a change of heart within the government. No doubt the League's work for the past six years had unbarred the door; but it was the Irish famine which finally unlocked it, as Harriet Martineau explained:

The stealthy rain . . . generated some minute plague, of what nature nobody yet knows . . . a plague so minute that no microscope has yet convicted it, yet so powerful that it was soon to overthrow governments, and derange commerce, and affect for all time to come the political fate of England. . . . The minute plague spread and spread, till it blackened thousands of acres and destroyed the food of millions of men. In some wholesome region, the last to be affected, the inhabitants would hardly believe what they read. The newspapers were exaggerating shamefully for some political object; the League was trading on the rain and frightening the public. . . . But soon the change appeared even in these healthiest districts. A man might exhibit his green and flourishing crop to a stranger and say that he should take it up on Monday. On that night would come a thunderstorm and the next morning, if the owner stirred the soil of his blackened field with a pitchfork, up came such a steaming stench as showed him that his field was turned putrid.

The logic of the situation was obvious to all but the most besotted protectionists: if the staple food of Ireland was destroyed, to tax the only alternative to it was both cruel and lunatic. The League had always had a gift for the memorable phrase and now found a highly effective slogan, 'Open the ports.' Even Lord Ashley acknowledged to a meeting of his constituents in Dorset that the Corn Laws were now doomed and that the government should be considering how to 'break the force of an inevitable law' to the agricultural interest. On Tuesday 28 October 1845 more than eight thousand people — promised special late trains to take them home — assembled in the Free Trade Hall to hear Cobden declare that if Peel failed to act to avert the threat now hanging over Ireland 'he would be a criminal and a poltroon'. John Bright, who followed, declared in his peroration that his audience would be almost equally guilty if they failed to act.

How dreadful the abandonment of duty, how awful the crime, not less than that of those who made the Corn Law, if we step back from our place, if we fail in the work that we have set ourselves, which is to abolish the law that restricts the bounty of Providence and to establish the original and heaven-given law, which will give plenty to all the earth.

The Times predicted after reporting that the Cabinet had met on Friday 31 October 1845, 'Henceforth the League may cease to exist. . . . The "great fact" [a reference to the famous leader of 18

November 1843, quoted earlier] is hastening to become a *fait accompli.'* Other Cabinet meetings followed, on the Saturday, and on Monday 3 November and Thursday 6 November, but still the members of the League waited . . . and waited. 'I do not recollect a period in which there was so eager a desire to see the London papers. . .', wrote Prentice. 'Every morning and every evening witnessed the deep disappointment of thousands upon thousands who had been hopeful enough to believe that what was right to be done would be done.' A public dinner to Charles Villers in the Town Hall, Birmingham, provided an opportunity for further attacks on the government, but the first to announce his conversion was Lord John Russell, in an open letter from Edinburgh addressed to the electorate, on 22 November 1845:

> I confess that . . . my views have in the course of twenty years, undergone a great alteration. I used to be of opinion that corn was an exception to the general rules of political economy; but observation and experience have convinced me that we ought to abstain from all interference with the supply of food. . . . I have for several years endeavoured to obtain a compromise on this subject. . . . [But] it is no longer worthwhile to contend for a fixed duty. . . . Let us then, unite to put an end to a system which has been proved to be the blight of commerce, the bane of agriculture, the source of bitter divisions among classes, the cause of penury, fever, mortality, and crime among the people.

Lord Ashley, *The Times*, Lord John Russell, one by one the League's opponents were surrendering, but still Peel, who had done more to reduce protection than any politician alive, held aloof. On 4 December 1845, *The Times* announced that the government proposed to recall Parliament early in the New Year specifically to repeal the Corn Laws, provoking its rivals to fury. 'Some ministerial papers doubted and then indignantly denied this. . .' wrote Harriet Martineau. '*The Times* was scolded, insulted, jeered at, lectured; and everybody was warned not to mind *The Times.*'

On 5 December the *Standard*, still jealous of its rival's scoop, published a denial of the earlier story, headlined 'Atrocious fabrication by *The Times*,' but *The Times*, like the great newspaper that it was, stuck to its guns. 'We adhere to our original announcement,' it asserted on 6 December, 'that Parliament will meet early in January and that a repeal of the Corn Laws will be proposed in one House by Sir R. Peel and in the other by the Duke of Wellington.' As for the source of its information, it was — in the best journalistic tradition — not telling, but one colourful story

was, as Harriet Martineau sceptically recorded, that 'the Duke of
Wellington had come down to the Horse Guards in great wrath,
swearing, as he threw himself from his horse, at the pass things had
come to when the Corn Laws were to be given up,' and had been
overheard by an attentive passer-by. The story did probably contain
a grain of truth, for Wellington, though he held no portfolio, was by
far the most influential member of the Cabinet after Peel. On
Sunday 7 December 1845, rumours swept the capital that he had
given way, while in distant Osborne the chill December winds
whistled off the Solent and rattled the windows of the rooms where
the Queen was entertaining her Prime Minister.

Peel had arrived at Osborne, the Queen's seaside retreat on the
Isle of Wight, the previous day to offer his resignation, the sequel to
an earlier visit to Windsor to warn Her Majesty about the potato
disease in Ireland, and a letter, on 27 November, reporting serious
differences within the Cabinet. Victoria's chief concern was that the
government should stay — though on the Corn Laws she, too, had
become converted to repeal. 'The Queen thinks,' she wrote to her
Prime Minister, 'the time is come when a removal of the restrictions
upon the importation of food cannot be successfully resisted.
Should this be Sir Robert's own opinion, the Queen very much
hopes that none of his colleagues will prevent him from doing what
is *right* to do.' The news of irreconcilable differences which Peel
brought on 6 December was therefore highly unwelcome, but
Prince Albert urged Sir Robert to stay in office even if some of his
colleagues did resign. But this, Peel replied, would be impossible.
Too many influential peers, and members of the Royal Household,
would be against him, and the Tories in the Commons would desert
him. Peel pleaded to be allowed to go with dignity before his party
was rent by internal feuds and more ministers had committed
themselves to statements they might soon have to recant.

Discussion then turned on his successor. Could the
Conservatives, with their comfortable majority in the Commons,
not form a new ministry under Lord Stanley, a dedicated
protectionist, it was asked? But this, thought Peel, would
irretrievably identify the House of Lords with the unpopular
protectionist cause. 'I'm afraid,' he told his sovereign candidly, 'of
other interests getting damaged in this struggle about the Corn
Laws; already the system of promotion in the Army, the Game
Laws, the Church, are getting attacked with the aid of the
League. . . . But . . . I feel it my duty to your Majesty not to leave
you without a government.' As for the so-called *Edinburgh letter*,
in which Lord John Russell had announced his change of heart,
'Even if Lord John goes to the full extent of his declaration in that

letter (which I think goes too far), I will support him in Parliament and use all my influence with the House of Lords to prevent their impeding his progress.'*

Before catching the ferry back to the mainland, Peel helped the Queen to draft a letter summoning Russell to Osborne, and another for the information of the now retired Whig leader Lord Melbourne. Back in London, on 8 December 1845, Peel wrote a formal letter of resignation to be shown to Russell, in which he pledged himself to 'exercise any influence' he might possess to support Russell's policy. This handsome offer made, Peel seems to have experienced a great sense of relief at giving up the burdens of office. In the train on 10 December 1845, when the Cabinet travelled down to Osborne to hold its final council, he was untypically lighthearted, telling stories and jokes, and, the business done, he returned at once to London to avoid confronting his successor under the Queen's roof.

The railway network in 1845 was still incomplete. It took Russell until Thursday 11 December to reach Osborne, the same day on which the news of the government's fall was learned in London. He showed, however, little enthusiasm on finding the premiership about to fall into his hands, being dubious about his chances of gaining majority support in either the Commons or the Lords. Russell now approached Peel through the Home Secretary, Sir James Graham, to seek his ideas on the form of Bill which the less dyed-in-the-wool Tories might accept. Peel, not unreasonably, drew the line at telling the Whigs how to resolve the question which had led to his own resignation. He did confirm, however, that Lord Stanley, the only other potential Prime Minister in sight, was not prepared to form a government himself or join a protectionist ministry formed by someone else.

During the exchange of letters which followed it became clear how little now separated Russell and Peel on this issue. Russell, it emerged, had, like Peel, been thinking of a suspension of the Corn Laws to meet the immediate crisis, followed by their gradual repeal, but now only total and immediate abolition would satisfy the Whig backbenchers. The letters went back and forth while the Court returned to Windsor, where both Russell and Lord Lansdowne visited the Queen, and the League's leaders worked themselves almost to a standstill. 'Bright and I are almost off our legs,' Cobden told his wife on 4 December 1845. 'Five days this week in crowded meetings.' Bright's report to his sister-in-law, in which he followed

---

*Allegedly verbatim accounts of conversations are usually suspect. However, this one was noted down by Prince Albert at the time, in English, in a memorandum otherwise written in German.

the old Quaker custom of identifying the date by the day of the month alone, was equally revealing. 'On second day we got to Gloucester, fourth day to Stroud, fifth day to Bath, sixth day to Bristol, on the eighth of the month to Nottingham, ninth to Derby, eleventh Stockport' — a gruelling schedule that carried the two tireless travellers to nine counties in two weeks.

At a meeting in Manchester on Saturday 13 December 1845 the Council agreed to rescind a previous resolution against petitioning the present Parliament and recommended 'that petitions be sent from every Town and District in the Kingdom, as numerously signed as possible, praying for the *Total and Unconditional Abolition of the Corn and Provision Laws*'. On a motion moved by John Bright the Council also agreed 'that a subscription of a Quarter of a Million Sterling be immediately commenced, to meet the present emergency,' the appeal to be launched at a public meeting a week later.

With the Queen, the Prime Minister and the Leader of the Opposition all become repealers, the recantation of many prominent Chartists followed. Week by week the *League* and local newspapers in the industrial areas carried reports of meetings where the working men who had once clamoured for the Charter now assembled to petition against the Corn Laws. From Gateshead and Wakefield, from Leicester and Birmingham, the message was the same. Where was Chartism? Where? demanded one speaker in Newcastle, recalling how he had been howled down there three or four years ago, as the *Gateshead Observer* recorded that December. 'In response to his demand echo answered "Where?"'

On 18 December 1845, Lord John Russell at last announced his willingness to form a government and on the following day Peel wrote jubilantly to a colleague about leaving office. 'I heartily rejoice,' he declared, 'at being relieved from the thankless and dangerous post of having the responsibility of conducting public affairs, and being expected to conform not to my own sense of the public necessities, but to certain party doctrines, to be blindly followed whatever new circumstances may arise. . . . Whatever country squires may think, it is not safe to guarantee the continuation of the present Corn Laws.'

Peel had rejoiced too soon. The following day he heard that Russell had been unable to form a Cabinet; the reason, he learned later, was that Lord Grey had refused to serve if Palmerston was given the Foreign Office, while Palmerston would accept no other post. Since Russell considered the inclusion of both essential he had eventually to abandon his attempt, leaving the field to Peel. What was to have been the latter's farewell visit to Queen Victoria now became a triumphant return to power.

Unexpectedly invited by the Queen to form a new government, Peel instantly accepted, returning to London to meet the colleagues he had already summoned to a meeting at Downing Street that evening, Saturday 20 December 1845, like a man, as he wrote to a friend, 'restored to life after his funeral service had been preached'. A few changes proved necessary, for Lord Stanley, neither prepared to defend the Corn Laws nor to share the collective responsibility for repealing them, resigned. There was also one important addition to the government's ranks, W.E. Gladstone, who accepted the post of Colonial Secretary.

At a meeting with the Queen on 23 December 1845 Peel confirmed his intention to abolish the Corn Laws. The Conservatives' natural supporters in the country would, he hoped, be reconciled to the change by the government taking over from the counties financial responsibility for the cost of the rural police, the magistracy and the poor law, and, later, by government loans to landowners to help them improve their estates. At this stage Peel still hoped to repeal the Corn Laws merely as part of his general economic policy. 'My wish,' he wrote to his Chancellor of the Exchequer, Henry Goulburn, that day, 'would be not to give undue prominence to corn, but to cover corn by continued operation on the Customs tariff. . . . Let us put the finishing stroke to this good work.' This was a little optimistic, if not naive; the Tory Party might accept, indeed had accepted, the steady dismantling of the tariff barriers protecting British industry, but to abandon the laws protecting their own income and estates — with which they identified the national interest — was a totally different matter. Peel meanwhile had come to regard repeal as a simple matter of duty. His Conservatism rested — as generations of his successors were to claim that theirs did — on a belief in the possibility of a partnership between the poor and the privileged, a partnership in which the Crown itself could share. Victoria's support at this crisis was unwavering, and even her greatest favourite among her former advisers came in for the sharp edge of her tongue when he criticized Peel. 'Lord Melbourne, I must beg you not to say anything more on this subject now,' she told him sharply at a dinner party on 20 December 1845, when her guest had accused his successor of 'a damned dishonest act'.

The League was under no such inhibitions. The meeting to launch the quarter of a million pound fund, held on Tuesday 23 December 1845, took on the air of a victory celebration. When it was announced that the League's last special appeal, for £100,000, had been over-subscribed by £23,508 and that it was ending the year with £12,033 still in hand, cheers rent the air. A motion pledging everyone present not to rest until the Corn Laws were entirely abolished was then carried unanimously and the announcement of the setting up of the new £250,000 fund prompted a series of donations of £1,000, followed by others for amounts from £500 to £50. During a lull in the flow of promissory cards both Cobden and Bright were called on. It would have been difficult for any speaker that night not to be applauded, and Cobden was, Archibald Prentice noted, 'received with almost overwhelming cheers'. He warned against premature rejoicing, but promised that 'If Sir Robert Peel will go on in an intelligible and straightforward course . . . he shall have the support of the League and the country as fully and cordially as any other prime minister.' John Bright claimed that this was the most enthusiastic meeting Manchester had ever witnessed and by the time it dispersed, almost £60,000 had been subscribed in an hour and a half.

CHAPTER TWENTY-ONE

Our Cause is Won

'My heart feels light now that our cause is won.'
— John Bright to George Wilson, 26 June 1846

Few Prime Ministers can ever have faced a more daunting future than that which confronted Sir Robert Peel at the opening of 1846. He had first held office back in 1809 at the tender age of twenty-two; now, at fifty-eight, he faced the supreme trial of his life, with famine devastating one part of the kingdom and with his own party certain to oppose what he believed to be the only remedy. But, he believed, what he was proposing was also sound politics. 'The worst ground, on which we can fight the battle of true Conservatism,' he wrote to a friend, Charles Arbuthnot, early in January 1846, 'is *food*.' A week later he reminded his Cabinet colleagues that he had always aimed to lower the duties on 'everything connected with the clothing and subsistence of the People,' but they were unconvinced. His plan, one had warned him on accepting office, would be repugnant to the very people 'by whose constant support you can alone expect to be able to carry on the government,' while another, even more off-puttingly, remarked that 'it was . . . under no impression that I was joining a durable administration that I accepted your offer'.

At her home in Drayton, Lady Peel found her husband abused on all sides by neighbours and former friends, while her husband, preparing in Downing Street for the new session, was assailed by the Conservative press. The League, meanwhile, was riding high. The new year began, as usual, with a great meeting in the Free Trade Hall, into which, on 15 January 1846, nine thousand were squeezed by removing most of the seats. The new fighting fund already stood at £75,000 and soon afterwards it reached £150,000, much of the 20 per cent 'on account' which was required having already been paid. Four days later, on 22 January 1846, the Queen opened Parliament in person. The Speech from the Throne made much of the failure of the potato crop in Ireland but contained no direct reference to the Corn Laws, though it did refer to the recent removal of many customs duties and the possible extension of the same policy to other articles. The House of Lords at least was not deceived. Peer after peer thundered his denunciation of the League, and one old adversary, the Duke of Richmond, suggested sarcastically that the government should make Cobden a peer and invite him to join the government.

In the House of Commons the government's new policy had an even rougher ride. The mover and seconder of the address of thanks to Her Majesty both confessed that they had totally changed their minds on the Corn Laws, and received a cool reception. When the Prime Minister rose to face a crowded House, he was received in stony silence by the benches behind him, in painful contrast to the triumphant cheers from the Opposition side. Peel none the less made the best case he could. The earlier extension of free trade, he pointed out, had not harmed agriculture; the disaster in Ireland made it impossible to postpone tackling the Corn Laws; and true Conservatism required taxing those best able to bear the burden. This argument cut little ice with the government's backbenchers and during the whole two hours that Peel was on his feet the same almost uncanny stillness hung over their ranks. Only once did they break out into cheers, when Peel quoted the view of the recently-departed Lord Stanley that the whole crisis was exaggerated. Equally violent applause greeted Disraeli, who for sixty minutes attacked his own leader, and he was followed by an inarticulate but visibly sincere 'country gentleman' MP who warned that he and his friends would use every means they could to frustrate the government's intentions.

Peel's proposal, to reduce the duty on corn to a nominal level over the next few years as part of a general reduction in tariffs, fell short of the 'total and immediate repeal' which had always been the League's policy and on which some extremists thought it should continue to insist. Soundings taken by the leadership, however, soon showed that such hard-liners were in a minority. 'The great bulk of the merchants of Sheffield who are members of the League,' one MP for the traditionally Radical city of Sheffield told Cobden, 'anxiously hope that no impediment may be thrown in the way of carrying out the plan.' 'Peel's measure,' Cobden himself reported to George Wilson from London, 'seems to be universally well received here. Our most ardent workers receive it open handed. Today I met Gibson of Spitalfields at the office in Fleet Street . . . he said that was the opinion generally in the City.' Sensibly, the League recognized that it would be madness to risk Peel's fall, and resolved that its sympathizers in the House should give him all possible support.

The moment for which the League had laboured for six long years came at last on 27 January 1846, when Peel rose to deliver a speech lasting three and a half hours. He began unexcitingly by listing all the other articles on which duties were to be lowered or removed, from straw hats and cured fish to butter, cheese and foreign meat, but his proposals about corn were revealed at last. The duty on imported corn, would, under the new law, be lowered gradually over the next three years. It would be reduced immediately to a scale ranging from 4s to 10s when the price of domestic corn varied from £2. 12s to £2. 8s, and would drop still further until 1 February 1849, when it would sink to a nominal 1s, considered necessary to ensure that imports were properly recorded.

For practical purposes, as everyone realized, it was the end of the Corn Laws and Peel went on to spell out the 'sweeteners' for the rural gentry. The Law of Settlement* was to be relaxed, administration of the highways was to be improved, the cost of prosecutions and custody of prisoners was to be removed from the country authorities, along with much of the financial responsibility for Poor Law medical officers and school teachers, and public loans were to be provided for the improvement of agriculture. All this, however, failed to mollify Peel's critics. Their strategy for the moment was to try to scare Peel into having second thoughts, and a whole flurry of resignations followed. Three peers resigned from posts in the Royal Household; the first Lord of the Admiralty, the Chief Secretary for Ireland and two junior Treasury ministers also abandoned the threatened ship. And a whole series of Members of Parliament elected on a protectionist ticket resigned their seats on grounds of conscience or under pressure from their patrons, precipitating unwelcome by-elections, the most notable, though wholly voluntary, such martyr being Lord Ashley. The ministerial resignations were doubly unwelcome in that anyone appointed from the back benches to fill the vacancies also had to stand for re-election. The first signs from the resulting polls were not reassuring. Gladstone, having given up his seat at Newark on entering the government, could not find another to fight. The new First Lord was rejected by his constituency in February, as was the new Chief Secretary for Ireland. The only comfort for Peel lay in the disarray of his opponents, some of whom favoured immediate repeal, while others wanted Lord John Russell to join forces with the dissident Tories to overthrow the government.

On 29 January 1846, the Council of the League met in Manchester, as J.B. Smith reported to Cobden, in London:

> There was a meeting of the Council today and as there is great excitement and anxiety to know what the League intends to do it was crowded with folks who seldom attend. Greg [i.e. R.H. Greg] thought we should be cautious how we refuse what is offered and said he was satisfied if Peel's measure was carried we should not find the means to carry on the League agitation. . . .

*This enabled any place to send its paupers back to their parish of origin and worked to the disadvantage of rural areas — see my book *The Workhouse* for details.

We turned the tide a little and passed a resolution recommending petitions from all parts of the country for total and immediate repeal and then adjourned.

This was, however, little more than a sop to the militants for, as Smith commented, 'I wish *entre nous* that we may get it . . . I am doubtful if we could find means to carry on the League if Peel's measures are carried. Already people are . . . talking of not paying further subscriptions.' The die was finally cast when Cobden returned to Manchester to throw his weight on the side of those recommending support for Peel, and on 2 February 1846 he summed up the situation in a letter to a colleague. 'Your view of the Peel measure is precisely that which Villiers, Bright, Gibson and myself took of it and I found our friends here acquiescing in the same opinion. . .'. Shortly afterwards the League's position was made clear to its members. 'The League,' its weekly newspaper declared, 'will offer no factious or fanatical opposition to Sir Robert Peel's measure. Nothing will be done that can for a moment put in hazard the vast substantial benefits which the ministerial proposal offers to the country.'

Peel greatly eased the League's task by announcing that, if the House voted for it, he would accept its 'total and immediate' policy. No such concession proved necessary, though Peel faced serious opposition from his own side. A venerable riddle, first heard a few years before, now again made the rounds. 'Why are the Tories like walnuts?' it ran. 'Because they are difficult to Peel.' Diehards like Colonel Sibthorpe, MP for Lincoln, fulminated against the 'Potato Peel government', an odd echo of his father's nickname of 'Parsley Peel' resulting from the parsley-leaf design on the textile-printing patterns which had made the family's fortune. On Monday 9 February 1846, a formal motion to go into committee to consider the Corn Bill was opposed by two of Peel's backbenchers, who moved an amendment to postpone discussion of it for six months, and it was on this parochial, procedural motion that, in theory, debate raged for the next week. It was not till ten o'clock in the evening of the following Monday that Peel again rose, for another epic of oratorical endurance, lasting nearly three hours. Totally in command of the House, from time to time 'indulging himself', in Archibald Prentice's admiring words, 'in a sarcastic pleasantry, upon some of the absurdities of his opponents,' he several times provoked 'bursts of laughter'. 'He was,' thought Prentice, 'luxuriating in his newly acquired liberty, a man renovated by the touch of truth.'

Despite the length of his speech, Peel's essential message was simple: that the crisis in Ireland made immediate action essential:

> We saw in the distance the gaunt forms of famine and of disease
> following in the train of famine. Was it not our duty to the
> country, aye our duty to the party that supported us, to avert the
> odious charge of indifference and neglect of timely precautions?

As for the British mainland, the sufferings experienced there were
also too recent to be ignored:

> The memory of the winters of 1841 and 1842 never can be effaced
> from my recollection. . . . This time may recur. . . . If these
> calamitous times do come . . . will not our expressions of
> sympathy seem more sincere; will not our exhortations to
> fortitude be more impressive, if we can at the same time say, and
> with pride, that in a time of comparative plenty, urged by no
> necessity, yielding to no clamour, we anticipated all those
> difficulties and removed every impediment to the free circulation
> of the bounty of the Creator?

Such language could have come straight from a League
publication and next day John Bright paid the Prime Minister —
whom one of his own backbenchers had just accused of cowardice
and treason — a tribute more likely to embarrass than assist him.
'When the right honourable baronet resigned,' Bright told the
hostile faces opposite, 'he was no longer your minister: he came
back to office as the minister of the sovereign, as the minister of the
people and not again as the minister of a class who made him such for
their own selfish objects.' Cobden's turn came a week later, when he
warned the Conservatives not to look to a dissolution of Parliament
to save the Corn Laws. 'The members who came up under such
circumstances to attempt to maintain the Corn Laws, from your
Ripons and Stamfords, Woodstocks and Marlboroughs' — i.e. from
'pocket boroughs and nomination counties' — 'would hold those
opinions only till they found it was determined by public opinion to
repeal them. . . . If the country found that they would not give way
to moral force, they might think it requisite to place them in another
Schedule A' — the list of seats abolished under the Reform Act.
After two weeks' debate, an exceptionally full House voted, at
twenty to three in the morning, to go into committee by 337 votes to
240. The repealers had got their majority at last, of 97, though the
Parliamentary battle was but beginning, for 231 Tories had voted
against the motion and only 112 for it. Peel had got his majority only
with Liberal help: 227 of the Opposition had voted with him, 11

against. Prince Albert had watched the debate from the gallery — his presence was felt to be a discreet demonstration of the Queen's support. 'This does not look like a strong government,' he commented. The League, meanwhile, drew comfort from the supposed strength of the free-trade cause in the country. Government supporters returned by boroughs represented nearly 300,000 electors, those voting against it only 30,000.

The League still did not feel certain of victory, and when — on Monday 1 March 1846 — Charles Villiers moved his traditional motion calling for immediate repeal he was beaten by 267 to 78, a decisive majority of 189. Peel, it seemed, had better judged what was acceptable to the Commons, and on 27 March 1846 he obtained a decisive majority on the key second reading of his Bill, when the House endorsed its general principles by 302 votes to 214, a majority of 88. But there was still a last ditch fight on third reading, which was only carried, at 4 a.m. on Saturday 16 May 1846, by 98 votes: 327 to 229. If his opponents in the Tory ranks were for the moment outnumbered, they were far from reconciled and about Peel's winding-up speech there was the feeling of a farewell message. 'You have a right,' he acknowledged, 'to taunt me with my change of opinion on the Corn Laws,' though on free trade, in general, he insisted, he had always been consistent. He ended by reaffirming his basic political philosophy:

> My earnest wish has been during my tenure of power, to impress the people of this country with a belief that the legislature was animated by a sincere desire to frame its legislation upon the principles of equity and justice. I have a strong belief that the greatest object which we or any other government can contemplate should be to elevate the social conditions of that class of the people with whom we are brought into no direct relation by the exercise of elective franchise. I wish to convince them that our object has been so to apportion taxation that we shall relieve industry and labour from any undue burden and transfer it . . . to those who are better able to bear it.

As for the results of this policy, the state of the country spoke for itself:*

Where there was disaffection I see contentment; and where there

*The words anticipate those of a later Conservative Prime Minister — Mrs Margaret Thatcher, who, before entering 10 Downing Street on 4 May 1979 quoted St Francis of Assissi: 'Where there is discord may we bring harmony; where there is error may we bring truth; where there is doubt may we bring faith, and where there is despair, may we bring hope.'

was turbulence, I see there is peace; where there was disloyalty, I see there is loyalty. I see a disposition to confide in you [i.e. to trust Parliament] and not to agitate questions that are at the foundations of your institutions.

No institution was more valued, at least by its members, than the House of Lords and here the government still faced a stern struggle, though the Duke of Wellington warned his fellow peers they risked alienating themselves from both Commons and Court. At a great meeting in London on 21 May, attended by backwoodsmen from all over the country, a curious alliance of highly intelligent Tory MPs like Disraeli, and singularly dim ones like Sibthorpe, united to denounce the traitor who had betrayed the landed gentry. Some of the Whig peers, with equally great estates, were also unhappy about Peel's Bill, but Lord John Russell summoned them all to Lansdowne House to warn them that he would resign as Party leader if the government fell over the Corn Laws, a threat which proved effective; the Whigs in the Upper House agreed to support Peel.

Already the body principally responsible for the coming change in the law was preparing for its dissolution: 'I have been plagued for several days with sitting to Herbert for the picture of the Council of the League,'* grumbled Cobden in a letter to his wife on 23 June 1846, 'and it completely upsets my afternoon.' As for the final passage of the measure to which most of the past six years of his life had been devoted, it was, he complained, proving a long-drawn-out affair. 'I thought the Corn Bill would certainly be read the third time on Tuesday (tomorrow), but I now begin to think it will be put off till Thursday. There is literally no end to this suspense. But there are reports of Peel being out of office on Friday next and the peers may yet ride restive.' But the peers did not prove restive. On 25 June the Bill completed its passage through Parliament with an unopposed third reading; those peers who disliked it were not prepared to divide the House. On the following day, 26 June 1846, henceforward a red-letter day in every League member's calendar, the measure officially known as 9 & 10 Victoria Cap.XXII, *An Act to Amend the Laws Relating to the Importation of Corn*, finally reached the statute book.

That joyous Thursday Richard Cobden broke the news to his wife in a jubilant letter:

June 26. My Dearest Kate,
Hurrah! Hurrah! The Corn Bill is law and now my work is done. I shall come down tomorrow morning by the six o'clock train in

*This historic picture appears as illustration 16 of this book.

order to be present at a Council meeting at three and shall hope to
be home in time for a late tea.

The mails to Manchester also carried a letter from John Bright to
George Wilson:

The assent is given. It was five o'clock before the words were said
which completed our labours. . . . We have not seen the last of
the barons, but have taught them which way the world is
turning. . . . My heart feels light now that our cause is won.

Punch rubbed salt in the wounds of the Conservatives with a
mocking parody of a speech from *The Tempest*, under the heading
The Knell of Protection:

Full fathom five, Protection lies:
On her bones are carols made;
Those are cut that were her ties;
Nothing of her that doth fade,
But doth suffer a PEEL-change,
Into commerce free to range.

From the moment he announced his conversion Peel had been
living on borrowed time, and a few hours after the Lords had given
the Corn Bill its third and final reading his government was defeated
by a combination of Liberals and anti-Peel Tories over a familiar,
almost routine, issue — an Irish Crimes Bill, giving additional
powers to the Lord Lieutenant. Early the following morning Peel
scribbled a resignation note to the Queen and it was despatched by
special train. On Monday 30 June 1846, having been cheered by
great crowds all the way from Whitehall Gardens to the Palace of
Westminster, he formally broke the news to the House of
Commons. With remarkable generosity his final speech as Prime
Minister paid a warm tribute to the man whose work had ultimately
brought him down.

The name which ought to be, and will be associated with the
success of these measures, is the name of the man who, acting, I
believe, from pure and disinterested motives, has, with untiring
energy, by appeals to reason, enforced their necessity with an
eloquence the more to be admired because it was unaffected and
unadorned . . . the name of Richard Cobden.

As for his own fate, Peel accepted it with equally becoming
dignity, in words which were constantly to be quoted in later years:

In relinquishing power I shall leave a name severely censured I fear by many who on public grounds deeply regret the severance of party ties . . . from the firm conviction that fidelity to party engagements . . . constitutes a powerful instrument of government. I shall surrender power severely censured also by others, who from no interested motives, adhere to the principle of protection. . . . I shall leave a name execrated by every monopolist who, from less honourable motives, clamours for protection because it conduces to his own individual benefit; but it may be that I shall leave a name sometimes remembered with expressions of goodwill in the abodes of those whose lot it is to labour and to earn their daily bread by the sweat of their brow, when they shall recruit their exhausted strength with abundant and untaxed food, the sweeter because it is no longer leavened by a sense of injustice.

Peel was cheered as he sat down, and left the House by a side door to avoid the crowds. He was soon recognized and, between a corridor of cheering citizens, hats doffed in his honour, made his way home and into private life, being succeeded by Lord John Russell.

For the League it was a time of rejoicing. When the news that the Bill had been passed reached Rochdale a jubilant band of Bright's supporters forced their way into the church tower, against the opposition of the vicar, to ring a victory peal. On 8 July a giant procession marched through the town, bearing silk flags inscribed with triumphant slogans, and displaying a giant loaf with the names of Cobden and Bright carved upon it. The celebrations ended in a victory dinner, where John Bright hailed the occasion as a day of deliverance and predicted a new understanding between master and man in the years ahead.

The League, unlike so many bodies formed for a single purpose, resisted the temptation to linger on once its task had been accomplished. On 2 July 1846 a meeting of the League Council, attended by members from all over the country, met to put their own demise in train. It was a time for thanks and congratulations. George Wilson recalled the League's turbulent history; Cobden praised his colleagues, Lord John Russell, and, most fervently of all, the leader of the Conservative Party who, elected to maintain the Corn Laws, had lived to repeal them. 'If he has lost office,' said Cobden, 'he has gained a country. For my part I would rather descend into private life with that last measure of his, which led to his discomfiture, in my hand, than mount to the highest pinnacle of human power.'

The Manchester men, business-like to the last, then wound up the formidable organization they had created, as briskly and efficiently as they had built it up. Fittingly, Cobden moved the formal resolution and John Bright, his faithful henchman to the last, seconded it:

> That an Act of Parliament having been passed providing for the abolition of the Corn Laws in February 1849 it is deemed expedient to suspend the active operation of the Anti-Corn-Law League; and the executive council in Manchester is hereby requested to take the necessary steps for making up and closing the affairs of the League with as little delay as possible.

A few formalities were still to be completed. It was agreed that only a fifth of the vast £250,000 fund, i.e. the instalment already due, should be collected, and there was a vote of thanks to the Executive Council, plus a well-merited gift of £10,000 to George Wilson. A sub-committee was set up to decide on how the other most active members of the Council should be rewarded; ultimately they each received a silver tea and coffee service. For Richard Cobden and John Bright a special subscription was raised. Cobden was ultimately presented with £75,000, sufficient, had he wished, to have kept him in idleness for life. More than £5,000 was raised for John Bright, who purchased with it a 1,200-volume library, housed in an oak bookcase on which designs symbolizing free trade in corn were carved, commemorating the great struggle which had made his name.

And so it was all over. As they cast their minds back to that March day in 1839 when it had been decided to set up a permanent Anti-Corn-Law League, as they recalled the time when their emissaries had been greeted with stones and fire-hoses and the Chartists had wrecked meeting after meeting, the members of the League Council would have been less than human if they had not experienced something like regret. 'An air of grave solemnity had spread over the meeting as it drew to a close,' felt Archibald Prentice. 'There were five hundred gentlemen who had often met together during the great contest and, notwithstanding their exultation over a victory achieved, the feeling stole over their minds that they were never to meet again.' George Wilson, a model chairman to the last, tidily wound up the proceedings. 'As no other gentleman has anything to address to this meeting, it is now my duty to say that the Anti-Corn-Law League stands conditionally dissolved.' Still those present remained reluctant to disperse, as Henry Ashworth described:

> A deep silence followed this announcement for a few seconds,

when someone called out for 'three cheers' and Mr Cobden, rising, said, 'I don't think we can get up a cheer for, as I have just been observing to my friends on my right and left, I never felt so "flat" in all my life. I never heard speech that fell so flat and never saw an audience that looked so flat as the audience of today. It is right it should be so, for we have been celebrating the obsequies of the League. We began in solemnity, and we end in solemnity. The world will see, at all events, that whatever else we may be, we are earnest men who have engaged in this work. If you would like to have a cheer, let us try if we can't get up a few sepulchural ones. Come, I'll be your fugleman.' The honourable gentleman then led off and was followed with right goodwill by the meeting, in very loud, prolonged and effective cheering.

The final three cheers were for the Queen and five hundred sober, triumphant, deeply-affected Victorian businessmen and politicians, not without a damp eye here and there, and perhaps a sentimental tear trickling down into side-whiskers and beard, shook hands with their neighbours and dispersed, conscious of a great undertaking honourably completed.

CHAPTER TWENTY-TWO

After the Battle

'I am deep in mangolds and pigs.'
— Richard Cobden writing from retirement in
Sussex, July 1857

The effect of the repeal of the Corn Laws on the price of bread was neither immediate nor striking. The gradual lifting of duties ensured that there was no sudden flow of corn through the ports and in any case no other country had in 1846 vast stocks of its own to spare. The price of bread did not fall dramatically in June when the repeal Bill became law. The quartern loaf (which for some curious historical reason actually weighed 4 lb 5 oz [1·96 kg]) in fact cost considerably more in 1847 — 11½d — than in 1846 when it had been only 8½d, and in 1845 when it had been cheaper still: 7½d. In 1849, when the duty on imported grain finally fell to a nominal 1s a quarter (28 lbs or 12·68 kgs), the price of bread at 7d was little lower than in the previous year. For the next thirty years it varied, reaching a low of 6¾d in 1850 and a peak of 10¾d in 1855, the average price of this period being around 7½d. On a farm labourer's budget, in which bread was the principal item, even a farthing made an appreciable difference, but no reduction in price which occurred sufficed by itself to make the poor comfortable or the destitute self-supporting, and it was not until 1869 that the absurd 1s-a-quarter levy retained by Peel was finally extinguished by a Liberal Chancellor. 'It is,' he observed with unchallengeable common sense, 'no more difficult to register the arrival of corn without levying a duty of 1s per quarter on it than it is to roast a pig without burning down the house.'

Long before this sensible pronouncement put the seal on the League's work it had seemed, for a few dizzy weeks, that it might need to be revived. At that last meeting in 1846 it had been agreed that 'In case any serious attempt be made by the protectionist party to induce the legislature to retrace its steps, or to prevent the final extinction of the Corn Law in February 1849, the gentlemen who have hitherto so ably fulfilled the duties of the Executive Council be hereby authorized to call the League into renewed existence'. No one at the time had seriously anticipated that this might happen, but in February 1852 the Conservative Lord Derby took office and, in the words of Henry Ashworth, 'formed a Ministry which was protectionist to the backbone'. On 27 February 1852 Derby told the Lords that the 'fiscal system . . . was fairly open to revision' and that while imposing duties upon other articles of import, 'there was no reason why the single one of corn should be omitted'. Immediately, from the old headquarters in Newall's Building, George Wilson signed an invitation to attend a meeting to all the League's former activists, who poured in from all parts of the country to hear him on Tuesday 2 March 1852, from his 'old chair' as Ashworth nostalgically observed, call on Cobden, Bright and other familiar names to address the faithful. A resolution was unanimously carried calling on 'the Council of the League . . . to put themselves into immediate communication with their friends in all parts of the kingdom, urging them to immediate action to prevent the return to Parliament of candidates in favour of the re-enactment, under whatever pretence or form, of any duty upon the imports of foreign grain'. A subscription to finance the new campaign brought in promises of £26,000 on the spot, largely in £1,000 donations, and raised £70,000 by the end of the month. It was like old times all over again and soon lecturers were being hired, meetings were being held, and the Queen, who must have hoped she had heard the last of the Corn Laws, was once again receiving addresses on it from her loyal subjects. The General Election which followed in July, however, put the issue beyond doubt. Derby had said he would not re-introduce the Corn Law until the country had given its verdict and this it now did in a decisive fashion with the return of a solidly anti-protection majority. That December Lord Aberdeen took office, presiding over a Cabinet of six Whigs, including Palmerston, Gladstone and Lord John Russell, six Peelites and one Radical. The taxation of imported food ceased, for at least half a century, to be a major issue in British politics.

What of the long-term effects of repeal? As already mentioned, the price of bread did not plummet until every man could eat his fill. Instead, despite soaring demand as the population increased, prices failed to rise. For twenty years from 1849, while Great Britain was completing its transformation from a basically rural to a mainly industrial nation, the price of a quarter of wheat remained on average about £2. 12s; taxation on the pre-1846 level could have pushed it up, at least in some years, to £3. 13s, almost half as much again.

That the price stayed steady was due to the increase in imports, which in the three years before repeal had been around a million quarters; in the nine years from 1846 to 1854 they reached nearly five million. There were, too, new suppliers. In the pre-repeal period three-quarters of the imported grain had come from

Germany and Prussia; in the subsequent nine years much of it arrived from France, Italy, the Middle East and North America. This last was to become the granary of Great Britain from the 1870s onwards, as the great trains thundered across the newly-ploughed prairies of the Middle West and the giant steamships bore their produce across the Atlantic.

The economies of scale made possible by the steam engine, whose potential had been undreamed of by Malthus, were sufficient by themselves to confound his pessimistic predictions. In 1860 the United States had had about 30,000 miles of railways; by 1870 this had risen to 53,000 miles, by 1880 to 94,000 miles, while the cost of shipping a ton of grain from Chicago to Liverpool by water dropped from £3. 7s in 1873 to £2. 1s in 1880 and then to £1. 4s in 1884, a saving of 9s. 9d per quarter on transport alone. Malthus's assumption that the earth's capacity to support life was finite and man's ability to reproduce almost infinite, was soon shown to be false. Great technical improvements in the mechanics of sowing and reaping speeded up and cheapened the whole process of wheat production. The self-binder attached to the mechanical reaper, introduced in the late 1870s, alone enabled one man to do the work of two, and the repeal of the Corn Laws meant that it was the British workman who reaped the benefit.

And yet, such are the ironies of history, while the League was proved right the protectionists were not proved wrong. With no barrier against foreign competition the price of home-grown wheat slumped from £2. 6s. 9d a quarter in 1877 to £2. 6s. 5d in 1878 and £1. 11s in 1886. The effects were marked from around 1869 onwards: the 3,600,000 acres under wheat in that year had by 1879 fallen below three million and by 1895 below two million; by 1904 it dropped to its lowest ever figure, of less than 1,400,000, though the output of other cereals, like barley and oats, remained more steady and in some years actually rose; it paid the British farmer better to grow food for his animals than for his fellow-citizens. The last quarter of the nineteenth century was in any case a bad time for British agriculture, but the depression was most marked in relation to corn. In 1831–40 the country had imported only 2 per cent of its grain. By 1861–70 it was importing 24 per cent, by 1880–89 65 per cent. Only two successive worlds wars were to reverse the trend — but war was not a contingency that Cobden and Bright had envisaged in their rosy, free-trade future.

The decline in agriculture was demonstrated not merely in the falling incomes of farmers but in the accelerated flight from the land. By 1881, although the population as a whole had risen sharply, 100,000 fewer labourers were employed in agriculture than in 1871.

By the end of the century agriculture was no longer the largest single employer, being surpassed by engineering and transport. The Anti-Corn-Law League was not responsible for the economic and social revolution, but by destroying the old belief that the farming coommunity *was*, in some special sense, the nation, it had contributed to it.

Although reference to 'the bread tax' and 'the breadstealers' had possessed a unique propagandist value, Cobden and his colleagues had always insisted that their real objective was universal free trade which, they claimed, would bring prosperity to the whole community. In 1876 one of its former leaders, Henry Ashworth, in publishing his recollections of Cobden, attached, as a tribute to his hero's memory, a detailed analysis of how the pattern of trade had changed in the generation since the League's great victory. 'It has,' he wrote, 'become my pleasing duty to supply, from the evidence of the Board of Trade, what have been the anticipated results, namely, an enormous increase of our national commerce, as donated by the published returns of our Imports and Exports . . . affording as they do a very accurate measure of our national prosperity.'

Ashworth looked first at agriculture where, he recalled, Peel, before his conversion, Sir James Graham, the League's most bitter opponent, and 'His Grace the Duke of Wellington, who appeared to know less of economic science than about fighting', had all asserted that, if protection were removed, 'the English farmer . . . would be ruined'. What in fact had happened to British agriculture now that imports of wheat and flour had soared by more than 300 per cent and those of other types of corn by 2,400 per cent? Far, it seemed, from such competition laying a blight upon the countryside, it had stimulated the home industry to new exertions:

> Our farmers, no longer affrighted by the cheap farming of foreigners, have embarked their capital, drained their land, improved their agricultural machinery, and thus the produce of the homeland has been largely increased; meanwhile they have also increased the wages of their labourers; and . . . although the population of the country has increased by about 17½ per cent since 1841, the extent of pauperism has been diminished by upwards of 25 per cent during the same period.

In addition to corn, imports of foreign cattle and sheep, of beef and bacon, of butter and cheese, of potatoes and eggs, had all increased by from 250 to 700 per cent between 1840–41 and 1873–74, and the rise in some cases had been spectacular, as in the instance of rice, where imports were up 1,329 per cent and lard, 'no longer "spoiled" at the Custom House,' up 4,374 per cent.

From these changes the ordinary family had benefitted enormously. To those whose memories went back to the family budgets of the 1840s, the improvement in eating habits was barely credible. Consumption per head of imported food had gone up between 1842 and 1874 more than three fold in the case of wheaten flour, sugar and tea; more than seven fold for butter and cheese; more than ten fold for rice; and nearly forty fold for bacon and ham, which had formerly been almost out of the poor man's reach. 'Every family in the country,' summed up Ashworth, 'is, on the average, indebted to the foreigner for about 2¼ lbs of bread stuffs and ¾ lb of sugar per day; for ⁴/₅ lb of bacon, for ½ lb of butter, for 2½ lbs of cheese, for 1 lb of rice and for ½ lb of tea per week.' Raisins and oranges, cinnamon and pepper, formerly rare luxuries in most homes, were now beginning to appear, the statistics indicated, on a far wider variety of tables.

The essential preliminary to all this had been the removal of protection. Free trade had breathed new life into manufacturing industry and — contrary to the charges so often made — it had not been the cotton-masters who had benefitted most. Imports of raw cotton had risen, by 179 per cent over the same thirty-year period, but hemp and jute, used in many trades, were up by 310 per cent, and metals, the basic requirement of the engineering trades, by no less than 4,436 per cent. All told, the value of imports, a mere £62 million in 1840, had multiplied nearly six times, to £365.3 million, by 1872–4.

With the restrictions on the sale of their products removed, foreign countries were also buying more British goods. 'The value of the exports of British produce in 1840,' wrote Ashworth, 'was £51,308,740, and the average for each of the years 1872–3–4 was £240,326,690, showing an increase of 387 per cent.' Wherever one looked, it was the same story, as Great Britain and other countries, in theory competitors, in practice enriched each other. British citizens grew plump on the agricultural produce of other countries and rich on their own labours as the workshop of the world, while foreign homes were enriched by British 'haberdashery and millinery,' 'hardware and cutlery,' 'boots and shoes,' 'earthen and china ware,' all showing enormous increases in exports, and foreign factories were resounding to the clatter of 'steam engines,' 'hoops, sheets and boiler plates,' 'tinned plates' and 'brass of all sorts' made in the Midlands and the Black Country. Free trade, declared Ashworth, had effected this transformation and had brought the tonnage of cargo vessels cleared through British ports from less than 5 million in 1840 to well over 22 million in 1874, with the volume still increasing. 'How manifestly,' he wrote, 'do these facts indicate that the human race constitute only one family, that we are all necessary to each others' comfort, that there is only one Father, and that the whole world is kin.'

By that time most of those involved in the League's struggle had vanished from the political scene. Sir Robert Peel, having resigned in June 1846, was never to hold office again. In 1847 a General Election left the Whigs in office, for though the Conservatives outnumbered Russell and his allies by 330 to 325, they were fatally split between Peelites and the protectionist majority. Peel himself was comfortably returned for Tamworth but the dissident Tories looked first to Lord Bentinck to lead them, then, in 1848, to Disraeli. Disraeli's future adversary, Gladstone, was meanwhile moving steadily, like other Peelites, towards active support of the Whigs and in December 1852 finally accepted office in a Whig-dominated Liberal-Peelite coalition. The Corn Laws, in their death throes, had produced one of those rare but traumatic upheavals which periodically reshape the face of British politics, though Peel did not live to see the final consequences of his actions. On Saturday 29 June 1850 he was thrown from his horse on Constitution Hill and on the following Tuesday, aged 62, he died from his injuries. All over the country, as the sad news spread, flags were flown at half-mast and shops put up their shutters. The nation, which had rejected him, was conscious it had lost a leader of rare integrity and courage. 'I little thought,' wrote the Whig historian Macaulay, 'that I should have cried for his death,' but, not long after, cheap copies of Peel's portrait were to be found hanging in the homes of farm labourers and factory workers, while everywhere statues of him were erected, often bearing the words about the Corn Laws with which his resignation speech had closed.

The epitaph was apt, the tributes deserved; but if it was Peel who finally destroyed the Corn Laws it was Cobden and his colleagues who had made this possible. Cobden's business, which he had neglected, had by 1846 come close to foundering. He used the £75,000 memorial fund to pay off his debts and to enjoy a recuperative fourteen-month tour of the Continent. Cobden's known passion for travel gave Lord John Russell an excuse to leave him out of his Cabinet, and on his return Cobden had enough money left to buy back his childhood home at Dunford, in the parish of Heyshott in Sussex, less than two miles from what he described as 'the quiet little close borough of Midhurst', i.e. one where no candidate unacceptable to its patron would have a chance. He continued to sit in Parliament, where he constantly opposed British military involvement overseas, but when his opposition to the Crimean War and a punitive expedition against China cost him his seat, in the General Election of 1857, he settled contentedly back into rural life. 'I am deep in mangolds and pigs,' he wrote that July. 'When I saw the other day that the House sat till half-past four, I hugged myself and looked out on the South Downs with a keener relish.' In 1859 he was returned unopposed, for John Bright's home town of Rochdale, and was offered the post of President of the Board of Trade, but turned it down on the grounds that having been a 'systematic and constant assailant' of Palmerston's foreign policy as 'warlike, intermeddling and quarrelsome,' he could not now serve under him. In 1860, however, he was responsible for negotiating, at first as a backbench MP and then as a government emissary, a major commercial treaty with France, a notable service to the nation rewarded by a second public subscription, which raised £40,000. A preferred baronetcy he declined. He died in 1865, aged sixty, after having come up to London, though ill, in bitter weather, to oppose the building of fortifications in Canada.

John Bright also achieved *his* full status as a politician only after the League's campaign was won, but his career continued after 1846 to be deeply intertwined with that of Cobden. In 1849 they were united in the National Parliamentary and Financial Reform Association, a basically middle-class movement like the Anti-Corn-Law League, and he opposed the Crimean War even more passionately than Cobden. As a result he was burned in effigy in his own constituency, in Manchester, and when the General Election came in 1857 he was abroad, leaving Cobden to campaign for him. 'I don't believe there is a thought, I don't believe there is one aspiration in the minds of either of us that the other is not acquainted with' (one biographer has noted that only twice in their long parliamentary careers did Cobden and Bright vote in different lobbies), Cobden told an audience in the Free Trade Hall — not the scene of their former triumphs but a new and more imposing building bearing the same name. Appropriately enough they were now defeated together, though in August that year Bright got back into the House, being elected unopposed for Birmingham.

Bright possessed one blind spot as a reformer; he opposed the Factory Acts relating to adults as interfering with the relationship between master and man, though he recognized the need for the legislative protection of children. In most respects, however, he was a radical through and through. As early as 1848 he opposed the death penalty and in 1861 urged the restriction of the powers of the House of Lords after they had rejected a Bill to abolish one of 'the taxes on knowledge', the duty on paper (they later climbed down). His greatest service to the country came that December when his behind-the-scenes efforts helped to prevent the great catastrophe of great Britain going to war on the side of the slave-owning Confederacy during the *Trent* crisis.*

Like Cobden, Bright was reluctant to accept office, but finally became President of the Board of Trade in Gladstone's first ministry in 1868. Later he held other office, but without distinction; opposition had suited his temperament better. In 1882 he resigned from Gladstone's second Cabinet in protest against its military coercion of Egypt. He still missed the advice of his former ally, dead these seventeen years. 'My dear friend, Cobden,' he confided to his diary that day, 'how often I have wished him here for his counsel and help.' Bright finished badly. The young Beatrice Webb, who heard him speak to a public demonstration, found 'something nobly pathetic in the old old story of Tory sinfulness told by the stern-looking old man,' and in his last public speech he allied himself with the Conservatives against the first Home Rule Bill in 1886. Three years later he died, aged seventy-seven, at Rochdale. As he lay, informally, in state, his workpeople, his daughter noted, 'came from the mill in their working clothes' to file weeping round the coffin.

The story of the other men who had combined to destroy the Corn Laws can be more briefly told. J.B. 'Corn Law' Smith, after withdrawing from the Presidency of the League in 1841, suffered ill-health and from the collapse of a local bank, and dropped into near obscurity. George Wilson, his successor as the League's nominal head, devoted his later energies to promoting Parliamentary reform, ended his commercial career as Chairman of the Lancashire and Yorkshire Railway, and as a director of the Electric Telegraph Company, which provided the natural complement to the penny post. He declined all invitations to stand for Parliament and died relatively young, at the age of sixty-two, in 1870.

With the Corn Laws safely repealed, 'the keeper of the League's conscience', Joseph Sturge, was able once again to concentrate on preaching peace. After 1846 he travelled, with naive optimism, to peace congresses in several foreign countries, and died, as he would surely have wished, while preparing to attend the annual meeting of the Peace Society, of which he was president, in 1859. Charles Villiers, now forty-four, found after 1846 his occupation gone, and — a little hurt by the acclaim, which Cobden now received on all sides — he declined a public 'testimonial', pointedly remarking that

*The *Trent* was a British merchant ship from which some Southern envoys were removed by force. War was averted thanks to the Prince Consort toning down an offensive despatch and John Bright privately urging Lincoln's government to be conciliatory.

'the reward of public service is public confidence and I will accept nothing else'. He later served as Judge-Advocate-General and as President of the local Government Board, proving a notably reforming minister in a notoriously backward department. He finally became a Parliamentary institution, and died in 1898 at the age of ninety-six, still Member for Wolverhampton.

Compared to Villiers, Colonel Thomas Perronet Thompson had opted for early retirement, having withdrawn from Parliament at the age of seventy-eight, but he continued to write articles under the apt pen-names of 'An old reformer' and 'A Quondam MP' and only death caused the old warrior finally to lay down his pen in 1869.

His fellow MP, Sir John Bowring, had a more adventurous life. He survived an attempt to poison him while serving as governor of Hong Kong, and a shipwreck in the Red Sea on his way home. When approaching eighty he 'addressed an assemblage of three thousand persons at Plymouth with all the energy of youth,' but died soon afterwards, in 1872.

The enlightened mill-owner MP, Robert Hyde Greg, often called to the chair at League meetings, and one of the first to demand repeal in the House of Commons, lived on to become an equally enlightened farmer, being followed to his grave, in 1875, at seventy-nine, by five hundred mourning tenants and employees. Notable among the League's supporters outside Parliament had been Henry Ashworth, a close friend of Cobden and Bright. It was said of him that, though belonging to the Society of Friends, he 'had a most unquakerly passion for the gun, which he used with great dexterity on the moors . . . and . . . at eighty he was as sure in his aim as at twenty'. At eighty-five, in 1880, he was still indomitably travelling in Italy, but caught a fatal chill and died, far from his murky native Birtwistle, in sunny Florence.

The League's paid employees and lecturers also mostly survived for years into a Corn-Law-free world. Abraham Paulton, the former medical student, used his work for the League as a springboard to a new career. Having, at the age of twenty-seven, become editor of the *Anti-Corn-Law Circular*, he later bought Prentice's *Manchester Times* — renamed the *Manchester Examiner and Times* — and edited it as an organ of the Radical wing of the Liberal Party. Paulton made a good marriage and, still active in politics and still renowned as a talker, died a country gentleman in Surrey, aged sixty-four.

James Acland, who had so often suffered violence and lack of money as a League lecturer, was found a post by George Wilson, when the League was wound up, with the Electric Telegraph Company, but it proved short-lived for Acland used the information he acquired through handling business messages to gamble on the Stock Exchange. A natural survivor, he bobbed up again and earned his living later in life as a Liberal Party agent. The League's covert publicist, the golden-voiced William Fox, used his work for the League to help him into Parliament, in 1847, where he campaigned for an extension of the franchise and compulsory education. By League standards he was short-lived, dying at a mere seventy-eight in 1864.

In some ways the saddest fate was suffered by Archibald Prentice. He had sacrificed his own prospects as a journalist to the cause, until, after 1846 — as already mentioned — he had to surrender his editorial and proprietorial chair to Abraham Paulton, a former League employee. Prentice's misfortunes caused some indignation among his admirers, one of whom protested to Colonel Thompson:

> I have known him more than thirty years, a faithful, earnest, principled man, and he never forfeited a principle. He was the father, the intellectual and moral guide, of the League through its childhood and youth into manhood and I should like to know what Cobden and Bright would have done on many a stormy day without him. . . . But now that they are become machines for working Reform-Club tactics and Prentice does not, as he never did, go into that groove, the insolence of factory-system wealth swaggers in his face with an opposition paper and ten thousand pounds.

Prentice found consolation in a modest appointment in the Manchester gas office, while he continued writing, especially about teetotalism, his new enthusiasm. He died in 1857, having left every later student of the subject in his debt with his sometimes inaccurate but wholly indispensable two-volume *History of the Anti-Corn-Law League*.

The League was rich in chroniclers. Several memoirs were written of both Cobden and Bright. The future Sir Edward Watkin, for example, was only twenty when the League began its work, though he was to make his name and fortune as a railway manager and promoter, and as a Liberal Member of Parliament. So deep was the impression Cobden made upon him, however, that in 1891, long after his hero's death, he published his *Alderman Cobden of Manchester*, a work which approaches hagiography; Watkin himself lived on into the present century.

There were to be no tributes from the Chartists, though the League's contention that repeal would have had to wait an unconscionable time if it had to follow electoral reform was proved right. In 1848 the Chartists' last effort to intimidate the government confirmed only that the movement had shot its bolt, as was already clear in Lancashire. At Mossley, near Manchester, once a Chartist stronghold, the former Chartists' assembly room had, the *Manchester Guardian* reported in May 1846, already been closed and 'the boards which comprised the floor . . . are now converted into a resting place for swine. Some ill-natured people say they were never used for a better purpose.'

What, then, had the Anti-Corn-Law League achieved during its six years of active life — apart from securing its great objective? The answer in the long term lay, surely, in the demonstration it had provided of what, against all the odds, determined, intelligent and industrious men could accomplish when they concentrated their efforts on a single, comprehensible objective and refused to be diverted from it, either by the hostility of the conservative or the taunts of the progressive. The League showed that the path to solid achievement in Great Britain lay in moderation, that common sense, well-marshalled evidence and administrative efficiency could challenge privilege and defeat it. The repeal of the Corn Laws, without bloodshed, was a triumph for sanity and — as its advocates would not have been ashamed to say — for decency and justice. Here is the true significance of what happened in 1846, a judgement which history can with conviction record all too rarely: the right side won.

THE BRITISH LION IN 1850;

OR, THE EFFECTS OF FREE TRADE.

Punch, loyal to the League to the last, published this cartoon on 7 February 1846, shortly before the repeal Bill was finally passed. In a few years' time, it suggested, the British people would be able to take their ease, grown plump on untaxed bread and British beer.

A Note on Sources

The place of publication is London unless otherwise stated. The publisher is identified only in the case of relatively recent books or where the company still exists. The dates shown are those of the edition I used; where this is not the original, this is indicated by 'f.p.' for 'first published' and the earlier date. Where the source of a quotation is obvious from the main text the information is not repeated below. The list is arranged alphabetically under the names of authors or editiors, *not* of subjects, but where appropriate (e.g. where there are several biographies by different authors) this is indicated by a cross-reference. Non-hyphenated names are listed under their final component (e.g. for W. Cooke Taylor, see Taylor). Pamphlets and reports not attributed to a named author or authors are listed separately. In addition to the titles listed below I made extensive use of the *Annual Register* for the years referred to, *Hansard*, and the *Dictionary of National Biography*.

Books, Pamphlets and Articles Consulted

Apjohn, Lewis, *Richard Cobden and the Free Traders* (1881)
Ashworth, Henry, *Recollections of Cobden and the League* (1877)
Ausubel, Hermann, *The Life of John Bright* (Wiley, New York, 1966)
Axon, W.E., *The Annals of Manchester* (Manchester, 1886)

Bain, Donald, *The Egregious and Dangerous Fallacies of the Anti-Corn-Law League* (Edinburgh, 1843)
Barnes, D.G., *A History of the English Corn Laws, 1660–1846* (Routledge, 1930)
Bisset, Andrew, *Notes on the Anti-Corn-Law Struggle* (1884)
Briggs, Asa (ed.), *Chartist Studies* (Macmillan, 1962)
Bright, John, *Speech at Free Trade Meeting, Liverpool, on Wednesday 30 August 1843* (Pamphlet) (1843)
Speeches on Questions of Public Policy (1868)
Speech in Bradford to inaugurate the Cobden Memorial, 25 July 1877 (Pamphlet) (1877)
(See also: Hirst, Read, Robbins, Smith, Trevelyan, Walling.)
and Rogers, Thorold (eds.), *Speeches (by Richard Cobden) on Questions of Public Policy* (1870)

Brock, Michael, *The Great Reform Act* (Hutchinson University Library, 1973)

Buckley, J.K., *Joseph Parkes of Birmingham* (1926)

Burn, W.L., 'The Underworld of Victorian Politics,' article in *The Listener*, 25 February 1954

Byron, Lord, *The Poetical Works of Lord Byron* (f.p. 1823; Oxford edition; Oxford University Press, 1903)

C., S.S. [It is unclear whether these initials stand for author or publisher], *Corn v. Cotton. An Attempt to Open the Case between the Manufacturers and the Landlords, by the S.S.C.* (1843)

Cardwell, E., and Mahon, Lord (eds.), *Memoirs of the Rt Hon. Sir Robert Peel* (Vol. 2, Part III)
(See also: Gash, Peel.)

Cayley, E.S., *Reasons for the Formation of the Agricultural Protection Society* (Pamphlet) (1844)

Cecil, Lord David, *Lord M.* (Constable, 1954)
(See also: Sanders, Torrens.)

Clark, George R. Kitson, *Peel and the Conservative Party* (G. Bell, 1929)
'The Repeal of the Corn Laws and the Politics of the 1840s,' article in *Economic History Review*, 1951.

Cobden, Richard, *The Corn Laws. Speech of Richard Cobden in the House of Commons on 24 February 1842* (Pamphlet) (Manchester, 1842)
The Land-Tax Fraud. Speech of Richard Cobden in the House of Commons on 14 March 1842 (Pamphlet) (Manchester, 1842)
Tenant Farmers and Farm Labourers. Speech on 12 March 1844 on moving for a Select Committee to inquire into the effects of protective duties on imports upon the interests of tenant farmers and farm labourers (Pamphlet) (Manchester, 1844)
(ed.), *The Corn Laws. Extracts from the Works of Thomas Perronet Thompson, Selected and Classified by Richard Cobden* (Manchester, c. 1845)
(See also: Apjohn, Ashworth, Bright and Rogers, Morley, Read, Watkin.)

Cole, G.D.H., and Filson, A.W. (eds.), *British Working Class Movements: Select Documents, 1789–1875)* (f.p. 1951, Macmillan, 1965)

Conklin, R.J., *Thomas Cooper the Chartist* (Phillipines' University Press, Manila, 1935)

Cooper, Thomas, *Life of Thomas Cooper by Himself* (1872)
Thoughts at Fourscore (1885)
(See also: Conklin.)

Craig, F.W.S. (ed.), *British Parliamentary Election Results, 1832–1885* (Macmillan, 1977)
  British Electoral Facts, 1832–1980 (f.p. 1968, Parliamentary Research Services, Chichester, 1981)
Curtis, John, *America and the Corn Laws* (Pamphlet) (Manchester, 1841)

Day, G.C., *The Defeat of the Anti-Corn-Law League in Huntingdonshire. The Speech of Mr George Came Day at Huntingdon, 17 June 1843* (Pamphlet) (1843)
  The Effects of Free Trade. The Speech delivered by Mr George Came Day at a public dinner in the Town Hall, Huntingdon, 29 July 1851 (Pamphlet, 1851)
Dunckley, Rev. Henry, *The Charter of the Nations* (London and Manchester, 1854)

Elliott, Ebenezer, *Poetical Works* (Edinburgh, 1840). (This includes *Corn-Law Rhymes* f.p. 1831)
  More Verse and Prose by the Corn-Law Rhymer (1850)
  (See also: Searle, Sheffield.)
Encyclopedia Brittanica, The (7th Ed., 21 vols., Edinburgh, 1842)
Ensor, R.C.K., *England 1870–1914* (f.p. 1936, Clarendon Press, Oxford, 1946)

Faucher, Leon, *Manchester in 1844* (Translated by 'A Member of the Manchester Anthenaeum,' London and Manchester, 1844)
Fay, C.R., *The Corn Laws and Social England* (Cambridge University Press, 1932)
Fisher, H.A.L., *History of Europe* (f.p. 1936, Edward Arnold, 1946)
Fitzwilliam, Lord, *First, Second and Third Addresses to the Landowners of England on the Corn Laws* (Pamphlets, various dates to 1839)

Gammage, R.G., *History of the Chartist Movement* (London and Newcastle, 1894)
Garnett, R., *Life of W.J. Fox* (1910)
Gash, Norman, *Mr Secretary Peel. The Life of Sir Robert Peel to 1830* (Longmans, 1961)
  Reaction and Reconstruction in English Politics, 1832–1842 (Clarendon Press, Oxford, 1965)
  Sir Robert Peel. The Life of Sir Robert Peel after 1830. (Longmans, 1972)
  (ed.), *The Age of Peel* (Edward Arnold, 1968)
Gaskell, Elizabeth, *Mary Barton. A Tale of Manchester Life.* (A novel.) (f.p. 1848, numerous editions since)
Gordon, Strathearn, *Our Parliament* (f.p. 1945, Hansard Society, 1958)

Greg, W.R., Hope G., and Morse, A., *Three Prize Essays on Agriculture and the Corn Laws* (Pamphlet) (Manchester and London, 1842)
Greville, Charles, see Reeve

Halévy, Elie, *The Liberal Awakening, 1815–1830* (f.p. 1923, Ernest Benn, 1949
Hayes, Louis M., *Reminiscences of Manchester and Some of its Local Surroundings from the year 1840* (London and Manchester, 1905)
Hirst, Margaret E., *John Bright* (Headley Brothers, 1945)
   (See also: Ausubel, Bright, Read, Robbins, Smith.)
Holyoake, George J., *Sixty Years of an Agitator's Life* (2 vols., 1892)
Hovell, Mark, *The Chartist Movement* (Manchester University Press, Manchester, 1925)

Johnson, Leonard G., *General T. Perronet Thompson, 1783–1869. His Military, Literary and Political Campaigns* (Allen and Unwin, 1957)
   (See also: Cobden, Thompson)

Kingsley, Charles, *Alton Locke* (A novel.) (f.p. 1862, numerous editions since)
Kohl, Johann G., *Ireland, Scotland and England* (1844)

Leader, R.E., *The Life of John Arthur Roebuck* (1897)
Longford, Elizabeth, *Victoria R.I.* (Weidenfeld, 1964)
Longmate, Norman, *King Cholera* (Hamish Hamilton, 1966)
   The Workhouse (Maurice Temple Smith, 1974)
   The Hungry Mills (Maurice Temple Smith, 1978)

Mackie, J.B., *The Life and Work of Duncan McLaren* (Edinburgh, 1888)
Magnus, Sir Philip, *Gladstone. A Biography* (John Murray, 1954)
Malthus, Thomas, *First Essay on Population* (f.p. 1798, Macmillan, 1926)
Martineau, Harriet, *Dawn Island* (Pamphlet) (Manchester, 1845)
   A History of England during the Thirty Years Peace 1816–1846 (2 vols., 1849–50)
McCord, Norman, *The Anti-Corn-Law League, 1838–1846* (Allen and Unwin, 1958)
Mitchell, B.R. and Deane, Phyllis (ed.), *Abstract of British Historical Statistics* (Cambridge University Press, 1962)
Morley, John, *The Life of Richard Cobden* (f.p. 1881, 2 vols., 1903)
   (See also: Apjohn, Ashworth, Bright and Rogers, Read, Watkins.)

Napier, Macvey, *Selections from the Correspondence of Macvey Napier Esq.* (Oxford 1879)

O'Connor, Feargus, *The Trial of Feargus O'Connor and Fifty-eight Others* (London and Manchester, 1843)

Patterson, A.T., *Radical Leicester* (Leicester, 1954)
Pearce, John, *The Life and Teachings of Joseph Livesey* (1886)
Peel, Arthur George Villiers (ed.), *The Private Letters of Sir Robert Peel* (John Murray, 1920)
    (See also: Gash.)
Pool, Bernard (ed.), *The Croker Papers* (f.p. 1884, Batsford, 1967)
Prentice, Archibald, *History of the Anti-Corn-Law League* (2 vols., 1853)
Pease, Sir Alfred E. (ed.), *The Diaries of Edward Pease* (1907)

Read, Donald, *Cobden and Bright. A Victorian Partnership* (Edward Arnold, 1967)
    (See also: Apjohn, Ashworth, Ausubel, Bright, Cobden, Hirst, Morley, Robbins, Smith, Trevelyan, Walling, Watkin.)
Redford, Arthur, *Manchester Merchants and Foreign Trade 1794–1858* (Manchester, 1934)
Reeve, Henry (ed.), *The Greville Memoirs* (f.p. 1874–87, 8 vols, Longmans 1888)
The Letters of Charles Greville and Henry Reeve (1924)
Richard, Henry, *Memoirs of Joseph Sturge* (1864)
    (See also: Sturge.)
Robbins, Keith, *John Bright* (Routledge, 1979)
    (See also: Ausubel, Bright, Hirst, Read, Trevelyan, Walling.)
Rose, Mary B., *The Gregs of Styal* (Pamphlet) (Quarry Bank Mill Development Trust and National Trust, 1979)
    (See also: Ausubel, Bright, Hirst, Read, Smith, Trevelyan, Walling.)
Rosenblatt, F.F., *The Chartist Movement in its Social and Economic Aspects* (Columbia University Press, NewYork, 1916)

Sanders, L.C. (ed.), *Lord Melbourne's Papers* (1889)
    (See also: Cecil, Torrens.)
Searle, J. (Pseudonymn), *Memoirs of Ebenezer Elliott* (1852)
    (See also: Elliott.)
Sheffield Free Public Libraries, *Ebenezer Elliott, The Corn-Law Rhymer* (Pamphlet, Sheffield, 1949)
    (See also: Elliott, Searle.)
Slosson, P.W., *The Decliñe of the Chartist Movement* (Columbia University Press, 1916.)
Smiles, Samuel, *Autobiography* (1905)
Smith, George Garnett, *The Life of the Rt Hon. John Bright MP* (Hodder and Stoughton, 1889)
    (See also: Ausubel, Bright, Hirst, Read, Robbins, Smith, Trevelyan, Walling.)

Solly, Rev. Henry, *These Eighty Years* (1893)

Somerville, Alexander, *The Whistler at the Plough* (1852)
   Free Trade and the League (1853)

Sturge, Richard, *Life of Joseph Sturge* (1864)
   (See also: Richard)

Surtees, R.S., *Hillingdon Hall* (A novel.) (f.p. 1844, numerous editions since)
   Handley Cross (A novel.) f.p. 1843, numerous editions since)

Taylor, William Cooke, *Notes of a Tour in the Manufacturing Districts of Lancashire* (f.p. 1842, Frank Cass, 1968)

Thompson, Thomas Perronet, *A Catechism on the Corn Laws* (1827)
   (See also: Cobden, Johnson.)

Torrens, W. MacCullagh (ed.), *The Memoirs of Lord Melbourne* (Vol. 2, 1878)
   (See also: Sanders)

Trevelyan, G.M., *The Life of John Bright* (Constable, 1913)
   (See also: Ausubel, Bright, Hirst, Read, Robbins, Smith, Walling.)

Villiers, C.P., *Free Trade Speeches* (2 vols., 1883)

Waddington, John, *Congregational History. A Continuation* (5 vols., 1869–80)

Wallas, Graham, *The Life of Francis Place* (1898)

Walling, R.A.J. (ed.), *The Diary of John Bright* (Cassell, 1930)
   (See also: Ausubel, Bright, Hirst, Read, Robbins, Smith, Trevelyan.)

Watkin, Sir Edward W., *Alderman Cobden of Manchester* (Manchester, 1891)

Whibley, Charles, *Political Portraits* (Macmillan, 1917)

Willmore F.W., *A History of Wallsall and its Neighbourhood* (Walsall, 1887)

Young, G.M., and Handcock, W.D. (eds.), *English Historical Documents Volume XII (I), 1833–1874* (Eyre and Spottiswoode, 1956)

Zilliacus, Laurin, *From Pillar to Post* (Heinemann, 1956).

Pamphlets Published Anonymously
(all except those marked 'Not League' were published by the Anti-Corn-Law League in Manchester)

A Dialogu on the Corn Laws between a Gentleman and a Farmer (1845)

A Reply to the Prize Essays on Agriculture and the Corn Laws, by
    A Lincolnshire Landowner (Not League. London, 1842)
  (See also: Greg in main list above.)
*An Address to Farmers on the Way in which their Families are
    Provided For* (1842)
The Anti-Corn-Law League to the Duke of Wellington (1842)
Authorities against the Corn Laws (1842)
*Directions to be Observed by all Persons Engaged in the Registration
    of Electors for Cities and Boroughs* (1844)
Facts for Farmers (n.d., c.1842)
The Great League Fund (1842)
*The National Anti-Corn-Law League. The Quarter of a Million
    Fund* (1846)
*Practical Instructions for the Annual Registration of Voters in
    Counties* (1844)
*Report of the Proceedings of a Meeting of the Landowners, Farmers
    and Others Resident in the County of York for the Establishment
    of the Yorkshire Protective Society, held in the De Grey Rooms,
    York, 22 February 1844* (Not League. 1844)
*Report of the Statistical Commission appointed by the Anti-Corn-
    Law Conference held in London 8–12 March 1842* (1842).

Anti-Corn-Law Periodicals (all but *The Struggle* were official
League publications.):

The Anti-Bread-Tax Circular, 21 April 1841 – 26 September 1843
    (Manchester and later London)
The Anti-Corn-Law League Circular, 16 April 1839 – 8 April 1841
    (Manchester)
The Bazaar Gazette (London, 1845)
The League, 30 September 1843 – 4 July 1846 (London)
The Struggle (Preston, n.d., but c.1841–1843).

Other Periodicals Consulted

Durham Advertiser, later the *Durham Chronicle*
Glasgow Argus
London and Westminster Review
Manchester Times, later the *Manchester Examiner and Times*
Morning Chronicle (London)
Punch (London, from 1842)
Sun (London. Ceased publication 1871)

Tait's Edinburgh Magazine
The Times (London)
Parliamentary Papers
Reports of Select Committees. 1833 (612) v 1; 1834 (517) vii 1; 1835
(289) xiii 441; 1836 (189) viii Part 1 225; 1836 (465) viii Part II 1; 1837
(464) v 1; 1843 (447) xi 33; 1843 (511) xi 125; 1846 (139) viii 125.

Principal Sources

The outstanding contemporary source is Prentice, though his book
is not indexed and has the infuriating fault, common to so many, of
giving detailed dates while not making clear to what year he is
referring — an omission I have tried to remedy in my own work.
The most useful recent book is McCord, to whom my debt will be
obvious to all familiar with it, though it is also inadequately indexed.
The primary sources I used were the League Letter Book, George
Wilson's papers and J.B. Smith's papers in the Archive Section of
the Manchester Central Reference Library and the Francis Place
collection in the British Library. I did not consult the Cobden
papers, which are, however, extensively quoted by McCord.

1 The Price of Corn
The epigraph is from *The Poetical Works of Lord Byron*, Oxford
edition, O.U.P., 1904. On the Bolton meeting see Prentice (Vol.I,
p. 64). On the early history of the Corn Laws see Barnes pp.2–3
9–11, 26 and 46, this last containing Pelham's speech at Lewes. Fay
p.34 contains the quotation from Charles Smith. Barnes p.38 refers
to imports from the colonies and pp.44 and 48 to Pownall's Act and
Adam Smith, who is also quoted in Barnes p.7. See in addition Fay
pp.7–8 and, on Malthus, Fay p.28 and Malthus pp.iv and viii–ix. On
the Acts of 1773 and 1791 see Barnes pp.49–51 and Fay pp.35–7. On
'M' bread and the Speenhamland system see Barnes pp.74–5 and 84,
and on the 1834 Poor Law Amendment Act my book *The
Workhouse*, p.73. On the post-1802 period see Barnes pp.85 and
89–91, and Fay p.30. On prices in 1813–14 see Barnes pp.122, 126
and 130–1. On reaction to the 1815 Bill see Barnes pp.134–7 and Fay
p.42, on price levels 1815–1820 Mitchell and Deane p.487. The
Lords protest is in Fay p.43. On the effect of price fluctuations see
Barnes pp.158, 166–8 and, on the 1822 Bill, p.174. On Peterloo see
Halévy p.65. On the sliding scale see The Statutes pp.593–614 and
Barnes p.200. On the *Catechism*, Barnes p.218.

2 Stable and Regular Government

The *Morning Post* is quoted by Brock p.318, import figures come from the *Encyclopedia Brittanica* and the Prentice quotation from Vol. I p.1. The 'contemporary historian' is quoted by Apjohn p.781. On the 1832 Reform Act see Gordon p.56, Woodward, pp.78–9 and 84, and Craig's *Electoral Facts* Table 8. On events in Manchester see Prentice Vol. I pp.13, 20 and 24. On the effects of the election Brock p.356 and Craig Table 2. On Prentice on the King's Speech see Vol. I pp.32–3, on the Anti-Corn-Law pledge and the merchants' meeting Vol.I pp.36–7, on wheat prices Mitchell and Deane p.488, on the House of Commons debate Prentice Vol.I pp.37–40, on the 'draw the curtains' quotation Vol.I pp.42–3 and on parliamentary opinion in 1835 Vol.I pp.43–5. On Cobden's literary debut and the first Anti-Corn-Law Association see Prentice Vol.I pp.47–8, on the 1837 Election Vol.I pp.54–7, on the 1838 Bill Vol.I, pp.,59–61. For the Villiers letter see Sturge p.270.

3 Vile and Silly Laws

The epigraph is from Sturge p.271, the extract from Bowring's speech is in Prentice Vol.I pp.65–9 and the quotation from Bastiat on pp.71–2. On Bowring's career see the *D.N.B.* and on the work of the Provisional Committee and the first public meeting Prentice Vol.I pp.74–5. 'Mad Smith' is mentioned by Read p.21 and 'Corn-Law Smith' by McCord pp.35–6. On Sturge see the *D.N.B.* and on his relations with Villiers Sturge p.270. Brougham's letter is in Sturge p.271, the 'eternal principles' and 'abstract truth' tributes on p.275. On the wet autumn see Prentice Vol.I p.63, on 'smouldering discontent' p.77; on Paulton's debut and the other early lectures J.B. Smith's *Papers, Corn Laws* Vol.I and McCord p.38, which, along with Prentice Vol.I pp.59 and 78–9, also cover events in the Manchester Chamber of Commerce. The petition text is in Prentice Vol.I pp.86–7. On Melbourne's letter see Sanders pp.387–8.

4 The Great Object

The epigraph is in Prentice Vol.I p.125, the account of the January 1839 meeting in Vol.I p.90; the royal toast is mentioned on pp.97–8, the petitions on p.103. On the 'gradualists' and the Manchester Association's aims see McCord p.42. Melbourne's views are in Sanders pp.388–9. On Spencer see the *D.N.B.* and Sanders p.394. Reluctance to travel on Sunday is mentioned by McCord, p.45, and Wood's downfall by Prentice Vol.I pp.108–11 and McCord p.47. Woodward pp.99–100 explains the Bedchamber Crisis, while on Russell's inconsistency see Martineau Book V p.415; Walker's letter is quoted by McCord p.48, his expenses and the League's practice of subsidizing newspapers is described on p.50. The 'noisy agitators' quotation is from Smith's Papers, *Corn Laws* Vol.I. Prentice's despairing comment is in Vol.I p.113. For the Hanseatic League see Martineau Vol.V p.416 and H.A.L. Fisher, *A History of Europe* (Edward Arnold, 1946 edn.). 'One journalist' is quoted by Martineau on the same page. Villiers's efforts are in Prentice Vol.I pp.123–4, Martineau, *op. cit.*, and McCord p.53. See Prentice Vol.I. p.125 on the resolutions setting up the League, and on its officers McCord p.36.

5 The League is Manchester

The epigraph is from McCord p.80. On Manchester in 1838 see Axon pp.202–4, on the importance of the cotton industry Read pp.7–8, which also quotes from Disraeli's *Coningsby* (f.p. 1844). The 1841 visitor is Taylor, who is quoted by Faucher on pp.17–9. On Cobden's house see Read p.11, on Manchester's religious affiliations p.9 and Axon pp.208–13, on the Quakers' architectural pretensions Faucher p.26, for the *Manchester Guardian* and 'men . . . not big enough' Faucher p.72 footnote. Faucher pp.26–31 describes the social composition of Manchester and pp.60, 61 f.n., and 72, the local rates of pay. The League publication mentioned is the *Report of the Statistical Commission* pp.8–9. On recent improvements and the city's real needs see Faucher *Preface* pp.xi–xiv. On Newall's Buildings see Hayes pp.158–9 and on the League's unimpressive office Somerville, *Free Trade* p.376.

6 What Plans for London?

The epigraph is from the Place Papers Add. Mss.35.151. On the League's financial problems see McCord pp.65–8 and on the *Circular* Somerville, *Free Trade* p.513. On the Working Men's Association see Prentice Vol.I p.139, on Poulett Thomson p.132, on the Manchester election p.135, on press references p.136, on the *Morning Post* leaderp.139, on the Peterloo site p.141, and on the description of the Free Trade Hall in the *Manchester Times* and the first meeting held there pp.143 and pp.149–50. Place's reaction when first approached is in the Place Papers Add.Mss.35.151 as is his progress report to Cobden. The printed Report of the Association is in Vol.I of the Papers. The 'pistol' letter and the 'set afloat' letter are quoted by McCord pp.73 and 77, and the 'contemporary newspaper' account—in fact in the *Morning Chronicle* of 31 March 1840—is in the Place Papers Set No.7. Prentice's estimate is in Vol.I p.150, and his account of the deputations to Melbourne and Baring on pp.152 and 155. On the former see also Place Papers Set No.7. On the Brown's Hotel meeting see Prentice Vol.I p.158. Place's letter to Warburton is in Add.Mss. 35.151. On the London office see McCord p.76 and for Sidney Smith's letters of 2 and 4 May the League Letter Book. Prentice's indignation is in Vol.I pp.160–1 and the work of Place's Committee is described in Appendix A of the Metropolitan Association Report in the Place Papers Set 7, Vol.I. On Place's Statistical Committee and his letters to Cobden see Add.Mss.35.151, on the Business Committee's Report Set No.7 of the Place Papers. Prentice's summing up is in Vol.I pp.173–4.

7 It Never Can Be Worse

The epigraph can be found in the Place Papers, Set No.7, Vol.I. On the sanitary movement see my *King Cholera*, p.148. The Manchester Statistical Society's findings are in Woodward p.458 f.n. The family budgets for 1836 and 1840 are in the Place Papers Set No.7, Vol.I and that for 1841 in Set No.7 Vol.III. The 'fraction of a penny' quotation is from the Report of the Statistical Commission of the League pp.8–9. The investigator quoted is Bisset pp.228–9, and he described 'the cottage worse than any of these' on pp.234–5 and the higher price of bread in the countryside on pp.232–3. On Quarry Bank see Rose pp.7–14, on the transformation of Styal Rose pp.27–8 and Hayes pp.98–102, where the 'founding of a colony' comment appears, and pp.112–3.

8 The Great Engine of Repeal

On Paulton's demerits as a speaker see Smiles p.88 and McCord p.37. Shearman is quoted by Briggs p.355 and Walker by McCord p.48. On Grieg see McCord p.59, on Shearman Briggs p.353, on Sidney Smith McCord pp.59 and 64, on his need of textbooks p.21. On the Huntingdon meeting see the League Letter Book (Shearman No.198 and 199) and McCord p.61. Prentice Vol.I p.128, McCord p.62 and the League Letter Book (Shearman No.205 and 208) describe events at Cambridge. On Shearman's expenses and Scottish tight-fistedness see McCord pp.64–6, on Paulton and Acland's experiences McCord pp.57–9 and 65–6. Briggs p.355 quoted Bowring's letter, the League Letter Book (acland No.254–6) lack of 'the needful' in Sussex, and McCord p.67 the scale of fees. The letters from Birmingham are in the League Lettr Book (Acland No.337 and 340), while Acland No.614 is from near Woodbridge. On the *Essex Mercury* see the Place Papers Set No.7 Vol.1 and for the correct date League Letter Book (Acland No.548), which also includes the 'triumph everywhere' letter. The plan for Saxmundham is in Acland No.552, the report from Docking is Acland No.615, from Swaffham No.571, 'the dank localities' are in No.548, the letter from Saxmundham in No.587, from Halesworth and Framlingham No.603, from Ipswich No.638. 'The Immortal Acland' letter is quoted by McCord p.57, the *Northern Star* by Briggs p.355. On Finnigan see McCord pp.72, 126 and 225, Briggs p.355 and the Place Papers Set 7 Vol.I, which quotes the letter to Cobden. Sidney Smith's letter is in the League Letter Book (S.Smith No.531), Place's in Place Papers Add.Mss.35.151, and 'W.P.'s' letter in Set No.7 Vol.1, which also includes the Metropolitan Association report. For Murray and Griffiths see McCord p.73, and for Griffiths's letter the League Letter Book, not numbered but c.580.

9 Upset by Chartists

The epigraph is quoted in Briggs p.37 and p.342 mentions the 1819 opposition to the Corn Laws. Cole and Postgate pp.280–1 describes the People's Charter, Briggs p.106 includes the 'forcibly if we must' quotation, p.135 working class distrust of the factory-owners, p.4 carries the 'grasping capitalist' quotation, pp.35–6 the 'liberal manufacturers' one. O'Connor's attitude is described by Gammage p.270, the Leicester Chartist is quoted by Briggs p.137, C.P. Villiers by Briggs p.348, Cobden by Smiles pp.108–13 and pp.116–8. The first clash in London is described by McCord p.45 and the uproar in Manchester by Prentice Vol.I pp.116–8. O'Connor's advice is in Briggs p.3, Chartist fly-posting in Prentice Vol.I p.214. Griffiths's letter is in McCord p.54, the Operative Associations are in McCord p.75, pp.97–8 describes the peaceful rally, and the 'Irish lambs' are on p.99. The Chartist take-over of meetings is in Briggs p.37 and McCord p.100, which includes the Stephenson Square meeting, on which see also Prentice Vol.I pp.217–8 and Place Papers Set No. 7, quoted by McCord p.102; the latter also mentions the 'pitched battle' of March 1842. On the *Manchester Guardian* quotation see the epigraph source, *op. cit.*, on the *Standard* one, McCord p.103, on the Chartists' unscrupulous tactics in Huddersfield, Place Papers Set No. 7 Vol.1. (This meeting was in fact on 4 February 1839, not on 4 March as stated by McCord p.51.) On Chartist disruption see Briggs pp.359 and 343, and, on their contempt for Samuel Smiles, p.344. On Baines see Smiles pp.94–5 and Briggs pp.66–7. Place's letters are in Place Papers Add.Mss.35.151, Blackmore's amendment in Set No. 7, as is the Young Men's Anti-Monopoly Association. On Leicester see Briggs pp.108–9, Patterson pp.312 and 315, and Conklin pp.77–81, which carries the *Illuminator* quote and describes Conklin's acceptance of money from a Tory and from *The Times*. Conklin pp.103–4 carries the *Northern Star* report of 19 February 1842 and his prison sentence; Briggs p.138 describes the

Midland Counties Charter and pp.84 and 357–8 'the Fox and Goose Club' in Leeds. On the Council meeting of November 1841 see Briggs pp.364–5, on Sturge's essay Cole and Filson pp.381–2 and p.390, on the Birmingham meeting and its aftermath Sturge p.270, McCord pp.97 and 114–6 and Conklin pp.107–8. On the second conference see Cole and Filson p.382, on Cobden's conclusion Briggs p.367.

10 Educating a Nation
For the epigraph see Prentice Vol.I p.174. On the Metropolitan Anti-Corn-Law Association see its *First Report* in the Place Papers Set No. 7 Vol.1. 'Enlightening the public mind' is quoted by McCord p.180. On 'silent missionaries' see Prentice Vol.II p.21, on the distribution arrangements p.119 and McCord pp.180–1; on Bright's letter to Cobden McCord p.148, on Cobden's letter to Smiles Smiles pp.110–1. Apjohn pp.62–4 describes the *Catechism* and quotes the 'Victorian admirer'. On Perronet Thompson's career see the *D.N.B.* 'The time is not far off' passage is in Cobden, *Corn Laws, Extracts* p.3. On the *Prize Essays* see Greg *seriatim*. See *A Reply* for the Lincolnshire Landowner's reaction. On other publications see Prentice Vol.I pp.125–7, on the burning of League literature p.128, on the *Almanack* p.173; on later expansion of the propagandist effort pp.390, 394 and 406, and Vol.I pp.281–2 for Bowring's poem. See also the various titles mentioned in the text. See Elliott p.106 for his background, *D.N.B.* for his career; Somerville, *Free Trade* p.361, was the 'contemporary observer' and p.376 recorded Lytton's admiration. For the 'incomplete fragment' and 'dead father' verse see Apjohn pp.76–80. On Cobden's view of Thackeray see McCord pp.69–70, on propagandist china and wafers see McCord p.181, Prentice Vol.II p.27 and an advertisement at the end of Greg, which also lists other League publications. Cobden's optimistic letter is in McCord p.136.

11 Between Friends
For the epigraph see the League Letter Book (Sidney Smith No.531). On the Finance Committee's first operations see McCord p.49, on the £5,000 fund p.54, on Cobden's 'real friends' letter p.81 and on his letter to J.B. Smith J.B. Smith's Papers. For Hickin's warning see McCord p.110. On George Wilson see the *D.N.B.*, McCord pp.129, 167 (on the 'Manchester contemporary') and 168 (on Cobden's assessment of him). On his career with the League see McCord pp.53 and 133, on the 1842 reorganization McCord p.134, on the ornamental membership card p.181, on attendance at Council meetings and Cobden's view of Prentice p.164, and on

Hickin's warning to Cobden p.109. On the League's general efficiency see McCord p.172, on the effects of cheap postage Read p.19 and Zilliacus p.143; on the organization of League headquarters McCord pp.174–6, on expansion at Newall's Buildings p.133. Kohl's impressions are recorded by Prentice Vol.II pp.25–7, while the work of voluntary helpers is praised in Vol.I p.189. On moving the *Circular* to London see League Letter Book (Sidney Smith No.531–2), on 'the Goths and Vandals' and Hickin's return to Manchester see McCord pp.140–1. On the later history of the *Circular* see Ashworth p.39, McCord pp.65, 91 and 120, Prentice Vol.II p.117, and League Letter Book (Sidney Smith No.531). On the *League* see that publication, McCord pp.65 and 181, and Prentice Vol.I pp.130–1. On the *Free Trader* see Place Add.Mss.27.810, on the *Struggle* see that paper's files, and Pearce lxxii, which gives Cobden's view of Livesey, and lx–lxxi. On Livesey's life see my book, *The Waterdrinkers* pp.38–40. On the 'poor woman' story see the *Struggle* No. 2, on Livesey's reply to the 'great convulsion' argument No. 5, on the 'dinner agitation' No. 54. On Somerville see *D.N.B.* and McCord pp.143–4 and 176. On W.J.Fox see *D.N.B.* and McCord pp.185–6; on subsidies to the press see McCord pp.182, on the *Economist* 184.

12 Millions of Signatures

The epigraph is from Prentice Vol.I p.394 and the figures for petitions in 1839 and up to March 1842 are on pp.160 and 328. McCord p.49 mentions printed petition forms. The Livesey family petition is quoted by Pearce p.23, the Children's Petition is described by Briggs p.360 and the approach to mill-owners by McCord p.74. The meeting of November 1841 is described by Prentice Vol.I p.273 and events at Epworth by the *Report* of the *Select Committee to whom the Petition from Epworth . . .* [was] *referred*, dated 19 July 1843, pp.32–5, 71 and 79. The similar report for Cheltenham is dated 23 March 1846 and I quoted p.iii. On the tea-party for George Thompson see Prentice Vol.I pp.231–4, on the *Scottish Patriot* McCord p.27, on the August 1841 clerical conference pp.105–6 and Prentice Vol.I pp.237–47, on its sequel p.252, on later conferences pp.290–1. Support by the nonconformists is described by McCord pp.73 and 107 and the opposition of the Anglican clergy on 26. The cartload of petitions is mentioned by Prentice in Vol.I p.268 and the special collect on p.122.

13 A Hustings Question

For the epigraph see McCord p.90 and for Cobden's letter p.82. On

the first Whig candidate at Walsall see Prentice Vol.I p.176 and on
the election as a whole pp.177–182, which include the quotations
from the press. McCord p.84 quotes the 'narrow-minded bigots'
gibe. Cobden's successive letters to J.B.Smith are in the latter's
papers as (Walsall) (50), 1 January 1841, (51), 2 January, (54), 4
January, (55), 5 January, (56), 12 January, (58), 18 January—not 16
January as stated by McCord p.87—and (59), 24 January. Bright's
letter is quoted by McCord p.85. On the Tory candidate's sponsor
see Willmore p.417. On extra Tory voters see Prentice Vol.I p.182,
on the Whig response McCord pp.86–7, which include the Sidney
Smith account, on Joseph Parkes's encouragement McCord p.88.
Cobden's 'ambiguous' position is indicated in letter (58) *op. cit.* On
the campaign meetings see McCord p.88 and Willmore pp.416–7,
on Joseph Livesey's participation Pearce p.24, on the result Prentice
Vol.I p.183 and J.B.Smith's Papers (Walsall) (79). Cobden's speech
of 18 February is in Prentice Vol.I p.187, the agent's comment in
McCord p.89 and the League's later victory in Willmore p.417. The
quotes from the *Morning Chronicle* and the *Farmers' Journal* are in
McCord p.90, and Prentice's later judgement is in Vol.I p.183. On
Lord John Russell see Prentice Vol.I p.203, on Melbourne
Woodward p.103 and McCord p.92. The ministry's fall is described
by McCord p.94 and Prentice Vol.I pp.209 and 224, and
J.B.Smith's defeat by McCord p.95.

14 The Mainspring of the Movement

The epigraph is from McCord p.171 and the tribute to Cobden in
the *Circular* from p.96. On Villiers see *D.N.B.*, on Cobden's early
years Read pp.1–5, on his first pamphlets pp.13 and 18, on his
connection with Rowland Hill p.19, on his speeches to the Chamber
of Commerce p.24, on his 'Gothic invader' letter pp.29–30.
Cobden's appearance is described by Read p.25 and his speaking
style on pp.26–7, which quote John Bright. The slippers are
mentioned by McCord p.170, Cobden's efficiency at business by
Bisset p.7; Elliott's verdict by Smiles p.88, Hunter's, by McCord
p.170. On Bright's origins and education see Read pp.69–71, on his
political development pp.72–6 and Trevelyan pp.24–54. On
Bright's involvement with the Anti-Corn-Law movement see
Trevelyan p.30, on his marriage p.33, on Cobden's call after his
wife's death and their developing intimacy pp.43–4. For the tour of
the country in 1842–3 see Robbins pp.39–41 and Trevelyan p.99,
which quotes the diary extract. Cobden's 'moral spirit' letter is
quoted by Trevelyan p.63, Bright's attitude to the Corn Laws is set
out by Morley p.26 and Trevelyan p.56. His combative
temperament is revealed in Read p.85, his emotionalism on p.87.

The 'mainspring' letter is quoted by McCord p.171. On their differing approaches see Read p.95, on Cobden's desire for Bright's help in Parliament Morley p.264, on Bright's first defeat Robbins p.40 and Smith (George Garnett) p.22; on Bright's subsequent victory Smith p.29 and Trevelyan p.111. On the Game Laws see Hirst pp.15 and 22 and Read p.94. On Sturge see Sturge pp.275–8.

15 Begging for Bread

For the epigraph see Briggs p.53; for the Queen's Speech of August 1841 Prentice Vol.I p.253, for Melbourne's and Cobden's 255–7, for the division and Harriet Martineau's account 260–2, for the Day of Humiliation and the petitions 248 and 268, for Prentice's 'uncharitable' quotation and conditions in Bolton 269–71. On the Leicester framework knitter see Briggs p.126, for the *Manchester Times* quote Briggs p.53 *op. cit.*, for Livesey's 'empty table' drawing the *Struggle* No. 61. On the Duke of Norfolk see Pearce p.lxiv; on the petitions Prentice Vol.I pp.273 and 295, on the Duke of Buckingham and the Queen's Speech of February 1842 302–3, on the mass lobby of the House 309–10, on the meeting at Brown's Hotel 314, on the subsequent campaign 316–8, and on Villiers's motion 328; for Peel's Bill see Barnes pp.251–3. The circular letter of June 1842 is in Prentice Vol.I pp.355–6 and Ashworth pp.75–80, the later conference in Ashworth p.94 and Prentice Vol.I pp.335–40. On the *Manchester Guardian*'s unwelcome observation and subsequent debates see Prentice Vol.I pp.368–9, on the deputation to Peel pp.346–62 and Ashworth p.89. On the end of the conference and the visit to Sir James Graham see Ashworth pp.93–8 and Prentice Vol.I p.365, which dates the latter as 26 July. On Melbourne's letter of 6 August 1842 see Sanders pp.514–5, on his private response Torrens pp.384–5.

16 A Middle-Class Agitation

The epigraph is from Briggs p.366. On employers who welcomed the 'turn-out' see Prentice Vol.I pp.370–1. On Sir James Graham see Briggs pp.386 and 390–1 and Pool p.186. On the first walk-out see Gash p.357, on later developments Ashworth pp.104–5 and Prentice Vol.I pp.372–3. Gash p.338 quotes Peel's letter of 11 August, Prentice Vol.I pp.374–5 mentions the peaceful Peterloo anniversary, Peel p.202 quotes the letter of 18 August, p.203 that of 20 August, p.204 that of 21 August. Gash p.344 describes the sending of the cavalry to Staffordshire, 343 the use of the police and the Guards, 344–5 the routing of the Chartists in London. Peel's letter to Graham of 26 August is quoted by Gash pp.354–5; Prentice's article is in Prentice Vol.I p.380, Bright's address 377–8, events in other areas 379 and Ashworth 110. For Cobden's speech of 25 August see Prentice Vol. I pp.384–7, for its subsequent quotation see Briggs p.367 and, for abuse of the League, 345. McCord p.64 gives details of its officers in Lincolnshire, Peel p.205 quotes the letter of 1 September, Gash pp.350–2 describes the government's distrust of the magistrates and its advice to the general restoring order. On the casualties during the riots and the subsequent trials see Woodward p.135 and the *Annual Register* for 1842, pp.133–4 and 150. On the £50,000 fund see Prentice Vol. I pp.393 and 398 and McCord p.138. Prentice Vol. I p.414 quoted the *Leeds Mercury* and 402, the smaller donations. The falling price of corn is from Gash p.360, Peel's attempt to discredit the League, pp.356–7.

17 A New Power in the State
On the Free Trade Hall and the inaugural meeting there see Prentice Vol. II pp.14–20, and on Harriet Martineau pp.36–7. Gash pp.364–8 gives the details of the attack on Peel and its aftermath, while Prentice Vol. II p.37 mentions Peel's bodyguards and pp.41–3 the scene in the House. Peel's unescorted walk home is in Gash p.369; Wilson's defence of the League is in Prentice Vol. II p.47, the Drury Lane meetings in pp.57–8, and the verses quoted, p.67. See Prentice Vol. II pp.80–1 for the report in the *Sun*, pp.89 for the *Morning Post*, 93 for the *Globe*, 94 for the rejection of the enquiry, and 105–6 for the speaking tours in the North. On Bright's victory see Robbins pp.44–5, on his maiden speech Prentice Vol. II pp.110–1, on the Covent Garden meetings pp.117–21, on S.J. Loyd pp.127–8 and 145, on the 1843 tour pp.128–31, on the League's pre-appeal finances p.120. *The Times* leader is also quoted by Prentice Vol. II pp.137–8, the *Morning Herald* on p.139, and the provincial papers and the *League* on pp.142–4.

18 Appeal to the Constituencies
The epigraph is from *Directions for Cities* p.13. For the start of the year's campaign see Prentice Vol. II p.146, on the look-back at 1843 p.119 and on the Queen's Speech 164–5. On the Agricultural Protection Society see Cayley, on the Yorkshire Protection Society see the latter's *Report*, on S.S.C.—no clue as to what the letters stand for is provided in the pamphlet—see that publication, on Cobden's speech see Prentice Vol. II pp.171–6 and on the *League's* response pp.179–81. The debate on Villiers's motion is in Prentice Vol. II pp.185–213. On electoral corruption see Burn, on Walsall McCord p.89, on Cobden's attitude p.158, on the League's guidance to its members *Directions* and *Practical Instructions*. For Wilson's speech see Prentice Vol. II pp.220–1, for Dudley

pp.237–41, low wage rates 217, the revision of the electoral lists and Cobden's speech of 24 October 1844 250–4, that of 12 December 261. On Savings Banks Halevy Vol.II p.170 and *Britain, A Handbook* (H.M.S.O., 1967 edition) p.387. McCord pp.152–4 describes the house purchase procedure; on Bright's speech of February 1845 see Prentice Vol.II p.298, on Wilson's and W.J.Fox's speeches of 15 January 1845 pp.276–7. McCord p.155 describes the 'model farm' plan and the *Report of the Select Committee on the Votes of County Electors* (Parliamentary Papers 1846 Vol. VIII) pp.iv, 192 and 213 the League's vote-challenging activities.

19 The Cooperation of the Ladies

The epigraph is from Prentice Vol.I p.386, his later view and the quote from M.Bastiat on 171–3. The Ashton anecdote is in Prentice Vol.II pp.132–3; the tea-party is in Vol.I pp.170–1, the 'memorial from the females' on 274, and 'unmanly attempt' to slander them on 284. The formal response is in Prentice Vol.I p.345, the committee of September 1841 on pp.297–8 and Somerville, *Free Trade*, p.516. For the Manchester Bazaar see Prentice Vol.I pp.299–300, on the pin-cushions, the proceeds of the Bazaar (which it wrongly dates at July 1842) and the *Quarterly Review* comment, see Fay pp.107–8; on Priscilla Bright's letter, Trevelyan p.107, which wrongly suggests it was in 1843. The 'cooperation' quote is from Prentice *op. cit.*, the *Leeds Mercury* one in Vol.I p.414, *The Times* one from Vol.III p.138; the 'beautifully engraved' card is in McCord p.139. For George Wilson's letter on the London Bazaar see the *Bazaar Gazette*. Cobden's new year speech is in Prentice Vol.II p.269, proceedings at Covent Garden on pp.271–82, Bazaar preparations 298–300, and the *Morning Herald* on 328–35. The total of contributing towns is in the *Bazaar Gazette* No. 1, excessive prices are mentioned in No. 3, Free Trade cushions in No. 7, handkerchiefs in No. 8, the continuing flow of contributions and the riddles in No. 15; recent inventions are described in No. 5, the visit of the design students in No. 11, the reduction in admission prices in No. 8, the extended hours in No. 7, and the *Morning Chronicle*'s summing-up in No. 16. Prentice Vol.II pp.336–7 and 340–1 quote the other periodicals mentioned, and 335 and 383 describe the Bazaar's financial success.

20 The Time is Come

For the epigraph see Gash, *Sir Robert*, p.555. On the Budget and Select Committee attempt see Prentice Vol.II pp.295 and 309, on Villiers's motion 377, on the meeting in Wiltshire 381–2, and on Harriet Martineau 394–5. Lord Ashley's conversion is in Prentice

Vol.II p.398, Bright's peroration on 401, the Birmingham dinner on 403, Russell's letter, 404. On Peel's resignation attempt see Gash pp.554–6—where a footnote records Prince Albert's memorandum—on Stanley's attitude see p.558, on Cobden and Bright's frenzied activity Read pp.94–5. The December meeting is in *Quarter of a Million Fund*, the recantation of the Chartists in Briggs p.370, Peel's premature rejoicing in Gash p.559, Grey's refusal to serve in Prentice Vol.II p.412, Peel's 'restoration to life' in Gash p.561, his meeting with the Queen and letter to Goulburn on pp.563–5, and Her Majesty's reproof to Melbourne in Longford pp.228–9. For Cobden's 'overwhelming' reception see Prentice Vol.II p.414.

21 Our Cause is Won

The epigraph is quoted by McCord on p.205. Peel's letter to Arbuthnot is in Gash, *Sir Robert Peel* (to which later references refer unless otherwise indicated) p.566 and his reminder to his colleagues on p.565. Prentice Vol.II pp.418–9 describes the opening of Parliament and Gash p.568 the cheers for Lord Stanley's views. Cobden's letter to Wilson is in McCord p.201 and Peel's proposals are set out in Fay p.99. MPs' resignations are mentioned by Gash pp.571–3, the League Council meeting by McCord pp.201–2, the riddle about Peel by Longford p.226, and 'Parsley Peel' by Gash in *Mr Secretary Peel*, p.21. On Peel's speech and the result of the debate, see Gash, *Sir Robert Peel* pp.580–1; on Cobden's see Prentice Vol.II p.431, on League support among electors p.434, on Peel's winding-up speech 438. Gash pp.591–3 describes the peers' attitude, Morley p.387 quotes Cobden's letters to his wife, the *Punch* verses appeared in June 1846 (p.27 of the bound volume), Gash p.601 describes Peel's resignation letter and p.604 his final speech. Prentice Vol.II pp.439–40 quotes his tribute to Cobden. Gash p.620 describes the split in the Tory Party, Robbins p.62 celebrations in Rochdale, Prentice Vol.II p.441 quotes Cobden's praise of Peel, Ashworth p.332 his look back at the League's early days. The subscription to Cobden is in Prentice Vol.II p.444, Bright's library in Robbins p.62, the last meeting of the League in Prentice Vol.II p.443 and Ashworth pp.334–5.

22 After the Battle

The epigraph is quoted by Read pp.138–9. On bread prices see Mitchell and Deane p.498, the end of the shilling levy Fay p.99, the revival of the League Ashworth pp.331, 341–2, 358 and 364–5. On the effects of repeal see Woodward p.119, Fay pp.117–9 and Ensor pp.115–6. On the acreage under wheat see Mitchell and Deane p.78, on employment in agriculture p.60 and Woodward p.117. Ashworth's assessment of the situation in the 1870s is in the Appendix to his book, the figures being drawn from various tables on pp.1–21, while the 'pleasing duty' quotation is on p.3, the 'our farmers' one on p.6, the 'value of exports' on p.8, and the 'one family' extract on p.9. On Disraeli's rise to power see Woodward p.157, on Peel's death Gash p.705. Cobden's refusal of office is described by Morley pp.403–4, his life in retirement on pp.467–70, his return to the House by Read pp.138–9, and his closing years by *D.N.B.* On Bright's post-1846 career see Read p.117, for his being burned in effigy p.135, and for the 'transparent intimacy' quotation pp.149–52 and 130–1. Bright's return from Birmingham is in Read p.137; his defects as a reformer appear in Hirst p.17, his attitude to war with the U.S. on 75–6 and in my book *The Hungry Mills* pp.61–6. For Bright's refusal of office see Hirst p.34, on Home Rule see Read p.198; on 'my dear friend, Cobden,' Beatrice Webb's disappointment, and Bright's death, see Read pp.232–3. J.B.Smith's later life is described by McCord on pp.87, 95 and 133, George Wilson's by the same source on pp.162 and 201 and also in the *D.N.B.*, which is the main source for the later life of Sturge, Villiers, Perronet Thompson, Ashworth, Paulton, Fox, Prentice and Watkin. On Acland see McCord p.57, and, finally, on the fate of the Chartists floor, Briggs p.60.

Index